the Church

in today's catacombs

the Church
in today's catacombs

Edited by Sergiu Grossu
Translated from the French by Janet L. Johnson

ARLINGTON HOUSE PUBLISHERS   New Rochelle, N.Y.

Library of Congress Cataloging in Publication Data

Grossu, Sergiu, comp.
    The church in today's catacombs.

    "Originally published in France in 1973 as a
supplement to the journal Catacombes."
    Bibliography: p.
    1. Persecution—Communist countries—Collected
works. 2. Communism and Christianity—Communist
countries—Collected works. I. Title.
BR1608.C7G7613   272   74-32251
ISBN 0-87000-260-0

Translator's Note

THIS DOCUMENTARY CONSISTS OF ESSAYS, STORIES, LETTERS, POETRY, APPEALS, and newspaper articles that testify to the religious persecution and harassment behind the Iron and Bamboo Curtains. Originally published in France in 1973 as a supplement to the journal *Catacombes*, it is designed to awaken Christians to the plight of men who have been denied the right to speak their minds, from an unknown monk in Pochaev, U.S.S.R. to the famous Solzhenitsyn.

In reading this translation, two aspects should be kept in mind. First, its uneven quality, intrinsic to a documentary culled from many sources. Second, the text basic to the current English translation comprised many sections translated from Eastern European languages into French. I have, therefore, referred to reliable English renderings of the same events and facts whenever available.

I am deeply grateful to the many people who have helped me with the work, especially the typist, who prefers to remain anonymous.

—Janet L. Johnson

Contents

the Church

in today's catacombs

I: Introduction

1. A Document of Accusation

This book is the logical sequel to the monthly periodical *Catacombes*, founded October 15, 1971 for the purpose of testifying on behalf of the Church of Silence. The same spirit of truth and justice, the same evangelical responsibility in the face of the totalitarian explosion of the anti-Christian forces of insurrection impel us today, as they did then, to begin a new adventure in Christ: the publication of this documentary.

It is impossible to give an exhaustive treatment to the countless aspects of human suffering that occur under the reign of the godless; we have tried to present the most important ones to show clearly the horrors of the world of concentration camps that crush, behind the Iron and Bamboo curtains, all individual and collective desire for religious and political freedom. This book, then, is an accusation against that subhuman world, marked by class struggle and the so-called dictatorship of the proletariat, against that dim world that is subjected to the reign of hatred, ideological coercion, and unrestricted tyranny.

We hope that this book will convince our friends that the existence of the Church of Silence continues; that this Church, savagely persecuted and tortured for its faithfulness to Christ in the midst of treason and apostasy is forced to live in modern catacombs; that the actual forms of persecution—practiced in thousands of prisons, hard-labor camps, and psychiatric asylums across the Soviet

11

empire—exceed all methods of degradation and torture that man has known; and that the long list of Christian martyrs of all faiths honors the children of God who, despite their chains, remained faithful to him "unto death."

The amazing spiritual tenacity of our brothers under the cross should cause us to revise our thinking, our plans, our daily behavior and, especially, the direction of our lives so that we may be true Christians, always ready, as the Apostle Paul exhorts us, to remember those who are mistreated as though we were "of one body." Thus may we heed the cry of these innocent victims who from the depths of their social pit incessantly entreat the political and religious leaders of the free world.

We wish to draw our readers into "the good fight for the faith" against the flagrant atheism of our day and to ignite in each the spark of active approval that may grow into enthusiastic participation in this apocalyptic confrontation. "Communism has declared all-out war on Christendom," an enlightened French believer has said. "Christendom will wage war against it, or perish." This is the war of the free spirit against the revolt of atheistic materialism that was unleashed to corrupt even the authorities of the Church and to transform the world into one vast death camp.

Let us not smooth over the facts or seek shelter in empty causes. Instead of ignoring the gravity of the hour, let us put on anew the armor of the Holy Spirit, laying aside all arrogance and humbling ourselves so that Jesus may grow in us until we reach the spiritual stature of the Christian martyrs of the East: those Christians to whom the articles, testimonies, and documents of *The Church in Today's Catacombs* bear witness and to whom this book is dedicated.

—Sergiu Grossu

2. *The First Streaks of Dawn*

Recently I lamented to a friend the indifference of French public opinion toward religious persecutions in the Soviet Union. He pointed out that, for most of our fellow citizens, Christianity in Russia is dead. There is probably truth in that remark, to which I shall return. But even if it is well-founded, alas, it does not explain everything. It must be said first that, because of the atrocities reported to us daily by newspapers, radio, and television, what one may call the general conscience has reached its saturation point. It is interesting to note that this applies especially to such collective dramas as Biafra, Bangladesh, and today's Burundi. We must admit, of course, that men of enormous good will—doctors, in particular—offer their services and that public appeals for assistance are not without response. Yet, real emotion is much more readily mobilized by a news item about an individual, such as a kidnapping, or the rape of a young girl, or a son's stabbing of his father's murderer. In this last case, 40,000 signatures to a petition to have the son provisionally released were collected within a few days.

Persecutions, however, are of a completely different nature. They cannot be discovered by observers in helicopters; although they certainly deal with individuals, they are not classed as news items that can be verified and up to a point reconstructed. Hence, they enjoy an unfortunate and scandalous impunity.

But if the French are ignorant of a revival of the Christian faith among many young people in the Soviet Union, that fact may generally be attributed to the deceitful propaganda carried on by the Kremlin and, we may be certain, conveyed by the French Communist party. The latter, slave to indoctrination, will not fail to spread abroad the idea that only old women muttering prayers before icons attend church services. How can the members of the Communist party conceive what is in fact the truth, that young workers, before the factories open, meet together in barns to celebrate the Lord's Supper?

What we must especially guard against in our country is the fact that the intellectuals who connect Marx, Freud, and sometimes Nietzsche imagine that they have thereby established a kind of solid ground for dialectical exercises—the sum total of philosophy for those who have lost the capacity for what was, up to the Second World War, the practice of reflection worthy of the name.

But for us, who have had the privilege of hearing once again a Bergson, or even a Brunschvicg or a Delbos, the thought of those young Christians emerging slowly from a tortured world not only brings us comfort but also confirms us in the unfading assurance that between faith and freedom there exists a bond that only party spirit can deny. Moreover, in the sporadic news that reaches us of this awakening, how can we fail to see the first streaks of a dawn that doubtless, one day when we have left this world, will renew and enlighten the West—a sick world, victim of its own victories, where the "Betrayal of the Clergy" is fulfilled in a way the poor Benda was unable to discern.

—Gabriel Marcel

3. *The Church of Silence*

They are grains and then more grains
in dark husks of silence
crushed in nights of suffering
for the shame of human kind

They are grains of heavy anguish
grains of corn, grains of rice, wounded
millions of believers wrung
in chains of sordidness

Sweat of blood dries at the bars.
Hearts on fire and eyes grown tired
in today's Gethsemanes
they weep for their vain tyrants

Vale of tears and vale of madness
vale of iron and bamboo
bread and wine until the end transformed
in prisons of dishonor

They are in the steps of Jesus
his true disciples on the earth
and true temples of his mystery
martyrs men no longer count

In the church of catacombs
holding tight the rose of faith
"and you," they cry, "and you,
are you not dancing on our tombs?"

They are grains and then more grains
in countries of the East . . . of the light . . .
crushed in Calvary's mill
omen of an alien hunger

Without dismay, are we, their brothers,
worthy of such holy bread?

—Jacqueline Delpy

4. *What Does the Church of Silence Mean?*

To me—as should be true for every Christian—the Church of Silence stands for persecuted brothers in Christ; that is—as Christ himself declared to St. Paul, a persecutor before his conversion—that *I am persecuted in them.* If I am a Christian, it means that Jesus Christ communicates his life to me and actually lives in me; the same life of Jesus Christ in me exists also in my brothers. Since we then share the same life—that of Jesus Christ—my brother's life is no longer apart from mine. And that means that I must consider all that happens to my brothers as though it were happening to me: rejoicing in their joys as my own, suffering in their sorrows as my own, serving their needs as my own, thus making myself, in the words of St. Paul, "all things to all men." It means that, according to what Msgr. Ghika called "the theology of need," I must consider any need of theirs that I encounter in circumstances willed by God as a call from him that I serve that need.

Thus, whatever happens to any Christian anywhere must resound in me as though happening to myself. My brothers in Eastern Europe and in Asia may be geographically removed from me; however, if they are persecuted Jesus Christ, through whom I live, is persecuted in them, and that persecution strikes what is deepest in me, the life of Christ within me. That is why one wonders how those who remain indifferent to the Church of Silence, who even smile upon its persecutors, dare to call themselves Christians.

But while I deeply mourn for them, I am struck even more deeply with joy over the prodigious work of the Holy Spirit that is accomplished in them through their sufferings: those churches are our glory and pride because they are on the cross with Jesus Christ, because Pentecost fulfills itself in them—and thus in them the future Church is being born.

—Jean Daujat
Doctor of Letters,
Laureate of the French Academy and
the Academy of Sciences

Churches Under the Cross

This title refers to churches which a political régime, despite its constitutional and official declarations, prevents from expressing themselves publicly—except in an extremely partial and supervised fashion—through practices normal for any community of believers: catechism for children, religious publications and books, public conferences, and meetings and congresses. Such means are part and parcel of "religious freedom" as proclaimed by the Synod and expressly recognized by almost all countries in the United Nations Declaration.

Sometimes it is even more: the churches of silence are the churches under the cross.

For us it does not relate to politics or to political opposition to legitimate public authority. It has to do with a human right, confirmed and rendered even more sacred as a divine right based on Jesus Christ, founder and ever-living head of the Church.

—Yves Congar
Theologian and author

Nature of this Church

The Church of Silence is the church of the most living, the most loving, and the most striking eloquence.

—André Piettre
of the Institute

The Church of Hope

Paradoxical though this statement may seem, the Church of Silence is for me the Church of Hope. For in silence the Holy Spirit always operates in the unspoken meditation of souls that do not doubt, but remain faithful. And it is always at the moment of utmost abandonment, as in the third hour on Calvary, that all is ready to rise again, that the Resurrection is near.

For me, it refers not only to a change for the better in the conditions of life and expression for the Christian communities in Eastern Europe. Having directly observed it in the U.S.S.R. and in what are commonly called the "popular democracies," I know the profound faith and the heroic virtues of those who publicly confess their zeal for Christ through attendance at church, daily behavior, and sometimes even through their writings. Christianity there is as a life-giving underground stream that could suddenly erupt and spread wide its waters to the sun.

—Achille Dauphin-Meunier
Member of the Academy of Agriculture
Dean of Independent Faculty of
Economics and Law in Paris

Christ Crucified in Mao's Land

We keep silent about that Church of Silence, whether it be behind the Iron or behind the Bamboo curtain. We have our lips sealed concerning it, much as the Chinese do concerning their own system and their own suffering.

Television—and with it all other means of public communication—emphatically extols famous artists, movie stars, champions . . . we don't readily talk about martyrs of various ages, whether they be of Nero's time or of Mao's.

Now, in Red China, Christ is crucified afresh . . . Is it possible to sleep and to keep quiet? . . .

—André Athenoux

The Christian Obligation

We live upon this earth that we may love and glorify God, our Creator and the Creator of all things, and that this love for God may express itself and bring forth its fruit in love of one's neighbor.

The moral worth of a country's institutions is measured according to the degree of liberty that they allow to fulfill this obligation.

Corrupted by secularism, materialism, and the surrounding immorality that flows from these, the liberty of western countries favors evil above good. Its comforts generate languor. But the faith, even if it cannot always make itself heard, can in principle be expressed.

In Communist countries, although worship is theoretically free, the only propaganda permitted is that of an antireligious and atheistic nature. The Church is legally required to keep silent, which is unthinkable for the Christian unless he denies his baptism. Hence persecution generates heroism and holiness. That is the Church of Silence.

The two types of constraint, one by indirect stifling, the other by policed tyranny, are essentially the same, and differ only by degree of violence. Indeed, both intend to establish a society that does not consider God. Both oppose, one practically, the other legally, obedience to the injunction of the prophet Isaiah against keeping silent: "Cry aloud, spare not, lift up your voice like a trumpet; declare to my people their transgression . . ." (Isaiah 58:1).

—Admiral Auphan

Prayer for the Church of Silence

May our prayer be helpful to the persecuted; may our brotherly solidarity cause them to feel that they are not alone, and that their example is one of edification for the whole Church, especially for us who remember them with so much affection.

Grant, oh Lord, that their days of trial be shortened and that soon they all—with their converted oppressors—may serve you freely.

—Pius XII

Two Churches

In an age when freedom is proclaimed as the supreme good, when the rights of man are universally, solemnly defined, there is a division between two churches: the Church of the Word, of the free word, and the Church of Silence.

I hear the voice of Pascal: "Here you can profess your faith without any trouble. There you can be faithful only through much labor and under constant threat."

—Jean Guitton
Catacombes, Nov. 3, 1971

2: The Church and Its Modern Catacombs

1. *A Spiritual Profile*

We have now witnessed for some time a kind of spiritual estrangement, a decay of the life of the Church, a surrender to the political and ideological decay of the life of the Church, a surrender to the political and ideological attack of Marxist-Leninist atheism; this is indeed a form of treason against the cause of Jesus on the part of a number of churchmen more or less highly situated, more or less madly won to the cause of those who "want to pervert the Gospel of Christ" (Gal. 1:7). Ignoring the Word of God and the injunction to defend it against any contrary wind of doctrine, perverting the official documents of their own hierarchy, trying even to reconcile Christianity and Communism, doctrinally as well as sociopolitically, these progressives in cassocks do not heed the Lord's continuing accusation: "The priests did not say, 'Where is the Lord?' Those who handle the law did not know me; the rulers transgressed against me; the prophets prophesied by Baal, and went after things that do not profit" (Jeremiah 2:8).

This explains the appearance of the theology of violence and revolution; the disastrous tendency to "politicize" the Gospel and "demythologize" the Bible; the story of the emotional approach, the anti-evangelical drift of many priests and bishops toward the enemy of Christianity; indeed, even the desire to collaborate with the French Communist Party, the assistant general secretary of which said, without embarrassment and in spite of his strategically "extended hand": ". . . between Marxism and Christianity there is no theoretical accord, no ideological convergence possible."

While the church of the Free World accepts compromise and continues to sleep, satisfied with its moral lethargy, its obtuseness and unforgivable silence toward the believers who suffer behind the Iron and Bamboo curtains, the Church of Silence continues to live, to fight atheism and to testify to Christ, despite persecution and the daily threat of police, despite the assault of Red propaganda against the spiritual resistance of the children of God, despite prisons and hard-labor camps. For this church in chains, the cry of the Apostle Paul is engraved across a forbidding sky: "Who shall separate us from the love of Christ? Shall tribulation, or distress, or persecution, or famine, or nakedness, or peril, or sword? . . ." (Romans 8:35) Overjoyed with the new dimensions of life that the Gospel grants to everyone hidden with Christ in God, the religious author A. Krasnov-Levitin writes in his disturbing "Song of the Eagle": "I have never felt happier anywhere than in camp . . . God was so close that I felt Him at my side, and in those moments I would cry out: 'My God, may this time, the happiest of my life, last as long as possible' . . . Thus I found happiness in distress, inner freedom in the worst of captivities."

The members of the underground church, whether they live in the U.S.S.R. or in Rumania, want to know only this: "Be faithful unto death, and I will give you the crown of life" (Revelation 2:10).

They are always ready "to make a defense . . . with gentleness and reverence" to anyone who calls them "to account for the hope" that is in them (I Peter 3:15), specifically before the political watchfulness of the Communist authorities, represented in every factory or institution by the inflexible "chief of personnel," the eye of the party and of the secret police. In all those countries under Soviet jurisdiction, where the Bible, while not officially prohibited, has been banished from bookstores, libraries, and universities and replaced by Marx's *Das Kapital* and by the dogmatic works of Lenin, believers still make use of God's Word, the indispensable tool for spiritual labor, the "sword of the Spirit" in the evangelical battle, their daily food, a devouring "fire" and a "hammer that breaks the rock." According to this Word, they are persuaded that carnal man is powerless and must be completely renewed in Jesus Christ by reclothing him with Christian armor, in order to be able to resist and react Scripturally against enemy attacks, exactly according to the description of the Apostle Paul, "through great endurance, in afflictions, hardships, calamities, beatings, imprisonments, tumults, labors, watching, hunger . . ." (II Corinthians 6:4, 5).

I well remember the difficult, almost indescribable trials that I endured in Rumania with my brothers in faith and hope, in the miserable circumstances of a ruthless existence. Because we condemned injustice and lack of freedom, we suffered afflictions; while accusing the institutions of aggressive atheism, and refusing all idolatry, we lived in hardship; because we did not give in to Marxist-Leninist teaching, we frequently met calamity. In openly deploring the régime's terror and the brutalities that oppressive authorities tolerated, we suffered beatings; for fighting beneath the banner of truth; while lies and hostility to God's work increased, we were imprisoned; in our preaching to people in churches or illegal gatherings of the need for an inward, Christ-centered revolution, we strengthened the vacillating consciences of those who otherwise would have been drawn into political *tumults,* and we showed them the narrow way of death to sin and resurrection by grace. While giving ourselves body and soul to a life of missionary combat for the regeneration of man and society, we were not exempt from labor as true soldiers of the Lord; suffering because of great social evils, we tried to remain watchful and unravel the source of evil to discover, denounce, and prevent its ravages. We claimed a pure life among our equals and strove to keep ours above reproach in hunger and active asceticism, in order to "commend ourselves in every respect."

"Beware of men . . . ," Jesus would tell us at every moment, in every dilemma. This did not mean to run from people, to isolate ourselves, to begin to hate men and thus by distrust of "suspects" break our ties as brothers with the world. But we were to keep ourselves from "some," from those who slipped in among us and tried to "pervert the grace of our God into licentiousness and deny our only Master and Lord, Jesus Christ" (Jude 4); from those who, taking advantage of the political darkness in a subjugated country, easily sowed the tares of atheistic materialism and of the so-called proletarian morality.

The Church of the Catacombs is not some recent catchword of anti-Communist propaganda. Neither is it the suspicious trademark of a few petty critics who have taken refuge in the West or of those who broadcast "false reports of religious persecution" (to quote Metropolitan Nikodim) and "jeopardize and undermine peaceful coexistence."

The Church of the Catacombs is a reality too little known, neglected, and disputed in the Free World. A painful, burdensome reality, it does not only turn its back on peaceful coexistence; it actually accuses the comfortable, coexisting Western church of cowardice, as well as the "children of light" who wrap themselves in the silence of their own shame.

To the honored representatives of the World Council of Churches, I put this question once and for all: Which is the member of the Body of Christ that actually suffers and with which all other members must suffer—the church of believers persecuted under Communist governments or the terrorist movement for Palestinian liberation? And when the Apostle Paul warns us: "Remember those who are in prison, as though in prison with them; and those who are ill-treated, since you also are in the body" (Heb. 13:3), has this to do with prisoners of white racism, with guerrillas of world revolution, murder, and vengeance, with those who are mistreated because they have returned evil for evil, *or* does he mean our brothers imprisoned for their faith, mistreated for their faithfulness to Christ, who love, bless, and pray for, despite their chains, those who persecute and torture them?

Paraphrasing the Gospel, I would say that the Church of Silence is a treasure hidden in fields of hate, a pearl of great price rejected because of misunderstanding and lack of enthusiasm on the part of the free church; it is the true, the incomparable bride of the Lamb. Its uncommon heroism brings it close to the *Ecclesia* of the first centuries, whose members suffered and died for Christ. From that church of tears, from that barred world where darkness "mixes everywhere with light," as Victor Hugo wrote, often come testimonies, cries, and letters that adorn from afar the disfigured face of a shameful Christianity.

In the April 15, 1972 issue of *Catacombes*, we published a plea that Christian-Baptist V. I. Kozlov addressed on October 23, 1970, to the Soviet leaders Brezhnev, Podgorny, and Kosygin. Long a prisoner under common law, condemned many times for theft, robbery, and gangsterism, Kozlov was brought to a genuine conversion by the example of Nikolai Khrapov, a Christian prisoner whom he met in 1953 in one of eastern Siberia's numerous camps. (Khrapov spent more than 28 years in prison and hard-labor camps, always because of his faith.) Although we cannot reproduce in its entirety this overwhelming letter that honors the Church of Silence, we must extract a few lines, so that "whoever has ears to hear, let him hear!"

"The transforming power of Christ and of the Gospel," Kozlov writes, "has overcome not only my own heart but the hearts of thousands of those who, like me, were poisoned by atheism and vice. The Russian prisons and camps have become a place of spiritual rebirth for many, and there their souls have met Christ. In 1953 I completely renounced my guilty past and the world of sin. I became a Christian. Yet thousands remain in prisons and camps; they are not changed, since the educational methods of the penal system

are of no value and do not improve them. Truly, they all go from bad
to worse because what they need is not an atheistic morality; they
need Christ. If believers currently imprisoned were not forbidden
to speak of Christ to these miserable persons, how the lives of thousands of sinners would be transformed! You would not need to
maintain a million public speakers to support an atheistic morality; you would not require police and more police. The money that
you spend to wage war against God would be put to better use in
publishing Bibles and Gospels for our Soviet people; then we would
have fewer drunkards and thieves, fewer crimes; then camps would
empty, and you would be able to change the prisons into museums
of former savagery and human cruelty . . ."

—Sergiu Grossu

2. Why Are the Christians Persecuted?

The behavior of the Communist authorities toward the Christians
is motivated by an atheistic ideology that of necessity incorporates
religious persecutions. To understand it properly, we need to consider briefly what the Marxist ideology is and discover the attitude
of modern Communism toward the Church and religion.

Karl Marx, regarded with Friedrich Engels as the founder of modern Communism, drew up the two most important treatises on
Socialism and Communism: *The Communist Manifesto* (1848)
and *Capital* (1867-1894).

Three factors underlie Marx's negative attitude toward religion:
his dialectical materialism, his deterministic view of history, and
his ethics. Marx was very much influenced by Ludwig Feuerbach,
who considered all religion as a fateful illusion, opposed to cultural
progress and sapping man's activity and self-confidence. On these
premises, Marx built a whole philosophic system that was both
atheistic and materialistic and excluded all belief in supernatural
truth. His statements are clear: "Religion is the opium of the
people;" "Communism begins with atheism;" "The critique of religion is the basis of all critique;" "I hate all Gods."

In his view of history, Marx attempts to be scientific. According
to him, individuals cannot influence the course of history; only economic and material factors can do so. Marx owes this deterministic
idea to Georg Hegel. According to Hegel, all things in history are
necessarily linked together; evolution in one direction is always

followed by evolution in a contrary direction. Finally, a third stage unites the best elements of the two preceding ones, according to the pattern of thesis, antithesis, and synthesis.

According to Marx, historical evolution will end when Communism will have reached its goal and created a classless society. Until then, however, the conflict between the classes will continue; workers will unite to wrest capital and the means of production from the ruling class and to establish the dictatorship of the proletariat, which is the best possible societal form before the total abolition of classes.

For Marx, the Church is an obstacle to be swept away because it is opposed to that necessary evolution: it is reactionary. In the conflict between classes, he said, it sides with capitalism and must therefore be fought by all possible means. Marx, of course, underestimated the spiritual force of the church and was unable to destroy its influence.

In Marxist ethics, all that hastens the evolution of history toward Socialism is good and just, all that counteracts this course is bad. In a Socialist world the state is everything and the individual nothing. That is why the Communists "in good conscience" sacrificed several million persons on the "altar of the state," using methods of torture more cruel than those of the Inquisition or of Nazism.

V. Lenin developed Marx's theories and adapted them to the twentieth century. The official Communist ideology became Marxism-Leninism.

Concerning religion, Lenin followed Marx's doctrine: religion is only "bourgeois prejudice" that makes man "the slave of gods he himself has invented;" and he adopts Marx's famous formula: "Religion is the opium of the people." It is under this same pretext that Christians are actually arrested, since they have willingly "inoculated their children with the poison of religion." For it is in fact forbidden to teach children and adolescents any form of religion. This "crime" of "leading minors astray" is punishable with several years of imprisonment.

After Lenin's death in 1924, J. Stalin took over. His was a long, bloody dictatorship. He "liquidated," tortured, or deported millions of people. Preoccupied first of all with consolidating Communism in the Soviet Union, he then directed Russian politics toward world domination by annexing a large section of Eastern Europe after the war of 1939-1945 and by ushering in the "cold war."

No doubt we should note Stalin's more lenient attitude toward the church during World War II, when he needed to revive the old traditions and seek the support of the church in his patriotic propaganda. For this reason, in 1943 the Russian Orthodox church was allowed to elect a patriarch, but Stalin saw to it that this church did not attain true autonomy; although persecutions let up for several years, the trials it faced did not disappear.

After Stalin's death, relations between church and state were redefined by decree of the Central Committee. The edict, signed by the new party chief, Nikita Khrushchev, was to forbid infringement upon the rights of believers in order not to strengthen their "prejudices." By this leniency, however, Stalin's successors intended only to consolidate their position. Further, Khrushchev's attitude toward the church was no less negative, as shown in the wording of the decree: "The Communist Party leans . . . upon Marxism-Leninism and its foundation in dialectical materialism; it therefore cannot be neutral toward religion, the ideology of which knows nothing of science . . . Religion dulls the mind of Man and condemns him to passivity in the face of the forces of Nature . . ."

Toward the end of 1958, a violent offensive of atheistic propaganda was launched. The newspaper *Communist* deplored the fact that so many Russian workers were still believers and that young people continued to suffer "the influence of religious prejudice" that reached even party members. Atheistic progaganda must be intensified.

At Easter in 1959 the entire Soviet Union celebrated a "week of atheistic scientific literature." A chair for atheism was established at the University of Moscow. Also created was a "House of Scientific Atheism" numbering 500 offices and 15,000 propagandists.

Pravda recently reported that a boat was traveling the waters of Vologda Province for the propagation of atheism with missionaries holding lectures and showing films reinforcing atheism. This is a typical example of atheistic propaganda as practiced today in all of the Soviet Union.

Such propaganda is actually considered the most powerful means to stamp out Christianity and other religions. Bolshevism will succeed in killing religion by alienating the young from the church through a godless education and through atheistic propaganda.

Communism is in fact itself a religion that demands man's total commitment. That is why it cannot tolerate another religion, and it is vain to pretend that Communism and Christianity can be compatible.

This is why thousands of Christians behind the Iron Curtain carry on "illegal" activities in an "underground" church. It is they who up to now have been imprisoned, martyred, eliminated . . .

—Nils Tonnesson
Martyrer unserer Zeit

◍◍◍

3. Modern Forms of Persecution

There are two kinds of persecution in the Soviet Union: a brutal form consisting of the arrest, deportation, even the massacre of the faithful; and another softer one that attempts, through various means, to prevent or limit the exercise of the faith.

Open persecution has almost totally disappeared in the Soviet Union. There are still exceptions, such as the case of Msgr. Velich-kovsky, underground Catholic bishop in the Ukraine, who was arrested and sentenced to three years of hard labor. Moreover, there are others not made known to the West. If, however, we compare the situation today with the great waves of repression that accompanied the civil war at the beginning of the régime or the dreadful massacres of the Collectivization (1928-1932), then we can say that bloody persecution has ended.

Nevertheless, persecution takes place in other, more secret ways. Less visible, it is just as abominable. There is, first of all, persecution directed against the leaders of the Orthodox church. We do not mean those who have been deported, but those who remain. For years now, these men are actually forced to sing the praises of the régime—that is, to proclaim the merits of those who destroy the faith, to affirm that religious liberty is fully accorded (an absolute lie), and to participate in various such propaganda campaigns as those of the "Peace Movement." These same men, in return, keep silent about the harassment of believers.

One thing is certain: Orthodox bishops are subjected to constant supervision and pressure from Soviet leaders. It is an artful but terrible form of repression.

Of course, it is the mass of the faithful who suffer above all from this permanent offensive against the faith. Without claiming to give a complete picture, we may cite a few of the most flagrant cases.

For about fifteen years, bulldozers have been demolishing innumerable houses of God throughout Soviet territory on the pretext that, since there are no more believers, there is no reason to maintain buildings for worship. (They know very well, of course, through numerous testimonies, that this is false.) Thus only about 15 churches remain open for worship in Leningrad, 20 or so in Moscow, and about 10 in Kiev, most of them downtown. It is almost impossible to learn the situation in the countryside.

Another method consists of limiting recruitment of priests. The entire Soviet Union has only two seminaries, counting 500 students, a minute number for a population of believers that still numbers perhaps 40 million persons, although an exact figure is unavailable, since all religious statistics are prohibited.

Thus the people of God find themselves deprived both of places of worship and of priests.

Believers are, besides, heinously persecuted in the exercise of their faith. Their children are, of course, subjected to the official materialistic and atheistic teaching. When their parents have them baptized, that act is registered and communicated to the authorities, a policy that has been going on for a number of years. If the believer holds office or works in a Soviet institution, he is likely to be accused, subjected to slander from his superiors, and even demoted or dismissed.

One example is very telling. About ten years ago, the Soviet press made a great case over the rehabilitation of a woman called Valentinova, accused of having had her daughter baptized. The little girl, it seems, was baptized by her grandmother without her mother's knowledge. Valentinova, having been able "to justify herself," was reestablished in her position after a reprimand for her "slight fault." Praising this gesture as an outstanding act of tolerance, the Soviet press added that the little girl could no doubt be placed again in the day-care center from which she had been expelled. Remarkable, isn't it! A child had been turned out of her nursery because she had the blemish of baptism!

I know of no instance in which Msgrs. Marty, Matagrin, and Gand, who claim to oppose totalitarianism, ever raised their voice against this behavior of tyrants. Tyrants yesterday named Khrushchev and today Brezhnev!

An exception? Not at all! Rather, permanent repression. I read in *Le Figaro* in an article by M. Boudarias—who is hardly a cowardly hyperconservative—that some workers had not been paid in full. Their offense? They had received the sacraments.

Thus countless abuses are inflicted upon believers regardless of their affiliation: Catholic, Jewish, or Baptist. Religion is subjected to systematic suffocation.

And yet, the faith continues. It is a treasure shared and fiercely defended by the most humble peasant of Lithuania or the Ukraine and by the great Solzhenitsyn.

—Roland Caucher

4. *Christmas in the Ukraine*

It wasn't the first time that Parasia had opened her home for secret meetings. Her husband, killed in war, had been a forest ranger. Her only son had gone underground; then, betrayed by a friend, he was caught by the Reds and hanged. From that time on the rumor spread that Parasia had gone mad with grief.

That served the cause. The old woman lived a solitary life and spent her days praying. After a terrible crisis of despair, God had opened her eyes. She never lost the sense of his presence and believed that she had been invited to climb Calvary's mountain with him. The night they brought her the corpse of her son, retrieved from the common grave, one voice said to her, "Blaspheme!" and another, "Pray for the hangmen."

"For a moment I was as though torn apart, then I chose."

The whole drama with its outcome hung on those few words. Parasia had nothing else to say. From then on her life was woven with silence.

On the pathway leading to the cottage, two women were waiting.

"Pod twoja milost,"[1] Parasia said.

"Spasi nas,"[2] a solemn voice retorted. Parasia bowed humbly, and according to custom, kissed the knees of one of the visitors.

"God bless you, Batyushka! Come warm yourselves a bit." They entered the cottage. In the hearth a good fire crackled.

"Wait till I light a candle," Parasia said, laughing. "I'm luckier than you, I don't need any."

The woman she had addressed took off her shawl. Father Dymitri had little trouble disguising himself! His emaciated features, regular and fine, lent themselves easily to disguise. He had even managed, though with some difficulty, to acquire an elderly falsetto and usually spoke with a quivering voice. All this helped him to get around. He even managed to procure a woman's passport.

"There are wolves in the Krasne forest. I had trouble getting through . . ."

An hour later, the stable was filled to bursting. The smell of tallowed boots, badly tanned furs, and perspiration was stifling. Everyone was kneeling, repeating over and over again, quietly yet with singular intensity:

[1] "By your grace" (*Sub tuum praesidium*, widespread prayer in the East).
[2] "Save us" (password)

"Hospody pomyluj! Hospody pomyluj!"[3]

Before beginning the mass, Father Dymitri spoke a few words:

"Beloved brothers, this is the time to rejoice! On this blessed night, our Savior was born. In a poor stable, like this one. Wretched beasts kept him warm with their breath. There is no donkey here, but there are plenty of lambs! Do not think for a moment that this happened once and for all 1951 years go. The Lord Jesus never ceases to be born in souls. For the one who loves God it is always Christmas. All you have to say to him is 'Come!' And he comes. Even if your soul is black and miserable, he does not give up. He comes to restore order inside. And love. More love! That is what makes us rich and happy. And with our whole heart we must pity those who are separated from love. Our enemies, those who persecute us, are much poorer than we . . ."

Parasia had taken her lookout position on the doorstep. Batyushka had given her good reason. It was up to her to watch. She couldn't hear the words, but the murmur of voices allowed her to follow the ceremony. The stable was only two stone throws away . . .

The sermon had begun! She crouches on the threshold, rapt in her precious inner light.

All of a sudden she jumps up. "Who's there?" A heavy hand falls on her shoulder, another covers her mouth.

"Old witch, shut up! So that is your 'madness', is it?"

Brutally pushed, she rolls on the beaten earth. Carefully the man closes the door. He mocks:

"Caught in your lair, I see! I'll make you talk! Come on! Where does the priest come from?"

Parasia had taken hold of herself. Her shoulder had been dislocated and hurt dreadfully. She fully realized the horror of the moment. How, but how, had she let herself be caught? "Mother of God, save them! Mother of God, have pity! Mother of God, take my life, but don't let one of them perish!"

"They have enough for the whole night," the man said, rubbing his hands. "My soldiers will be here in an hour. Meanwhile we can chat, eh? Tell me, what were you doing a while ago, on the doorstep?"

With her soul's ears Parasia distinctly heard words whispered to her. Gently, she repeated out loud:

"I was praying for you."

The man gave a start.

"Ah!" he said with a bitter laugh. "Now there's an honor I wasn't waiting for! So you were praying for me, you old pest? For me, who could wring your neck just like that?"

---

[3] "Lord, have mercy upon us."

She felt his hands squeezing her throat. She wasn't afraid, listening to the inner voice, repeating word for word what she heard. Suddenly he loosened his grip.

"I am not the one to pity. It's you! Why don't you pity your poor soul?"

They began to exchange words, like sword strokes.

"My soul, my soul! So you would have me believe in a soul!"

"Look then! Don't you see?"

"Witch! Let go of me!"

"I am not a witch! It's your soul! Do you see it? Like a child tied up. Like a starving child. Like an imprisoned child. Do you hear it cry? Your soul, have pity on your soul!"

The man before her seemed struck with amazement. They were standing up, Parasia with her back to the hearth, and he in the full light. His face, drawn, expressed an unspeakable terror. He was trembling and his teeth were clattering.

"I see your soul," she said with an authority not her own. "Your poor soul in the mud. The image of your God drowned in that mud. What mud! Lord Jesus, what mud! Listen . . ."

She continued to repeat only what was whispered in her ear. Engrossed in her vision, she had lost all sense of danger and of time. She saw all the sins of this man in precise detail, like a horror movie before her eyes. Even had she wanted to, nothing in the world could have kept her from speaking. Disgust gave her a kind of hiccup that she could barely control. She saw but one sin at a time, but in such a moving, swarming and darkened form that she felt faint with fear.

"That's what you did at age twelve, sixteen, twenty . . ."

Suddenly she screamed and staggered. Blood rushed to her face.

"It's you, Judas, I pray for. It's you who hanged my son!" she said in a choking voice.

She saw how it had happened. And she felt compelled to speak. Her Wania, her sweet child, her only son—so that's how they had treated him! Beaten unmercifully, unrecognizable, his face swollen, haggard, panic-stricken. "Mother!" he was screaming through the torture, "Mother!"

And they hanged him with a rope. On the branch of that tree, a birch tree. There were the sudden jerks of his whole body, then nothing. And this man, now prostrate before her, this Judas who had betrayed him and turned him in, this man was standing beneath the makeshift gallows, holding his sides and laughing . . .

She trembled. But the imperious voice would not let go! The death of her son was only an episode in that life of sin. Here was another nightmarish scene, and she must tell everything!

Up until this last night . . . he had managed to suborn the innkeepers's wife. In terror, she had spied on her husband. The entire plan for the meeting, the list of the faithful, it was she—that woman—who had turned them over to him. He hopes his deed will gain him a promotion, and he wants the honor all to himself . . . His police won't come, because they're waiting for him in front of the coal shed. They're waiting for the whistle that will alert them if the game is trapped. To cap his crimes, there's but that whistle to blow!

She stopped, worn out. The man was sobbing at her feet. All of a sudden, from the depths of her being arose an almost wild joy, like an immense torrent that sweeps away everything in its path. God had answered her! Her Judas, she was holding him.

Softly she leaned down and took him by the arms: "Peace, my child! It's a night of Peace!" He turned toward her a face still young, flooded with tears.

"What must I do, my little mother?"

"Come with me," she said, "Come, they're waiting for you."

Holding him by the hand, she led him to the stable and opened the door. Father Dymitri stopped short; all eyes turned toward the newcomers.

"He came as Judas," she said simply, "and now I bring you a brother."

—Maria Winowska
"Les voleurs de Dieu"
("God's Robbers")

3: The World of
Concentration Camps

1. *A Particular Style of Repression*

A little over a year ago a number of bishops of the Orthodox church outside the Communist camp admitted that "new atrocities" had begun in Russia. The régime, unable to mould a completely submissive "homo Sovieticus" through propaganda and terror, was now resorting to a special kind of psychiatric hospital in order to break, physically and intellectually, believers and those in general who think differently from what the Party dictates. The bishops condemned the methods, "medical" and otherwise, used in these "establishments" and pointed out that in the "traditional" asylums there are "special sections" for "treating" nonconformists and those who believe in God.[1]

In every stage of Soviet Communism, there has been a corresponding "style" of repression. On the morrow of the Revolution, there was Lenin, the creator and first organizer of the world of concentration camps. This revolutionary leader was in fact behind the decree that in April 1919 created the "Gulag," a term covering a gigantic administration of camps and the transformation of whole

[1] Orthodox prelates report special psychiatric hospitals not only in Kazan, Sichevka (in the Smolensk Region), Leningrad, but also in Moscow (where, according to the *Samizdat*, the control of a high officer of the K.G.B., Professor Lunts, is felt intensely), in Chernyakovsk, Dniepropetrovsk, and Orel. Doubtless others exist elsewhere, they add.

regions into convict prisons. We know that Lenin was also personally responsible for the liquidation of part of the peasant class, revealing another side of his character. When Stalin took over, the
structures ready to plunge entire populations into fear had already
been established. Childish, therefore, is the cry, "Lenin, help us!"
that marks the end of the film "L'Aveu," in which Stalin's methods
are denounced.

Stalin inherited a system that needed only to be perfected.
Marchenko, a convict of Stalin and post-Stalin times, for example
observed that in the Soviet camps an ordinary lawbreaker is in the
end less badly treated than a so-called "enemy of the people." In his
book, *My Testimony*, he shows that criminals or delinquents are
treated in accordance with certain rules, while prisoners in other
categories are left to the completely arbitrary actions of the administration and of the guards. Aleksandr Solzhenitsyn, another witness to the Stalin and post-Stalin nightmare, makes the same ob-
servation in his books, *One Day in the Life of Ivan Denisovich* and
The First Circle. He tells how penalties of 15, 20, and 25 years of
prison camp imposed upon actual or presumed "enemies of Socialism" are, at the end, suddenly extended so that often a prisoner
dies, never having regained freedom.

It seems that other world atrocities—the Hitlerite horror, numer-
ically less crushing, or in another realm the Biafra disaster—have
aroused more emotion. Yet Stalin indulged in a veritable genocide
of men and women of all classes, whether through mass execution
or deportations that were equally extensive. Agriculture was jeop-
ardized for lack of help; children by the thousands died of hunger.
Already at that time there existed establishments of a "special
type" for brainwashing and operations that often proved strangely
fatal—the mysterious death of Frounze, the no less mysterious death
of Mongolian leader Tsedenbal. The dictator's life can be summarized in one phrase: tens of millions of victims.

After Stalin's death in 1953 a new stage began. Khrushchev and
Leonid Ilichev, head of the Party's ideological commission, used
"special" establishments on a larger scale. The famous de-Stalin-
ization by Khrushchev was only partial, as evidence clearly indicates.
The antireligious campaign was in full swing: destructions of
churches followed one after the other, the clergy and the faithful
were rounded up. To cite but one example, the Pochaev monastery
was closed and the monks thrown into insane asylums.

But the establishments of Khrushchev's day served especially, it
seems, to eliminate the "intruder" for a time and thus avoid indictment for what had become more and more difficult to conceal: procedures that sometimes jolt Westerners from their passivity and

impede the mechanism of cooperation among countries with "different" systems. Ill-treatment, moreover, seems to have been less frequent than it is today.

Since the Brezhnev-Kosygin-Podgorny troika has come into power, trials have followed one another, camps have again become filled. Certainly, killings are not systematically carried out as under Stalin but, in view of the general use of the "special" psychiatric asylum and the placing of K.G.B. specialists on all its levels, we may speak of neo-Stalinism. We may also note that executions for economic offenses or "hooliganism" are increasing and, even if less frequently today than yesterday, scholars and writers do die in camps. At the beginning of November the writer Yuri Galanskov, who defended Sinyavski and Daniel, died from the "effects of an operation" in his camp at Potma in Mordovia. He was 33 years old.

Vladimir Bukovsky, before being sentenced to seven years of imprisonment under severe restrictions, had time to broadcast to the Western world the abominable treatments that are now common for the confined "asocial" population; Bukovsky knew the K.G.B. psychiatric hospitals from personal experience. The descriptions given by Natalya Gorbanevskaya, who protested against the invasion of Czechoslovakia and was therefore confined, are no less dreadful. We know at last through *Samizdat*[2] that the Calvary endured by another nonconformist, General Grigorenko, continues. We have no news, finally, of the historian Petr Yakir, who was arrested several months ago.

But the power of repression has met its equal today in the trend toward fundamental freedoms, already spelled out in the Soviet constitution, which is no trivial paradox. The political trials of the last several years have shown us defendants who refuse to plead guilty or who, like an Amalric or a Bukovsky, discredit the dictatorship. Through *Samizdat* we have been able to hear the voice of Krasnov-Levitin, the spiritualist philosopher who, before beginning a third period of imprisonment for "breaking the laws of separation between church and state," declared: "I am a believer and a Christian. The duty of a Christian is not limited to attending church. He must embody the commandments of Christ. That is why I defend human rights, whether those of the monks of Pochaev, the Evangelical Baptists, or the Tartars of the Crimea." Astrophysicist Kronid Lubarsky, condemned recently to many years of prison camp for supporting *Samizdat*, concluded his final declaration during his trial by expressing his faith in the triumph of freedoms in Russia.

---

[2] Underground publication

2. *Prisons, Labor Camps, Asylums*

On Imprisonment

Many of our relatives continue to languish in the camps; they have lost their health. Since the stiffening of camp regulations, the situation of our prisoners has become much more critical. The intervals between visits and between food distribution are much longer. We cry out in alarm, informing you that the health of the Christians in camps is subjected to great stress.

Once again we write to you, as we did for Pastor Afonin of the church in Uzlobaya, concerning today's sick and elderly, for whom the delay in release may end in tragedy and weigh heavily upon your consciences.

1. Golev, Sergei Terentevich of Riazan, preacher and member of the Council of Churches of the E.C.B., is serving his twenty-first year of imprisonment. Locked up for preaching the Gospel, he is seriously ill with diabetes and diseased in his legs; he is 74 years old. And if he was brought to trial already very sick, how can he be left behind barbed wire, waiting every day for his approaching end?

2. Guliuk, Vasily Nicolaevich of Bataiska, Rostov Oblast, born in 1901, second-class invalid, sentenced to three years of solitary confinement with hard labor.

3. Iskovskikh, Alexir Fedorovich, presbyter of the church of Devosk, Moscow Oblast, an elderly man of 78, sentenced to three years in a hard-labor camp.

4. The presbyter of the E.C.B. church in Rostov-on-Don, Rogozhin, Dimitrii Stepanovich, an elderly man of 70, ill with heart disease, languishing in a strict regime camp since September 13, 1969.

5. Popov, presbyter of the E.C.B. church of Omsk, an elderly man of 83, has been in hospital in a strict régime camp for three years; he has already undergone two leg operations. His condition requires his immediate release.

6. Miniakov, Dimitrii Vasilievich, a member of the Council of Churches, kept in a strict régime camp, contracted an open form of tuberculosis. He has been hospitalized since October 25, 1967. His condition requires his immediate release.

7. Zinchenko, Vladimir Petrovich from Kharkov, young man of 19, is ill with a liver disease and physically very weak. He was sen-

tenced on September 1, 1969 to a three-year term for directing a chorale and orchestra in the church. He is employed especially at hard labor in the rock quarries, without warm food from morning to night. With his weak, young body he cannot fulfill the work load required of him, which is that of a grown man. The prolonging of his labors is inadmissible, because his health will definitely be destroyed, perhaps even to the point of death.

—The Council of Relatives of Evangelical
Christian-Baptist Prisoners in the U.S.S.R.
March 16, 1970

In the Labor Camp

On July 7, 1972 the Presidium of the Supreme Soviet issued a decree, the first article of which may be summarized as follows: "It is ruled that for every illegal transmittal of objects to convicts—food products, money, alcoholic beverages and any other article or substance forbidden in reeducation work camps—or for all attempts at similar transmittal by any means whatsoever, in the measure in which such acts are not subject to judicial proceedings, the guilty party will be liable to an administrative fine from 10 to 50 rubles or else to measures of social action."

The Academicians Sakharov and Leontovich sent the following telegram to the president of the Presidium of the Supreme Soviet of the R.S.F.S.R., Academician Millionchikov: "Concerning the approaching ratification at the session of the Supreme Soviet of the decree of the Presidium of the Supreme Soviet of the R.S.F.S.R., No. 615 of 7 June 1972, we urge you to transmit the following declaration to the delegates:

"The issuance of this decree dealing with the illegal transmittal of food products to prisoners officially confirms the existence in our camps and prisons of a state of chronic famine. No one would risk illegal transmittal, if such were not necessary.

"By allowing convicts and their visitors to be searched, this decree makes even more severe the prisoners' tragic situation, which is well known to us through many reliable sources.

"We urge the delegates to vote against this shameful decree of June 7, 1972. We urge the delegates to stand for reforming our penitentiary legislation in order to stop the inadmissible torture of prisoners by hunger.

"Mikhail Dimitrievich, we want to believe that you will not remain indifferent."

This declaration was not brought before the delegates. The decree was, of course, ratified.

—*Chronicle of Events in Court*
No. 26, July 5, 1972

Camp Spirit

There are many of us at hard labor. Therefore, we do not suffer from isolation. Although the work is very grievous, our spirit is joyful and our heart is at peace. Considering the circumstances, this work will certainly last a very long time. But whether this period be long or short, we only need to pray the Lord that the labor may do us good, and that soul and body may profit.

—From a note sent to Hong Kong by a priest
Sept. 15, 1959

Hospital Morale

I have never felt happier anywhere than in camp. Today I still recall the hours of nightly prayers; I was working as male nurse in the camp dispensary. God was so close that I felt him at my side, and in those moments I would cry out: "My God, may this time, the happiest of my life, last as long as possible."

Actually, my whole subsequent life has been but a memory of those happy times. I found happiness in distress, inner freedom in the worst of captivity. Only there did I understand the meaning of the maxim, "The kingdom of God is within ourselves".

It depends on man and on him alone to be happy. There exists no greater satisfaction than that of the prisoner who suffers for his convictions.

Moscow, 1968

—A. Krasnov-Levitin

3. *Forced Labor in China*

Surely one of the high human costs which the Chinese people have paid for rule by the Communist party has been the system of

"Reform Through Labor Service," a euphemism for forced labor or slave labor. This has been a part of the Chinese Communist political system from the outset, although the formal 77 regulations—worked out with the aid of Soviet "experts" sent by Stalin—were not drawn up until June 27, 1952 and not officially promulgated until August 26, 1954.

During the early years Peking talked quite openly about this system, which it was confident would help to remould the class character of those former enemies whom it hoped to "save." It is an interesting commentary on Western wishful thinking about Mao's China that although forced labor is an organic and essential element of the Communist economy, it has received practically no attention for more than a a decade.[1] One can search the pages of the *China Quarterly* (the most important scholarly journal devoted to Communist China, now in its eleventh year of publication) in vain for a treatment of forced labor.

Part of the difficulty may lie in the curtailment of overt references to the system following the presentation to the Economic and Social Council of the United Nations in December 1955 of a report on forced labor, a major section of which was devoted to revelations about the conditions in China. Nevertheless, at the time of the celebration of the tenth anniversary of the PRC in 1959, there was an exhibition in Peking of the achievements of the corrective labor camps, and a subsequent one in Huhehot in April 1960.[2] Further, there have been many refugees who have found their way out of mainland China, who have testified to the continued importance of forced labor in the Chinese Communist economy. At the time of the Cultural Revolution outsiders were reminded once again of the importance of the labor reform camps. In the contending between factions in Canton in 1967, for example, one Red Guard publication reported on the disorders that Canton was "faced with a huge decisive battle" and noted that even "Labor reform camp prisoners are being set free."[3]

Since the early days of Chinese Communist rule, there has been little attempt to carry through any systematic study of forced labor and the conditions in forced labor camps. Following the airing of some of the details before United Nations bodies, with much of the

---

[1]The contribution of the Labor Camps was dealt with in W. W. Hollister: *China's Gross National Product and Social Accounts, 1950-1957* (Glencoe: Free Press, 1958), pp. 102-103. But little work on its role in the economy has been done since, largely because of the absence of Chinese Communist statistics.

[2]See *China News Analysis*, Hong Kong, No. 377, Nov. 16, 1961, p. 2.

[3]"Survey of the China Mainland Press," U.S. Consulate General, Hong Kong, No. 4019, p. 18.

evidence gathered from Communist publications, Peking played down its own discussions of "reform through labor service."

It is ironic that some of the more recent discussions of forced labor in Communist China have come from the Soviet Union. For example, Radio Moscow, on May 30, 1967, claimed that more than 18 million political prisoners were languishing in some 10,000 camps in mainland China, and it quoted a recently escaped Chinese as saying that in the labor camps the people were being treated like animals. Surely there is need for a more thorough scrutiny of this part of Mao's China, which is related to construction schemes and to the whole social and economic system, and we need more reliable information than the Soviets are likely to furnish if we are to understand the extent to which forced labor colors the whole of Communist China.

On the score of forced labor, as with casualties, figures are imprecise. The United Nations' report of 1955 listed some 20 to 25 million in regular labor camps and another 12.5 million in corrective labor camps. One scholar in the West estimated the number at about 14 million in 1954.[4] Certainly, as the years have passed, this institution, with its high human costs, has tended to be surrounded by ever denser fog. Most authors must, in the absence of adequate piecing together of hard evidence (and few seem inclined to that task), resort to imprecise phrases, but even the most cautious have commented on the "staggering number of persons involved."[5]

No estimate of the number of Chinese in forced labor camps for reform through labor service is less than 10 million. But once again, the issue is not one of precise numbers, but of the high cost in human terms of this degradation for political reasons or because of class origin or background. Those who have escaped and testified in the outside world allow no doubt about the subhuman and oppressive conditions in the labor camps, the hardships of separation from families, and the high mortality rates.[6]

[4]Karl A. Wittfogel, "Forced Labor in Communist China," *Problems of Communism*, 5.4 Jul.-Aug., 1956, p. 40. This is one of the very few scholarly articles dealing with this important subject. Wittfogel notes that his figure means that 1 of every 40 people in Communist China would be a slave laborer.

[5]Y. L. Wu, *An Economic Survey of Communist China* (New York: Bookman, 1956), p. 322. A. D. Barnett in his *Communist China: The Early Years, 1919-1955* (New York: Praeger, 1964), p. 65 is more cautious and says that the figure is "probably in the millions." He notes, however, the point being made here that the human element is undisclosed in the "dry bureaucratic and lifeless prose" of Chinese Communist publications (p. 67).

[6]Some compelling stories are related in *Forced Labor*, UNESCO, Document E/2815, December 15, 1955, pp. 92 ff. One personal tale is produced in an Appendix.

40

There is another high human cost in a system that, because terror is an essential ingredient, debases the very people who must perforce carry it through: the concentration and labor camp guards, as the following excerpt makes plain. Drawn from the testimony of Yüan Mei, an escaped prisoner from a labor reform camp, it was presented to the International Commission Against Concentration Camp Practices in Brussels in November, 1956:[7]

One wintry morning, as a chill wind swept in from the north, 170 laborers were marched to work as usual. On arrival at the work site, the supervisor on duty, a fellow named Fang Yu, nicknamed "The Star of Pestilence," ordered the men to wade into the cold water. He blew his whistle three times, but the workers were reluctant to move. He then fired into the air threatening to shoot to kill if the men dared ignore his order. My two friends and I had luckily been assigned to fell trees on the slope. But the shot scared both of them, and they took shelter under a dense cluster of bushes. I didn't follow them, but hid behind a sizeable tree-trunk and observed what happened subsequently.

Workers in threes and fives began to strip off their clothes and were driven into the icy water like cattle. But a few of them failed to get into the water fast enough. This enraged the supervisor, who grabbed a submachinegun from the nearest guard and let loose a barrage of fire which instantly killed several of them. A number of others leapt into the water with their clothes on. But the shooting was too much for them and they all stampeded, breaking away in all directions and running for cover.

The situation threatened to get out of control and the armed guards joined in the shooting. A short while later, the whole company of the border defense troops was rushed to the spot and deployed around the whole area. Order was quickly restored, at the price of more innocent lives.

The day's work was suspended. Those taking refuge behind the trees were then summoned and ordered to return to the camp. My friends, Liu and Tseng, were so scared that when they emerged from their hideout they looked more dead than alive. They asked me whether they had been wounded by the gunfire. I checked them over carefully and reassured them that there was nothing wrong with them. But their legs were too weak to move, so I had to drag them up to the top of the embankment along a path still slippery with blood.

The group was assembled for roll call. Some were plastered with mud, others were drenched. Everyone was ashen-white and shaking with fear.

[7]It is legitimate to wonder whether there are those so anxious to have the "privilege" of a guided tour in Mao-land that, as journalists or scholars, they are unwilling to report the many similar stories of violence available in Hong Kong almost daily.

Over 21 laborers were missing, killed, wounded, or, perhaps, escaped. No one could tell. But the would-be "escapees" were grouped together and one after the other were beaten up in front of the lucky ones whose assignments kept them from being directly involved.[8]

—"The Human Cost of Communism in China"
(U. S. Government Printing Office, 1971)

◊◊◊◊

4. Psychiatric Asylums

Letter Addressed to M. Boris Petrovsy
Minister of Public Health, U.S.S.R.

Dear Sir:

We possess numerous documents of unquestionable authenticity that reveal the treatment systematically applied by your department to those whose opinions are judged to be nonconformist. These persons are confined to psychiatric asylums, when it is clearly evident that they are normal, and are subjected to procedures that can only result in making them ill. Thus, nonconformity is classified as mental disorder.

I cannot conceal, Sir, the feeling of unanimous condemnation that such behavior evokes among my country's intellectuals. To us, it compares with Nazi methods openly condemned by the Nüremberg Tribunal, where the Soviet Union was represented.

If such methods are not ended, how can they not fail to severely affect the friendly relations that have for so long united our countries?

I dare hope, Sir, that you will seriously consider this request.

Respectfully,
Gabriel Marcel, Member of the Institute

◊◊◊◊

5. The Case of I. V. Lazuta

Dear Brothers and Sisters, Suffering Church of Christ!

We request that you bring before the Lord in your prayers our dear brother Ivan Vasilyevich, who is in very bad condition in the Jodichki psychiatric hospital in the Grodno Region. On May 24, 1970

---

[8]Reprinted in *The New Men* (Hong Kong: China Viewpoints, 1957), pp. 52-53.

we sent a special medical report regarding this to the government of the Soviet Union.

On February 11, 1970 our brother I. V. Lazuta was arrested and sent to an unknown address. Only after a prolonged search did his parents finally discover that he was under forced treatment at the psychiatric hospital of Jodichki, with neither warrant nor official medical report.

Before his confinement to the hospital, our brother had worked eight years as a highly skilled housepainter. Here is the testimony of the managers of the company where he worked: "The whole time he worked here he proved himself perfectly competent in his specialty and regularly performed at 110 or 120%. He was disciplined and modest. No one around him ever noticed the least trace of nervous imbalance."

His mother sent a complaint to Kosygin, signed by many residents of Lazuta's own village.

Upon his admission to the psychiatric hospital, our brother was placed in the section for lunatics, and after a preliminary medical examination the doctors began to treat him for schizophrenia, though his body and mind were perfectly healthy! They gave him a massive series of insulin injections. With the very first one, our brother fell sick, and the doctors were forced to decrease the dosage.

There were frequent conversations between the doctors and our brother. During one of these meetings, our brother asked: "What will happen if I reject my faith in God, if I cease to go to our prayer meetings, if I cease to pray? What will you do with me?" One doctor replied, "In such a case we will immediately let you go home."

All of this clearly shows their intentions and the new methods used by the atheists to repress believers. After discovering that trials, penalties, dispersing assemblies, and fines were futile, they decided to use a new method to break the resistance of the believers: confinement in psychiatric hospitals. Nevertheless, we can declare with Saint Paul: "For I am sure that neither death, nor life, nor angels, nor principalities, nor things present, nor things to come, nor powers, nor height, nor depth, nor anything else in all creation, will be able to separate us from the love of God in Christ Jesus our Lord."

We thank God for enabling our brother to keep his faith in the midst of such cruel tribulations. Observing that threats were ineffective, the doctor treating him asked this question after a series of insulin injections:

"So, Lazuta, do you still believe in God?"

After his affirmative answer:

"All right! But we will cure you yet of your fanaticism!"

A new treatment was prescribed that made him even more sick. May 11, his arms began to swell, and he suffered terrible pain in all his joints. Since May 18 he has been bedridden and so seriously ill that he cannot move without help. Nevertheless, praise God, his spirit is not broken! He is full of joy and says, "If the Lord wills, I am completely ready to die for his name, since I shall never deny him."

We believe that, thanks to his sufferings and trials, the Lord will call many others into the fellowship of his children. That is why once more we urge you to remember our brother in your prayers and to plead before the Lord that he remain faithful to the end.

We ask the Council of Relatives of Prisoners to bring a special report before our government. Truly the life of our brother is in extreme danger.

Signed, the least of your brothers and sisters in Christ, members of the fellowship of Borodichi.

—André Martin
"Enterrés vivants . . ."
(Buried Alive . . .)
May 26, 1970

6. *Antihuman Treatment*

I personally witnessed the treatment undergone by political prisoners in psychiatric hospitals when they tried to protest by refusing the food and the "treatments" inflicted upon them. They were tied up, injected with paralyzing sulphur and force fed. . . .

Christians! Your brothers in Christ are suffering! Defend my soul! It is not my body, it is my soul they want to nail to a cross. Better that they crucify my body! Christians! Do now allow them to administer to a holy being substances that destroy his soul! . . .

. . . The Communists have invented a powerful means to get rid of those who do not think as they do. Not only do they not hesitate to confine them in hospital-prisons, but they also compound their crime by injecting prisoners with chemical substances in order to destroy their personality and intellect.

—Vassili Chernikhov
"Appeal to the Soviet Society"
January 1971

7. *Notes from the Red House*

. . . May the will of the Lord be done in everything! Whether they make me crazy or whether they leave me my reason, all is good and beautiful under the sovereign heaven. I accept everything that God sends me, I accept it as a child accepts what is bestowed from his father's hands: sweetness and bitterness, folly and reason, light and darkness, all crime and all splendor.

In the asylum I often thought how everything in our universe is accomplished by the will of the Lord, a will so wonderful that it keeps man's freedom intact, all the while guiding man and all humanity by his mysterious ways. The mind cannot apprehend this phenomenon in its fullness, but one day you will discover it and you will believe in it.

They confined me like a criminal in an asylum, believing thus to terrorize me and prevent my "propaganda" for Christianity. One question naturally arises: Are they omnipotent? It would seem so at first sight . . . But they weren't able to terrorize me. On the contrary, they will once again be covered with shame before those who will read these notes. They will confine me again. With the same result. But if they utterly destroy me, what is of good in me will finally attain to holiness . . . not on the basis of my own merits—I have none—but because of the crimes of my executioners. And I still do not know what will be the worst for them: to kill me, to confine me to an asylum, or to leave me in peace. Where is the omnipotence in that?

This very short example does not explain the infinite mystery of everything, but is a telling illustration of the harmony between human freedom and the Grand Design.

—G. M. Shimanov

8. *Hecatomb of Church Structures*

In order to secure its ideological dictatorship, Communism crushes without mercy or shame all opposition. It seeks out all dissenting world views, ferreting them out rigorously and persistently, the more so as they declare or present themselves as incompatible with it.

Communism, wanting to operate only in a material world, has

a phobia of the spiritual realm. Its vision narrowed by sectarianism, it traces everything to sensible phenomena, and considers as hurtful or perverted all those who—moved by faith and aware of the spiritual—embrace a world bigger than theirs.

For Communism, the natural adversary and fitting obstacle is Christianity. Tangible signs such as religious structures are enemy fortresses. Doubtless this godless system does not inevitably stand for stupidity, anarchy, and uncontrolled resentment; rather than eliminate existing monuments, it strives for their reconversion, desiring to see them molded into its materialistic framework. Nevertheless, hatred often darkens it so much that to its list of shameful accomplishments may be added an impressive hecatomb of religious monuments.

Eastern Europe was rich in splendid churches, filled with icons, arsenals of a demonstrative piety and of faith of times past. Before the establishment of Bolshevism in the empire of the Tsars, the one Orthodox church counted more than 100,000 priests and nuns; about 75,000 places of worship; more than 900 monasteries for men or women; 40,000 schools and some 40 centers for clerical training. Add to that the work of other churches, and we may ask what happened to all those buildings raised to manifest the faith? Varied testimonies, writings, and facts are sufficient to inform us concerning the afflictions borne by our fellow believers in "screened" countries—that is, situated behind the different Communist curtains, and especially behind the Iron Curtain.

In order to remain true to its nature, the Soviet regime, born antireligious, can really never tolerate the free activity of the Christian communities, and all agreements with this regime are but a trap that results in their undoing. It abhors the Church, its leaders, and its doctrines. Seeking to destroy a world in order to rebuild it according to the standards of its political utopia, the régime leaves little room for moral scruples, and the sacred monuments are hardly the object of its admiration and care.

Since in Western Europe we still have the unappreciated privilege of unhindered worship either in temples that have survived the ups and downs of the past or in contemporary buildings, may we better avail ourselves of these! And may we think more often of the oppressed who do not have this freedom and yet fight and labor for God!

—Norbert Tournoux

9. *Destruction of the Russian Church*

Control commissions may at any time establish certified reports of "decay" and demand total and immediate restoration of a church—a legal procedure, though arbitrary and unjust. Parishes that cannot meet the high costs involved are forced to ask the authorities to close them down. That is how one of the two churches of Stanislav was closed. Frequently the proverbial generosity of the faithful can cause this financial strangling to fail. Then the authorities use other kinds of pressure. The existence of churches and cathedrals is declared to contravene Soviet laws. A particular church is too close to a school and constitutes an attack upon the secularity of education, a silent yet eloquent witness to the faith; such a case is frequent because the state schools are situated on the sites of the old parochial schools. Another church, considered a historical monument, must belong to all Soviet citizens and not believers only. Saint Nicolas's Cathedral of Novgorod was taken from the faithful; the only church in town opened for worship, it was exchanged for the little Church of St. Philip in the suburbs. Still another cathedral, like that of Perm, attracts too large a crowd and obstructs traffic. Paradoxically, to attract great crowds is more dangerous to the existence of a church than its more or less desertion. Trade unions and Komsomols are then sent out to collect thousands of signatures from peaceful citizens and workers demanding the disappearance of these vestiges of the past. As in 1930, the churches are then closed according to the wishes of the unbelieving majority, without any regard for the faithful, no matter how many there are. In another place the imperious needs of urbanization are invoked; this was the pretext recently advanced for demanding the destruction of the Patriarchal Cathedral of the Epiphany on Baumanovskaya Street in Moscow . . .

Encouraged by the government, the closing of places of worship became a veritable competition among local authorities and took in 1960-1961—at least in certain districts—a massive and brutal turn for the worse. In the evening the faithful were still at Vespers in their church, in the morning they found nothing but a vacant lot. During the night, commandos had come by to close the church, dynamite it, clean away the ruins, and level the land with bulldozers. The newspapers published triumphant reports: 180 churches closed in Volhynie, 68 in the province of Jitomir, 43 in Poltava, 40 in Cherkassy, 18 of 25 in the only district of Lipkan in Moldavia, 6 of 14 in Kotov, an average of 1 out of 6 in the Diocese of Perm. Twelve parishes were liquidated in the Diocese of Novgorod, a number in the

Urals in the Diocese of Kuibyshev and in Altai. Western tourists were able to glean several striking details on the spot: In Kiev there are only 8 of 25 churches left, 9 of 23 in Odessa, 1 of 5 in Ismail, 4 of 12 in Rostov-on-Don. The cathedrals of Orel, Brainsk, Chernigov, Riga, Kaunas, and elsewhere have been taken from the faithful. In Orel the relics of St. Tikhon of Zadonsk were desecrated for the second time and probably destroyed. A number of dioceses— Chernigov, Lugansk, Chernovtsy, and others—were destroyed. According to N. Yudin, an especially well-informed author of an antireligious brochure, at the beginning of 1962 there were only 11,500 active Orthodox churches of the perhaps 22,000 that existed before 1959. Thus, less than three years after the beginning of the persecution, nearly 10,000 churches had been closed. Since then, such closings have not ceased, and today many churches are in the process of being closed.

—Nikita Struve
Christians in Contemporary Russia

10. *Outrages Against the Churches*

The antireligious policy of the Russian Soviet government was intensified in the second half of the 1920s. It became particularly rigorous after 1929 when Stalin launched his campaign for the total collectivization of agriculture. The church and religion, as well as other "vestiges of the past" that hindered the "construction of socialism," became the subject of merciless attack. The closing and demolishing of churches, as well as the persecution of the clergy and of the faithful, were rapidly carried out. The heads of collective farms, named by the Communists, were encouraged or forced to close religious buildings located on their property, either because the people no longer needed them or because they were beyond repair. Innumerable acts of vandalism and outrages instigated by the Communists were committed against the churches. Most of the religious buildings were converted to secular purposes and transformed into clubs, cinemas, and stores or demolished with their interior ornaments and religious objects, often of considerable historic and artistic value. Wooden churches in many villages were transformed into granaries, barns, or even pigsties. Most, however, were simply demolished and the material used to construct sheds for collective farms or as fuel.

The famous Pechersk Monastery in Kiev, the oldest and most important in all the eastern Slavic countries, had in 1926 about

48

500 monks. After the arrest of their abbot, Hermogenes Holubynsky, the monks dispersed. When the monastery was closed, only seven were left. It was transformed first into a municipal museum in September 1926 and in 1933 into an antireligious museum. It was only after World War II that several of the buildings were returned to the monks of the Russian Orthodox church. Even that truncated monastery was finally closed in 1961 under the pretext of reconstructing the architectural complex.

In 1931 the famous Mezhyhirsky Spas Monastery near Kiev underwent an actual pogrom. Its baroque inconostases, painted by the famous Italian artist Antonio Scotti, and the library were destroyed. The church bells received the same treatment. The frescoes were ruined and "socialist-realist" scenes were painted over them. . . .

Professor M. Makarenko, archaeologist and member of the Academy of Sciences, tried to save the ancient religious monuments of Kiev by submitting a petition to Postychev, secretary of the Ukrainian Communist party and even to Stalin himself. He was arrested by the G.P.U. and exiled from the Ukraine to Russia, where he died.

—W. Mykula
"La religion et l'Église en Ukraine"
("Religion and the Church in the Ukraine")

The Paucity of Churches

For one church that remained open, twenty were ruined and irreparably destroyed, and twenty others were abandoned and desecrated. Is there a more heart-rending spectacle than those skeletons handed over to birds and to storekeepers? How many settlements are there where there are no churches within less than 100 or even 200 kilometers? And the North, which has always been the treasury of the Russian spirit and very likely represents the real future of Russia, is entirely deprived of churches.

—A. Solzhenitsyn

Failure of the Moscow Patriarchate

The 10,000 churches and the tens of convents closed recently are irrefutable testimony to the fact that the Moscow Patriarchate has not fulfilled its duty toward Christ and the Russian Church; for it is only by being assured that ecclesiastical leadership would keep silent that the atheists were able to close so many houses of God!

If the church's adversaries had not been sure that the Moscow Patriarchate would abandon the right to defend its flock, they would never have dared to deprive illegally so many Orthodox communities of their right to exist. The massive closing of churches, convents, and parish schools is, we repeat, flagrant testimony of the unreserved submission of Moscow's Patriarchate to the verbal "diktat" of the atheistic officials.

In all the immense expanse of our homeland, hundreds of thousands of Christian souls deprived of spiritual food will be witnesses before God of this iniquity.

—Nicolas Eshliman & Gleb Yakunin

Speech for the Defense

You see us here
neither as thieves nor bandits:
today, as in the days of Pilate
the Savior Christ is the accused.

Prophet most holy of Nazareth,
why do they judge Thee today?
Is it because Thou art source of light
of purity, goodness, and love?

Is it for bringing release
to the slaves of sin, the slaves of passions,
for salvation revealed to the nations
by holocaust of Thy love?

Turning your backs upon history
with fury you condemn
the freedom of conscience and faith
the right to serve the Lord . . .

No! You cannot crush the faith
in vain would you imprison Christ:
the triumph of his Passion
goes on and on in those he saves.

—H. P. Vintz

⬬⬬⬬

11. *Trials of Believers*

The Trial of Krasnov-Levitin

On May 19, 1971 the Moscow City Court, within the jurisdiction of the Lubin District Court, heard the case of the accused Christian writer A. E. Krasnov-Levitin (Articles 190, 142—Section 2, Criminal Code, R.S.F.S.R.). Judge: Bogdanov; Prosecutor: Biryukova; the defense: A. A. Zalesski.

Family and friends of Krasnov assembled in front of the Palace of Justice. Only his mother-in-law, G. A. Levintina, and the academician, A. D. Sakharov, were admitted to the courtroom.

The bill of indictment contained in its conclusions numerous quotations from Krasnov's writings upon which were based the accusation of calumny against the Soviet governmental and social régime; the author was also accused of having "urged the adherents of the cult to violate the law of separation of church and state" (Art. 142 of the Criminal Code). Krasnov was also accused of having signed in 1968-69 a whole series of appeals and petitions and, in particular, a letter to the Council of the Communist Party of Budapest and a petition to the U. N. in May 1969.

Krasnov-Levitin did not admit his guilt and asserted that the accusations were founded on an arbitrary and false interpretation of excerpts from his writings. He explained that his works contain some criticisms, but in no way slander the régime; that he expressed his real thoughts and not rambling generalizations. He also told the court that certain excerpts, presented in the final bill of indictment as examples of "anti-Soviet calumny," were texts from the Holy Scriptures.

The prosecutor, a Mrs. Biryukova, repeating the final bill of indictment, asked that Krasnov-Levitin be sentenced to three years of "re-education camp" at common labor.

The lawyer, A. Zalesski, after having refuted point by point all the arguments in the bill of indictment asked the court to accept the conclusion of his argument . . .

The jury condemned A. E. Krasnov-Levitin to one year of re-education labor at his place of work with 20 per cent deducted from his pay, according to Article 142-I, and to three years in a general regime camp, according to Article 190-I.

—*The Orthodox Messenger*
No. 55-56, 1971

Before a Hungarian Court

"Defendants, please stand."

Four priests, one seminarian, and a student stand and face the People's Court of Budapest. The president continues:

"Before the deliberation of the court and in conformity with the laws, you may speak. Do you have anything to declare or to add to the pleadings for your defense?"

Frigyes Hagemann, a priest, replies:

"We do not belong to any political organization, we do not want any change of régime, either from inside the country or from outside. . . . We want an up-to-date church based upon conciliatory ideas. As for my writings, I would point out that if you sift a hill of sand and find several stones, you cannot conclude that the whole hill is made of stones. In all that I have written, there has never been a hidden political motive. My writings had but one aim: to educate in a religious context."

Court verdict: Five years of prison, 5,000 forints in fine, and partial confiscation of the convict's belongings.

Sandor Somogyi, a priest, then speaks:

"After the success of the Yugoslavian Pact, I hoped that the situation here would become normal, as well. What I did was nothing but my priestly duty. It had no taste of politics, which would have been contrary to my priestly vocation."

Court verdict: Four years of prison, fine of 4,000 forints, and the partial confiscation of the convict's belongings.

A Priest's Defense

Lajos Tury, a priest, stands before the court:

"When I was arrested on September 10, I saw in it the finger of God and I said to myself: 'The Hungarian youth can no longer understand me. I am no longer worthy of them; I can no longer get close to them.' But afterward I became aware that I was mistaken. I do my duty only when I follow Jesus and observe his instructions, 'Go and teach all nations . . .' I have been teaching for thirty years, and since giving myself to young people I have never had one pupil convicted of a crime and thrown in prison. On the contrary, they all became honest citizens, respectful of society, living an exemplary family life. . . . I have done nothing besides what I promised and swore to do when I was ordained. What I did, I there-

52

fore did under orders, but under the order of Jesus Christ. I did not do or even desire to do anything against the state. That is why I do not admit to guilt."

Court verdict: Three years and six months of prison, fine of 4,000 forints, and partial confiscation of the convict's belongings.

Istvan Katone, a priest:

"I am not and have never been aware of any conspiracy or any organization hostile to the state. But I readily discovered that, according to radio and newspapers, youth is experiencing a serious moral crisis. And I was glad to be able, outside the church framework, to come close to young adults and deal with them on a moral and religious level, so that they could become honest workers, well-esteemed in their places of work . . ."

Court verdict: Two years and six months of prison, fine of 3,000 forints, and the partial confiscation of the convict's belongings.

—Paul G. Bozsocky
"Études" (Studies), July 1972

Lenin on Religion

The antireligious battle cannot be limited to abstract preaching; it must be tied to the concrete practice of class movement which tends to eliminate the social roots of religion . . .

Marxism must be materialistic, that is, the enemy of religion . . .

—Lenin

Report of Father Zdebskis on His Trial

. . . Let us now examine the very article of the law by which I am judged, which does not seem to have a clear contextual meaning. I remember an action of the same sort brought against me in 1964, when I was sentenced to one year of prison for the same reason: teaching children. Several months afterward, a decree was issued removing this judgment, and I was released, supposedly because it was discovered that "no constraint was used on the children." The court knew this when I was judged, but that did not prevent my being sentenced to prison. Not one word about "constraint" was mentioned during the trial or in the bill of indictment. And

Article 143 of the Criminal Code, as it applies here, was interpreted as follows: It is forbidden to provide religious teaching in schools (not in churches!).

It appears, then, that the court now judges me guilty of an offense for which I was previously acquitted. How can this be understood? Why am I judged again by the same article of the Criminal Code under the same circumstances, and for the same offense of which I was once declared innocent? Addressing a letter to the Soviet government, the parents themselves confirmed that religious instruction was given with their consent in a church. Can a law be differently interpreted under identical circumstances? Neither the investigator nor the Supreme Court at Vilnius have answered that question.

What can we conclude?

Today we are judged by the courts. One day we will be judged by the nation. And finally the Lord's hour of justice will come. It is his judgment that we fear.

I ask the court that it give its verdict in such a way that the faithful will have no reason to believe that a law written in the Constitution is meaningless and serves only as propaganda.

—Lithuanian Report *Elta*
June 1972

A Typical Trial

The accused are members of the Evangelical Baptist Church:
(1) Zheltonozhko Georgi Dimitrievich and (2) Troshchenko Nadezhda Tikhonovna.

The trial took place in the city of Nikolaev, in the Ukraine, from January 24 to 27, 1972.

The Judge: Zheltonozhko is indicted under Article 138, Section 2 of the Criminal Code, and also under Article 187. He is accused of having received and distributed literature: Bibles, New Testaments, and other religious books. Have you taken and distributed literature?

Zheltonozhko: Yes, I gave some to everybody.

Judge: Where is it printed?

Zheltonozhko: Praise God, I don't know.

Judge: Why did you do it?

Zheltonozhko: According to Lenin's decree, citizens are not only allowed to believe, they may also confess their faith and propagate it. Lenin granted us freedom, he did not limit it; the same is true of the Convention on Human Rights.

54

Judge: Were you at the meeting held in Varvarovka?

Zheltonozhko: Yes, Soviet officials also attended. Some were drunk; they behaved in a very gross manner, they insulted the believers, and they said that our meeting consisted of scoundrels. I told them they were acting illegally. You tell us to preach only in a prayer house. The Lord says: "Go into all the world and preach the Gospel."

Judge: You violate the law concerning worship services; your brothers and sisters in the official church have accepted that.

Zheltonozhko: The law about worship services contradicts the Gospel, Lenin's decree, and the Convention on Human Rights.

Judge: The Gospels were written long ago; they can change, just as our laws can, according to circumstances. When the Bible was written, it fitted those backward times. Today the authors would have written it differently.

Zheltonozhko: No, the Gospels cannot change. They are the Word of God. They do not need to be modified and completed, and they are accepted at all times and in all nations.

Judge: Do you plead guilty to having distributed literature?

Zheltonozhko: I certainly do not plead guilty. It is a duty of the Christian to do it.

Judge: Where do you actually worship and pray?

Zheltonozhko: True believers pray everywhere.

Judge: What do you do when you meet together?

Zheltonozhko: We meet to read God's Word and to pray, we sing hymns to the glory of Christ, in order to remain faithful to the Christian calling.

Accusation Against Nadezhda Troshchenko

Judge: You are accused for having assembled children and read the New Testament and poems to them, and for having taught them prayers. The laws on religion forbid this practice. Do you plead guilty?

Troshchenko: No! Didn't Christ say, "Let the little children come to me"? (Mark 10:14).

Judge: At 18 years of age children may freely choose, but you, you brainwash schoolchildren of 11 or 12.

Troshchenko: But before they can choose their own way, they should know both Communism and Christianity. I would like the children I know to be happy. No father or mother wants to abandon a child to ruin or to death.

Judge: Did you read the New Testament to the children?
Troshchenko: Yes, in the presence of their parents.
Judge: Do you intend to pursue such activities?
Troshchenko: I hope that I will no longer have to read them the New Testament but that they will read it to me . . .

⬥⬥⬥

Accusation and Confession

"They accuse me of having proclaimed the Word of God. Yes, I did so and I will continue to do so. It is no offense, according to current laws in force . . . Yes, I proclaimed the Kingdom of God and the witnesses confirmed it . . . I proclaimed it, I proclaim it before you today, and I will continue to proclaim it to the end . . . I know only one thing: never will he forsake me. The Christ himself suffered his Passion and never did he forsake those who followed him in the way of the cross. Yes, I rejoice in my lot, to be able to suffer for Christ!"

> —Vasylyi Tymtchak
> Speech for the Defense, Odessa Trial, 1967

⬥⬥⬥

12. *Torture and Its Accomplices*

Of all the sufferings endured by man, torture is the most detestable: first, because of its intensity; next, because it is inflicted by one man upon another. That is why its most symbolic manifestations obsess the memory of men: Jesus crucified by the Romans; Joan of Arc burned at the stake by the English; Callas beaten unmercifully by his judges. That is why one of the first measures of the revolutions in America and in France was to eliminate the practice of forcing confessions through torture. That is why the allies of the last war arraigned the Nazi torturers at Nüremberg.

After these pangs of compassion, one could hope that the race of monsters had been extinguished. Alas, that is not so! Millions still groan under torture, from the Oder River to the Pacific, from Murmansk to Hanoi, with an offshoot alive in Cuba. On a quarter of the globe, prisoners are made to stand day and night under a blinding light, their legs swelling until they collapse with cries of pain; others are struck until their limbs break; still others populate concentration camps, dark as hell, where suffering continues twenty-four hours out of twenty-four for twenty years. Not counting those buried alive in North Vietnam, and those priests in Communist China and in Rumania who were forced to eat excrement (according to David Rousset and Pastor Wurmbrand), and that Communist dissident in the U.S.S.R. under whose eyes his son was tortured, then murdered. Not counting the innocent Chinese villagers who were dragged to sinister "public trials" barefoot, with hands tied behind their backs and heads down, their abdomens twisted with fright, to confess outrageous crimes before a crowd spitting insults and cries of "Away with them!"; and then, following the verdict, led away to dig their own graves. And the young women sent off to hard labor for refusing the advances of some brute of the N.K.V.D., and who, if they survived, came back irremediably blighted and corrupted by the mixture of cruelties and sadistic assaults that a pretty girl inevitably undergoes in the world of concentration camps. Just read "Une goutte dans la mer" ("A Drop in the Ocean") in which Alla Alilova relates the attenuated torture, even more degrading than pain, that her own mother experienced. An encyclopedia would not exhaust the sadistic imagination of the Communist hangmen.

Torture becomes even more atrocious when it strikes the innocent. On this point the Communists offer nothing new. The history of wars, of religious fanaticism, of political intolerance is replete with tortures inflicted upon beings whose only fault was to displease or to be conquered. Nevertheless, the Communist barbarians introduced into the long history of torture the new practice of dealing torture not only to real opponents, to those who in fact do not think as they want them to, but to their own supporters as well, to the conformers, to faithful servants.

In Communism we find the first tyranny in history where even those loyal to the government are not protected. Whatever obscure and torturous plans are made in the secret machinery of the police or in the head of the secretary general, the most loyal supporter of the political system may hear, at four in the morning, the muffled knocks of the N.K.V.D. police; with fainting heart he knows that in a few minutes he will be taken away forever from the world of the living, without reason and without recourse. Recall the story of the "Accused," that great devoted leader of the Czechoslovakian Communist party, suddenly and inexorably accused of every heinous offense and tortured to the end.

It is the same in Cuba. His own sister told me that Fidel Castro had sent his most intimate friends to the grave, the very men who had helped him come to power. Such as the devoted friend who had hidden him in his house in Mexico and procured weapons for him at the risk of his life; such as the old man, his former teacher, whom he left to rot in chains in a pestilential dungeon. One after the other the companions of hard times, brothers in arms, family members, joined the long procession of useless martyrs, martyrs of a régime they had helped build. In the past the Romans tortured the Christians, who were mutilating the statues of their gods. The Catholics tortured heretics who were challenging their dogmas. The Mongolians tortured the princes who were resisting them. The Hitlerites tortured the Jews, who belong to a different race. These differences in no way justified such sordid cruelty, but at least they did exist. But Romans, churches, Mongolians, and Hitlerites did not torture their own followers. Communism has set this last precedent. It has killed with the worst sufferings ten thousand times as many Communists as have all the anti-Communist régimes put together. Even wolves do not devour each other. But Communists do. It is a madman's world.

Let us come to a proper understanding. It may have happened in the past that a tyrant put to death one of his own. But this was an exception, the result of personal intrigue. In the Communist world it is a matter of a governmental system. The leader consolidates his power by mass purges. He cuts off the heads of men who have become too prominent, creates scapegoats, recruits young Turks who quiver with zeal, submissive to their superiors and merciless toward their inferiors, ready for anything including the torture of their predecessors, in order to clamber up the rungs of a hierarchy that, in a suffocating and paltry régime, offers the only chance to live a little. And, instead of simply letting its old worn servants return to obscurity, this power-mad authority dooms them to Siberian camps or to bullets in the neck.

This saying of Stalin summarizes his character: "It is better to punish one hundred thousand innocents than to let one guilty person go free." And, with his elementary type of mind, he took that literally. But how does one dispose of a hundred thousand innocents? By falsely accusing them of totally imaginary transgressions and releasing upon their poor heads, which turn gray overnight, the cruelest secret police in history, the police created by Lenin. It is the Calvary of the mouse-man caught in the claws of the tiger-man, described most completely, truthfully, and hauntingly by Weisseberg. The longer the victim's denials last, the more oppressive are the nights without sleep in front of the floodlight; the interrogations while standing up and being beaten; the return to the cell with a bloody body that can no longer sleep; the separation forever from loved ones; the receipt of their letters of disownment forged

58

by the N.K.V.D.; and the despair, the fear, the great fear. And, as a last degree of insanity in this régime, when the accused makes the false confessions extracted from him, the one most relieved is often the policeman, for if he had not obtained those confessions, he would himself have been caught in the cogwheels of torture.

Communist terror has invented new methods. It has invented the supreme horror: confining prisoners to psychiatric asylums. In our age of science and permanent revolution, man tortures not only the body but the soul as well. Communism has decided that any opponent should be declared insane and shut up with other insane people. This has never been known before. Christ, Joan of Arc, and Callas, to their last breath could have called themselves— and were recognized as—of sound mind. This last refuge of their being, the sound mind, was left them, even under a torture that made them scream like animals. Communist justice could not deprive its martyrs of this last comfort. Writers, scholars, and proud opponents are thrown into lunatic asylums. They are made to take drugs that destroy the will or drive them mad, and day after day the wretched creatures feel humanity become dim in the torpor of semiidiocy.

Don't believe that, beyond this barrier of absolute evil, nothing can be worse. Don't be deceived. While classic torture was for centuries denounced by all enlightened minds as a monstrosity, torture one hundred times more detestable, carried on by the Communist dictators, is accepted today by all who consider themselves the advanced of our century. We have thus reached the depths of the spiritual abyss. Through party fanaticism, apathy, cowardice, fashion, base self-interest, and vile ambition, those who bow to Communism in the Free World close their eyes and stop their ears in order not to see and hear the terrible sufferings of martyrs hemmed in behind the Iron Curtain. When a publication such as *Catacombes* denounces them, these so-called advanced minds insult the publication and not the torturers.

This infamy cannot last forever. It will only be an episode in history. Future generations will pronounce a judgment upon Communism identical to the one our generation drew up for the executioners of Callas. Those who court Communism may be sure that in that future judgment they will appear as savages—as primitive, narrow-minded, and cruel as the judge that sentenced Callas to have his limbs pulverized. *Catacombes*, in contrast, will be considered the ensign of free man against the tyrants of the twentieth century.

—Suzanne Labin

(AYAYA)

13. *Methods of Degradation and Torture*

Brainwashing

The Communists have used many diabolic procedures, inhuman methods, "techniques of degradation" (to use the phrase of Gabriel Marcel), in order to abolish Christian thought, break the dignity and freedom of man, and reduce believers "to the condition of slaves and accomplices." One of the most monstrous of these despicable techniques is surely that of brainwashing.

Take the conclusive example of Red China, where the thought of Mao Tse-tung is supreme. Two Maoist phrases amply illuminate the problem: *"Wipe away all the old myths, free our spirit."*

On the emotional and intellectual levels, the cult of Mao was to replace once and for all the worship of Jesus and of any other deity. "The omnipresence of Mao Tse-tung was oppressive," Anthony Grey tells us in his book *Hostage in Peking*. "Every morning the guards woke me singing 'The East is Red!' the song that proclaims that 'China has given birth to Mao; he is the great savior of the people.' Then they began at once to read the famous little red book that everyone always carries. The chief guard exalted Mao, 'the great educator, the great chief, the supreme commander, the great pilot.' Then, he recited a short phrase that I ended up knowing by heart in Chinese and which means: 'Chairman Mao is the master who instructs us.' Lined up in two rows, eyes fixed religiously on the idol's portrait, all his fellow-guards chanted the same words after him. Then came sessions devoted to what they called 'the study of Mao's thought,' sessions that lasted all day and frequently extended until late evening."

The missionary priest Dries Van Coillie has the same memories of his imprisonment in China. He is the author of the disturbing testimony: "J'ai subi le lavage de cerveau" ("I Suffered Brainwashing"). To make him confess his crimes of "dirty imperialism," he was arrested, tortured, threatened, handcuffed, forced to stay awake a long time either standing or squatting, spit upon by prison "chums," struck with crushing blows on the chin, chest, and arms, and constantly exposed to the penetrating, nauseating sound of the loudspeakers: "The skies of the new China are clear-blue./The people of the new China breathe joy and happiness!" He had to listen continually to the guard of the inner court humming "The East is red—the sun is rising/China possesses a Mao Tse-tung/He is our life—he is our sun . . ." "That is their method," Van Coillie tells us: "Dull a man's mind, wear out his body and moral resistance, take away his means of defense," that is, bring him to the denial of his faith, to the abolishing of his human personality.

Another terrible yet convincing experience must not be overlooked: that of the missionary Clifford, author of the book *Facing my Enemies,* during his thirty-six months (1953-1956) in Maoist prisons. In his interview with French journalist Pierre Darcourt at the National University of Taiwan, Father Clifford emphasized the scientific technique of brainwashing as "an ingenious blend of practical psychology, Marxist philosophy, and force," that consists "above all, in breaking the will of the victim":

"In Communist China, Pavlov's theory, which at first was only a physiological study of animal behavior, has become the scientific foundation for human behavior. The use of the technique of 'conditioned reflexes' is found in all stages of brainwashing. The judges, the police, and the guards continually use threats of death and promises of pardon. They apportion violence, gentleness, cruelty, fury and kindness so effectively that the prisoner ends up not knowing what to expect . . .

"Relying on the results of these experiments, the Communist technicians decided that brainwashing was possible only through isolating the victims from all outside life. It is not so much imprisonment that weighs so heavily on shoulders of men, but rather the crushing feeling of not being able to escape from constant pressure . . ."

Father Clifford's decisive judgment is that "the victory of the man in chains is possible only under one condition: the complete, absolute, final refusal to cooperate, to agree, to submit. If he gives in one time, he is finished."

—Guy Serveux

Unveiling His Crimes

Those interminable days of sitting were spent, then keeping absolute silence in the regret of one's "sins" or for others drawing up endless letters of confession, or else discussing together the same old subject suggested fortnightly by the official prison radio . . . After listening religiously for two hours to this complete nonsense, we had to spend several days under supervision, three hours in the morning and five in the evening, in collective meditation upon the following points, always the same:

1. We must in total sincerity unveil all our crimes, even the most hidden, before the government of the people. The government knows them already, but wants proof of our loyalty. Anyone who hides anything will be, if not shot to death, at least kept locked up for life. Those who already have written an incomplete letter of confession and hesitate to make new admissions may be sure that the government will not grant them freedom until further information is forthcoming.

2. Each one must then become acutely conscious of his guilt. He will not be received by the people until he has shown profound regret for his errors.

3. As infallible proof of his contrition, each criminal must redeem himself by denouncing his accomplices, even though they be his closest relatives or most intimate friends. He will then obtain the "generous pardon of the government." . . .

Many wretched prisoners were torn between these two alternatives: either confess everything, or else conceal what the police perhaps does not know. In the first case, did they not risk being sent to the firing squad, despite the repeated promises of the government? In the second case, if the judges discovered their hidden crimes, wouldn't they be, if not shot almost immediately, at the very least be condemned to life imprisonment?

Since each convict had to "win merits" at the expense of his fellows, the poor "obstinate one" was exhorted for long hours by one or the other of his companions until, at nerves' end, he had decided to "spit it all out." Thus within three months one young workman confessed one after the other four murders and one rape.

"I am happy now," he told me. "The people's government is good: it is going to set me free. Long ago I was a Buddhist, but when my wife informed the police of my crimes and I was arrested, I—from the first hearing and in response to the judge's insistence—abandoned my religion. You too must do the same. Simply apostatize, and you will be set free." Another man spent hours proving to me the economic imperialism of America and of Wall Street bankers. And I was continually pressured to inform against the other priests.

"This morning," a fellow prisoner said to me one day, "I accused my father and my older brother. Why don't you silence your scruples and turn in the names of the enemies of the people!"

—Jean de Leffe
"Chrétiens dans les prisons de Mao"
("Christians in Mao's Prisons")

"Confession Cure" in Rumania

M. M., a student at the Faculty of Letters in Bucharest, was subjected to the following morally crushing trial. After all kinds of cruelty and beatings, his body had become almost insensible when struck; he was then forced to stretch out in the middle of the room. Seventeen students, subjected to the same confession cure, were forced one after the other, beginning with the most stubborn (the real "bandits") to lie on top of him. The leader then climbed on top of them all. Crushed by all that weight, the student was worn out. His abdominal muscles gave way under the pressure, and all that they kept him from evacuating in the toilet was released into the cell.

What followed this sinister incident borders on lunacy. Under the pretext that he had soiled the room and his clothes, which could not be washed during off hours, the wretched student was forced to clean his trousers with his mouth. His refusal to submit to an order of such beastliness infuriated the leader. They crushed his fingers with sticks and trampled on him; when he fainted, they awoke him with a bucket of cold water, the water they had refused to give him for washing his clothes. They pounded his head on the floor and against the wall, they dragged him across the floor by his feet until the blood started to pour from his mouth. Finally he gave in to their demands . . .

A. O., a student at the Faculty of Theology, one of the most "fanatic" mystics (believers) in the Pitesti prison, was forced to do his business in a mess-tin and then was given food in the same dish without washing it first. What he had to endure until his resistance and repulsion were overcome is beyond description. In the end he had to give in and eat . . .

By means of cruel torture, the convicts were made to forsake their faith, to deny God and especially Jesus Christ . . . To erase the least trace of respect for holy things, ritual parodies of Christian practices of all kinds were organized. Theology students had to modify the texts of prayers, substituting lewd words for religious terms.

Holy Week and Easter were choice occasions when the Organization of Communist Convicts went "all out." The ones "rehabilitated" often organized—sometimes on their own initiative—religious masquerades to make fun of Jesus. The scene related here took place at Easter 1950 in a cell for hard-labor convicts.

With several sheets and white shirts the "robe of Christ" (as the students called it) was improvised. From a piece of soap that was used to write declarations, a male genital organ was shaped. Then a

theology student was forced to tie this around his neck with a string.
The student represented Christ. He was walked around the room
while beaten with a broomstick to symbolize Golgotha, and finally
was made to stop near the window. Then all the students one after
the other were forced to pass in front of him, bow, and kiss the piece
of soap, declaring, "I bow in homage to your omnipotence . . . you
are the only true master of those who believe . . ."

There was one person, a mere high school student, who refused to
perform the sacrilege. He was treated savagely for hours to make
him act like the others, and fainted several times from blows with a
stick, but he did not give in. The "therapists" admitted defeat, although no one ever knew just why they quit. Did the boy's tender
age evoke in the arid and wretched souls of the torturers a drop of
pity? More surprising still is that this was the only time a demand
was not obeyed.

The one who reported this to me shared the same cell with B. and
participated as a victim in the sacrilege. I asked him what he felt
when he saw one younger and less educated than he resist and stal-
wartly refuse to the end. "At first," he said, "I felt pity for him because of the tortures they were inflicting, then a sort of irritation in
seeing him so intractable, and finally shame and self-hate. But I also
experienced a real shock to find myself feeling this way. If the one
who had betrayed me and who was still part of the cell group had
known what I was thinking then, he would have torn me to pieces."
"How could he ever know," I asked him, "since this went on in your
thoughts?" "But all he had to do was to put me in confession status
and demand that I disclose what I was thinking when B. so obsti-
nately refused. I am sure that in the end I would have told everything."

—D. Bacou
"Pitesti, Center for the Re-education of Students"
Translated from the Rumanian into French by J. G.

"The Torturers in White"

Some physicians in the service of the secret police do not conceal
the object of treatment they inflict upon their patients. The goal
is simple: reduce all "opponents" to ideological and political conformity no matter where they come from, no matter who they are.
"You are hospitalized for your political ideas," they admit to those
who demand their democratic freedoms or who protest against

the invasion of Czechoslovakia. "We are treating your ideas, it's because of them that you are here. Otherwise you are in good health. When you are cured of your political ideas, you will be set free."

The *Chronicle* of June 1970 declared: "It is difficult to state precisely the number of cases where the diagnosis is justified on medical and scientific grounds. Experience shows that each decision is made at K.G.B. level. It's up to Professor Lunts to form a medical conclusion."

The same organ gave several more details about the treatments inflicted on the nonconformists in special asylums: "At first they are locked up with the mentally ill and even the raving insane. If they do not give in and renounce their convictions, the doctors subject them to physical torture, injecting them with huge doses of aminasine and sulphasine, which cause depressive shock and other serious physical reactions . . . Sulphasine raises one's temperature to 40° C and causes extreme weakening, articular rheumatism, violent headaches, and pain in the places where the injections are given. In ordinary medical practice this drug is used as a last resort, in cases of extreme distraction. Intramuscular injections of aminasin prevent the sulphasine from dissolving and cause very painful abscesses that must be surgically lanced.

When the patient is not docile enough, the hospital assistants wrap him from head to toe in wet bandages so tightly that he can barely breathe. When the bandages begin to dry, the pain becomes intolerable. An attendant checks the person's pulse in order to loosen the bindings and prevent death. By way of punishment recalcitrant prisoners are tied to their beds for three consecutive days. Not one bit of sanitary care is provided. The miserable patient is not allowed to go to the toilet and is left to bathe in his excrement.

—André Martin
"Enterrés vivants dans les hopitaux-
prisons soviétiques"
"Buried Alive in the Soviet Hospital-Prisons"

Terror

All the governments of satellite countries of the U.S.S.R. (except Poland) use imprisonment, arrest, force, and threats in an effort to bring the young to their senses. This technique was brutally used in Hungary. On February 28, 1957, Magda Jorobo, Assistant Minister of National Education, declared before a general meeting of educators: "Members of our police units must, from time to time, show up in our schools." From February 9 on, teachers in a large secondary school were ordered to attend a course set up by the militia on "how to treat counter-revolutionary conduct among children." And the day before, a Hungarian newspaper had written: "It is necessary to take some children away from their families because relationship between parents and children has deteriorated." The plan was to place children in "children's towns where they can grow up mentally healthy and where they are taught socialism, patriotism, and discipline in a socialist atmosphere." The East German authorities would thus have received groups of several hundred Hungarian children.

Terror is also used to make people avoid visitors and thus facilitate propaganda. A Chinese man from Tien-Tsin confides: "Even among ourselves we don't dare discuss public affairs for fear of being denounced during a campaign of appraisal and self-appraisal. How then can a foreigner expect us to tell him the truth?"

When the enemy can add physical stress to moral weakening by undernourishment and hard labor, as in concentration camps, he accelerates the disintegration process since, for the materialists, "the spirit is but an offshoot of matter." Cardinal Mindzenty is one example. During his trial in Hungary, open to newsmen, he confessed everything the jailers desired; he had had a real personality change. And during the Korean War, eighteen American officers, one of whom was a colonel from the Pacific headquarters, were taken prisoner by the Chinese Communists and brought together without any physical force. At the end of several weeks of conferences, so-called free discussions and political re-education, all of the officers gave written testimony to their country's use of germ warfare. The group, psychically "disintegrated," had "undergone brainwashing and had been conquered." During the trial that followed in America, Professor Merloo, a Dutch psychologist summoned to testify, could say to the judges: "Sirs, if you had been in their place, no doubt you too would have signed."

—Colonel André Bruge
"Le poison rouge"
("Red Poison")

Lenin, the Instigator

Of course, we know by whom and why this general assault against the Russian church was organized. The instigator was none other than Lenin himself, as proven by an unedited letter published by the periodical *The Orthodox Messenger* in Paris in April 1970. We shall give a few significant excerpts: "For us . . . the present moment [in the decisive battle against the church] does not only appear particularly favorable but also unique. We can almost certainly beat the enemy thoroughly and secure an unassailable position for many decades. Now is the time to carry out the confiscation of the church's treasures with a last burst of power and without pity. For now, in the regions suffering from famine, cannibalism is taking place and hundreds, if not thousands of bodies lie strewn along the roads. . . . Without such a basis no government action in general, no economic profit in particular, and especially no defense of our positions in Genoa are possible . . . It is only now that we can achieve this [the seizure] with success . . . In conjunction with the famine we will crush the reactionary clergy as quickly as possible and without a trace of pity . . .

"The more representatives of the bourgeoisie and of the reactionary clergy that we succeed in shooting under this pretext, the better. Now is the crucial time to educate that world in such a way that for several decades, no one will have the courage even to think of opposition."

—Nikolai Grekov

A Plan for Psychical and Physical Liquidation

. . . Our situation is very difficult. We are here in the "jaws of the lion" of Cuba. All of us, political prisoners of Boniato, are presently subjected to the most brutal and most inhuman plan for physical extermination that America has known in all its history. For two years now we have suffered from total isolation, in cells where the windows and doors are hermetically sealed with steel plates. The total lack of light makes many of us semiblind. I write you this letter while lying stretched out on the floor, by the faint light coming through the crack at the bottom of the door . . .

"There are men here whom, from all evidence, one cannot possibly consider alive. They are specters. The government promised to reduce us to tatters with this type of prison in order to punish us for our decision not to be rehabilitated . . . It has already succeeded . . . we are already tatters, never again physically able to become men.

Many of us will die here. We are subjected to a scientific plan of psychical and physical liquidation, directed by Czechoslovakian doctors and Cuban and Russian Communists. They carry out biological experiments on us, they watch us constantly, they subject us to various stimuli.

—Letter from a political prisoner in Cuba

Annihilation

Then came the execution. I could only hear. I couldn't see very clearly. "Ten times, give it to him ten times!" Give what? I didn't know. A pause . . . to me interminable . . . then, as though by means of a pump with a tube inserted in the mouth, they seemed to be sucking the air from his lungs. "One." Then air forced into his lungs. His whole chest seemed to scream and then to crack, hoarsely. Again they sucked out the air. "Two." Could the man breathe? Did he try to breathe? What a horrible sound comes from all that vocal tubing! More pressure. Suction. "Three." The noise has deadened already, is no longer discordant. Unconscious already? Suction. "Four." Suction, pressure. "Five." It was no longer a human chest, it was a mechanical pump, lifeless. "Ten times!" they had said. They didn't finish.

"The curious guards went away in silence. The excitement was over. His course was finished. His liberation was complete.

—Gabriel Brossard
"Il fut un hôte du camarade Mao"
("He Was a Guest of Comrade Mao")

Murderers of Women!

At ten o'clock, two thousand prisoners stood on the main square of the camp, covered by machine guns. Naplouef and his men arrived, each holding a large police dog trained to kill.

Ten women, frail and thin, emerged from their prison. The convicts watched as they moved toward the center of the square, barefoot and dressed in long gowns. "Butchers! Women killers!" they yelled. Naplouef screamed back, "Silence, you scoundrels, or we'll shoot," then approached the nuns: "Citizens, this is my last warning. Sign, or you will be changed to blocks of ice in twenty minutes."

The two thousand convicts waited for the answer . . . "We refuse, our conscience does not permit it!"

"Good," Naplouef retorted, "we have time." He lit a cigarette. The sisters knelt on the snow and recited the rosary out loud. A quarter of an hour, a half hour passed by; the sisters continued to kneel in prayer.

Naplouef, unable to stand it any longer, cried out: "If you do not sign in five minutes, we will loose the dogs on you and they will tear you to pieces." With a loud voice, the sisters began to sing the Creed. Naplouef, in blazing fury, released the dogs. Barking ferociously, they bolted toward the sisters, who continued to sing. The prisoners were frozen in terror. Suddenly the animals, six feet away and set to attack, stopped and quietly lay down on the snow like sheep.

Then an immense clamor rose from the ranks of the prisoners, like a great cry of deliverance: "Miracle! Miracle! Praise to the heroic sisters! Shame on the butchers!" And the Ukrainians sang out their hymn, "O great God, the only God . . ."

Naplouef turned beet-red, then a deathly white. Drunk with repressed, powerless rage, he had the convicts break rank and sent them and the sisters to their barracks.

—"Stella Maris," Fribourg

◊◊◊

Death a Consequence of Violence

In an act signed on July 19 and 20, 1972 by twenty-three witnesses from the village of Volontirovka, Soviet Socialist Republic of Moldavia, can be read the following staggering lines concerning the tragic death of a young believer, Ivan Moiseiev:

"We the undersigned are witnesses to the fact that the condition of the body of Moiseiev Ivan Vasilievich, born in 1952, returned from military unit 61968 'T' in Kerch, does not confirm the diagnosis in the certificate of death indicating 'natural asphyxiation by drowning' (as stated in the rather illegible certificate). We affirm that death was the result of premeditated violence. We confirm this with photographs and documents: the heart was pierced through six times, the legs and head badly beaten, the chest burned."

The following information was given by Moiseiev himself (recorded on tape) during his leave from June 2 to June 12, 1972:

(1) December 1970. In Staryi Krym (Ancient Crimea): "No rest, day or night. Am summoned as often as fifteen times a day by different offices in order to make me change my convictions."

(2) Kerch: "Did not feed me for five days, then asked me: 'Well, have you changed your convictions?' "

(3) City of Kerch: "Stayed outdoors at night for five hours at 25 to 30 degrees below zero, in summer uniform, then a whole night. Then several nights. This lasted two weeks."

(4) "In January 1971, after brainwashing at the regiment in Kerch, they put me in a special truck for prisoners and sent me toward Sverdlovsk. First they placed me in a special cell by myself, then took me through a series of five other special cells for specialized tortures.

"The first cell had a cot, where I could lie down.

"Second cell, a small one, where I could stand up or sit on a bench.

"Third cell, where cold water showered continually from the ceiling. I could stand up.

"Fourth cell—a cold room, the walls of a refrigerator, frozen to the limit.

"Fifth cell, torture chamber, compression of the body, where they dressed me in a special rubber suit that they pumped up with air; they squeezed my whole body by increasing the pressure, and each time they asked me: 'Well, have you changed your convictions? If not, you will stay here seven years.' I declared: 'If such is the will of God, I will stay here seven years. If not, tomorrow you will stop the tortures.' This lasted twelve days, then I was brought back to Kerch."

—Bulletin No. 9 of the Council of
Relatives of E.C.B. Prisoners in the U.S.S.R.)

The Power Parade

. . . Armies
of butchers, of sbirros
pass, their pride rocking
in saddles of heroes;
pass also rocking
in sunlight, on horseback
rings of enslavement
performing;
handcuffs of iron glitter
victorious;
stakes, pales
triumphant
reclaiming
with cry and hue
their due.

The whip passes by
a lash in the wind
a dread to the world;
cudgel and bludgeon
swaying their banners
in rhythm to songs
in concert
with rope and guillotine
famous

assassin
scion of darkness and hatred;
in sumptuous array
an assortment
of flasks
perverse
with pitiless poison
pass;
then the pompous faun
the demi-god
the electric chair
of America.

Fetters pass by
scraping the ground
with nail-studded soles;
prison bars
gnash their teeth;
wheel-rims screech
their flagrant proofs;
latches and bolts
shout their feats to the mob;
hermetic wagons;
and with piercing cries
brutal bayonets
and secret-blade daggers.

At the rear, as prize
of the tyrant of fates
in ponderous dance pass by
chains
massive chains
dragging huge helmets
wielding coercion for parley

with vanity
bulging
convulsing
the city
bulging with self
with hate
with hard passion
they clank their sinister torture
and clasp in their links
bones, coffins, putrescence
in their armors of steel
carnage
barely quenched.
                              —Sergiu Grossu

14. *To Die for Christ*

A political figure at the beginning of the century answered someone
who claimed to have founded a new religion: *"Go then, and die on
the cross!"*

A quip, no doubt, but a significant one.

Nevertheless an objection soon arises: Is martyrdom really proof
for the truth of the faith?

How many certainly have given their lives, freely or by force, for
all kinds of ideals besides the Christian faith. Certainly . . . one may
die for many reasons, "but to die for the One who died for me in the
mystery of God: this exchange is unique and marks the unique character of Christian truth and life."

Saint Thomas Aquinas had already replied to this objection in
treating the question as to whether martyrdom is an act of the highest perfection.

To die as a martyr is certainly not. But if we consider the motive—
self-emptying love—it is a different matter. For then we no longer
consider only the subjective feelings of the one who offers himself
and the moral seriousness of testimony and commitment (which may
be as great in circumstances besides martyrdom), but also the object
that evokes such an offering and gives it its value. Then we may say
with Aquinas that "martyrdom more than any other virtuous act is
the greatest proof of love's perfection."

We all no doubt recall among the martyrs of the fifth [third] century the names of two very young women, Perpetua et Felicity, as well as the conversation between the latter and her jailer, while she was in labor and cried out in pain. The jailer said to her: "You complain? What will you do before the beasts?"

"*Today,*" she answered, "it is I who suffer; there, there will be in me someone who will suffer for me, because I, I shall suffer for him. . . "

That is a major statement of Christian anthropology. Indeed, in baptism our being becomes as though assumed by the Person of the incarnate Word. It is he who suffers through the Christian in the hour of martyrdom: the glorious Christ, the "standing" Christ whom Saint Stephen saw when he was being stoned by the Jews.

The martyrdom of Stephen was the beginning of the first expansion of the Church.

And today the sufferings endured, the persecutions undergone, the blood ever shed for Christ and his Church are the source of renewal for the Christian faith in the countries under Communist domination.

—Father Pierre Molin

Fate of the Bishops

We mention in the following lines the fate of fifty-two Russian bishops, although from 1927 to 1946 the number of persecuted or martyred bishops is much more than two hundred.

The unexpected testimony of a former Chekist informs us, for example, that in the concentration camps in Perm, there were in 1945 ten bishops, one of whom was set free under stated conditions.

The fate of at least two hundred bishops is unknown to us, but we may judge that some have already perished and that those who still live are dying in prisons and deportation camps.

—Archpriest M. Polsky

15. *List of Christian Martyrs*

Members of the Russian Episcopate, Victims of Religious Persecution

Vladimir (Bogoyavlensky), metropolitan of Kiev, killed January 25, 1918.

Andronic (Nikolsky), archbishop of Perm, killed June 4, 1918.

Hermogen (Dolganov), archbishop of Tobolsk, drowned June 19, 1918.

Basil (Bogoyavlensky), archbishop of Chernigov, shot in Perm.

Ephrem (Kuznetsov), archbishop of Selenga, vicar in Transbaikalia, shot August 6, 1918.

Theophanus (Ilchensky), bishop of Selikamsk, drowned in the Kama river, December 11, 1918.

Isidor (Kolokov), bishop of Mikhailov, vicar of Novgorod, killed in Samara (impaled on a stake, they say) about the same time as the above.

Ambrosius (Gudko), bishop of Sarapul, vicarage of Viatsky, stabbed to death with a bayonet in Sviyaga.

Mitrophan (Krasnopolsky), archbishop of Astrakhan, thrown from a high wall to his death.

Leontii (Vimpfen), bishop of Enotai, vicar of Astrakhan, killed and thrown into a pit. Burial prohibited.

Platon (Kulbush), bishop of Revel, killed in Iuriev, January 14, 1919.

Tikhon, archbishop of Voronej, who was in the Saint-Metrophane Monastery, hanged in the church in December 1919 at the Royal Portals that separate the altar from the rest of the sanctuary.

Joakim (Levitsky), archbishop of Njini-Novgorod, who had come to the Crimea, killed in his residence at Simferopol.

Nicodemus (Kononov), bishop of Belgorod, shot to death in 1918 at Christmastime.

Macarius (Gnevushev), bishop of Viazma, killed.

Laurence (Kniazev), bishop of Balakhnin, vicar of Nijni-Novgorod, killed.

Pimen, bishop of Viernenski, vicar of Turkestan, killed.

Herman, bishop of Kamyshin, shot to death as hostage in Saratov, after the attempt upon Lenin's life in 1918.

Varsanuphii (Vikhvelin), bishop of Kirillov, vicar of Novgorod, killed.

Justin, archbishop of Omsk and of Pavlogradka, died in prison in March 1920.

Methodius, bishop of Petropavlovsk, died in the spring of 1921 from a bayonet wound in the chest into which the executioners afterwards thrust a cross.

Simon (Shleev), bishop of Ufa, shot in his home, June 6, 1921.

Nazarius, metropolitan of Kutaisii, pulled from his sickbed and shot.

Benjamin (Kazansky), metropolitan of Petrograd, shot August 12, 1922.

Philaret, bishop of Kostroma, deported to the province of Arkhangelsk, where he died from exposure in 1922.

Seraphim, bishop of Eloturovsk in the diocese of Tobolsk, deported to Perm, where he died around 1925.

Ieropheus (Afonik), bishop of Veliky Ustiug, vicar of Vologda, shot during his arrest in May 1928, which the people opposed.

Peter (Zverev), archbishop of Voronij, died in the camp of Solovki in 1929.

Hilarion (Troitskyo), archbishop, vicar of the diocese of Moscow, died in prison in Petrograd in 1929.

Sergius, bishop of Efremovo, shot in 1929 at Buzuluk.

Seraphim (Meshcheriakov), metropolitan of the Caucasus, shot in prison at Rostov-on-Don in 1932.

Athanase (Sakharov), archbishop of Starobielski, shot in the prison in 1932.

Agapit (Vishmevsky), archbishop of Ekaterinoslav, died in prison.

Alexander (Belozerovo), archbishop, died in prison in Rostov in 1932.

Ambrosius (Poliansky), archbishop of Podolsk, deported, died en route in the "steppe of hunger" in the Kazakstan in 1934.

Philip (Gumilevsky), bishop, shot in prison at Krasnoyarsk in 1934 for not having recognized the agreement that Metropolitan Sergius made with the Soviets in the name of the church.

Arsen (Zhadanovsky), archbishop of Serpukhoo, shot in June 1935.

Damascinus (Tzedrik), bishop of Glukhov, vicar of Chernigov, died in Siberia in 1935.

Peter (Poliansky), metropolitan of Krutitsy, died in deportation in 1936.

Bartholomew (Remov), bishop and vicar of Moscow, shot June 26, 1936.

Anatole (Grisiuk), metropolitan of Odessa, died in captivity in 1938.

Joseph (Petrovykh), metropolitan of Petrograd, shot toward the end of 1938 for his moral support of the itinerant underground priests of the hidden Church of the Catacombs.

Dimitry (Liubimov), archbishop of Gdovsk, shot in 1938 for the same reason.

Alexis, vicar and bishop of Petrograd, shot in 1938 for the same reason.

Seraphim, bishop, shot at Aktyubinsk in 1938.

Pitirim (Krylov), archbishop, vicar in Moscow, former convict at Solovki, shot in 1938.

Juvenal (Maslovsky), archbishop of Riazan, shot in 1938.

Nikon (Purlevsky), bishop of Belgorod, shot in 1938.

Nikon (Lebedev), bishop, shot in 1938.

Nicandre (Phenomenov), metropolitan of Odessa, died in deportation.

Arsen (Stadnitsky), metropolitan of Novgorod, died in deportation in 1936.

Cyril (Smirnov), metropolitan of Kazan, died in deportation in 1936.

Each Must Choose His God

Two religions, two gods, confront each other today:
Christianity: God become man.
Anti-Christianity: Man become god.
God-become-man promises to men a kingdom that is not of this world. His weapons are poverty, weakness, love, his apostles, the martyrs.
The man-become-god promises to men the rule of this world.
His weapons are the power of falsehood, of violence, of hate.
His zealots, tyrants and police . . .
Each must choose his God.

—Marie Noel

The Three Virtues

Martyrdom is a sacramental act realized in privileged souls as a charisma, as a "grace of graces," whose supernatural effects spill to the entire community of the children of God. Absolute faith in Jesus, complete hope in the Promise, love raised to self-oblation. The three divine virtues are most fully realized in martyrdom. In the bloody sacrifice the whole Christian experience, moral and mystical, finds its most perfect expression.

—Daniel-Rops

"When the world will no longer see my body . . ."
—Beda Tsang

Father Beda Tsang, born May 17, 1905 in An T'ing, near Shanghai, received his doctorate from the Sorbonne. He was professor of litera-

ture and rector of Saint Ignatius College in Shanghai and dean of the
department of Sinology. Through his zeal, piety, and doctrinal beliefs,
he exercised a great influence upon youth and on the Legion of Mary.

August 9, 1951, about 1:30 P.M., policemen appeared at the re-
creation hall of the Fathers of Zikawei, where Father Tsang was playing chess with his colleagues. They asked to speak with him in the
hall. He went out and after a short exchange of words invited them
to follow him to his room. He took the small package that he had
prepared in advance and headed toward the car waiting for him outside. He climbed in and, smiling, waved for the last time to those
who had accompanied him to the door. . . .

The police did not announce the arrest. But before nightfall all the
Christians knew about it. His pupils and all the Catholic students
were greatly upset and wept. Not a week had passed before the Communists were announcing the approaching return of Father Tsang:
"He will make a public confession," they said, "and become head of
the patriotic church."

But Father Tsang still did not come back. He was kept awake and
subjected to all kinds of physical and moral tortures.

The Communists wanted him to appear before a large popular
tribunal. It was too late. His strength was declining rapidly, while he
repeated over and over: "Jesus, Mary, Joseph, save me!"

On October 30, they carried him to the prison hospital. He did not
regain consciousness, and on November 11, 1951, at 8:00 A.M., he
returned his soul to God.

—André Jany
"Les torturés de la Chine"
("The Tortured of China")

16. *The Martyrdom of Moiseiev*

The Council of Relatives of Prisoners of the Evangelical Christian-
Baptist Prisoners has received many documents, photographs, letters,
tapes, and eyewitness accounts concerning the death of a young
Christian, our dear brother Ivan Moiseiev.

This revolting despotic act, which we relate to you with deep sorrow, took place not in the Barnaul prison, as in the case of Nicolay
Khmara in 1964, but in the ranks of the Soviet army. As the documents prove, the secret hand of the murderer-torturers is the same
in both cases.

The reason for this report is not to stir up anger or revolt against the persecutors of Christ's Church in our country or against the atheists who support them, but first of all to call them to repentance (Ps. 2:10-12) and to help them understand that, unless they repent, they will have to appear before the Supreme Judge who will call them to account for all the innocent blood shed in our country and will render justice to each according to his works (Matthew 23: 32-33, 35).

Secondly, the Council of Prisoners' Relatives and the relatives of brother Vanya Moiseiev desire and pray to God that this death may urge many children of God, and all Christian young people, to witness more courageously to a world that hastens to its doom—of salvation through Christ . . . . Thus, the last sermon of the faithful child of God acquires a special power not only by the grace of the Holy Spirit but also by the blood of the martyrs for the Gospel.

Several facts concerning the execution of brother Vanya, which had been arranged beforehand, remain hidden to us, but for God nothing is secret that will not come into the open. And we believe that in the near future He will unveil for us everything that can still contribute to his glory and to the salvation of the souls that witnessed the death of the young preacher Ivan Moiseiev. It is the immutable law of spiritual warfare: the death of the first martyr—Stephen, a Christian—brought forth fruit a hundredfold for the Kingdom of God by inciting to the service of Christ, Saul the persecutor.

Before the end of his last military leave, brother Vanya agreed to be photographed, and said: "Remember me by this photo. As for me, I will never see it." This courageous warrior for Christ looks at us from the photo taken eight days before his tragic death. And next to it we have the photograph of his lifeless body carrying the marks of cruel tortures inflicted upon him by his executioners in order to wrest an unshakable faith in God Almighty from his heart. Thanks be to God, they could not hurt his soul. He died as a Christian. He died for Christ. He died for his church. He died carrying high the banner of Christian youth. By this glorious death, Jesus Christ crucified has again overcome the world, overcome our persecutors. They can wash away their shame only by the tears of deep repentance and by the blood of Christ. May the eyes of many Christians be opened to see this victory and may it stimulate them, by the grace of the Holy Spirit, to courageous preaching of the Word of God.

—The Council of Relatives of E.C.B. Prisoners
in the U.S.S.R.
Bulletin No. 9, July 1972

78

Cruelty of the Benefactors

You have divided the people into enemy camps and have thrown them into a fratricidal war of a cruelty unknown up to now. The love of Christ you have openly replaced with hatred, and under the guise of peace you have openly stirred up the class struggle . . .

No one feels safe; all live in constant terror of investigation, pillage, expulsion, arrest, execution . . . Bishops, priests, monks, nuns—innocent in every respect—accused wholesale of very general, vague counterrevolutionary action . . .

Is this not the height of useless cruelty on the part of those who call themselves the benefactors of humanity? . . .

Yes, we live in a terrible period of your reign, which will not be soon erased from the soul of the people, where the image of God has been obscured to imprint the image of the Beast.
Nov. 17, 1918

—Patriarch Tikhon

Death in a Soviet Camp

Afonin, Ivan Alexeevich, aged 44, presbyter of an E.C.B. church, died on November 22, 1969 in a camp in the Tula Oblast. A second-class invalid, suffering from both heart disease and rheumatism, he was illegally employed in work, where he died. Both we and his family wrote you concerning his severe condition; we warned you, but it was in vain. You took our letters lightly and thus tore out the heart of his widow and of his nine children, six of whom are very young. We discovered that the circumstances leading to his death were of a dubious nature: deprivation of his diet prescribed for a second-class invalid and the threats of the guards to let him "rot" in prison. Before the Most High God and all humanity, the death of brother Afonin will constantly cry out through the tears of the orphans and the sighs of the widow.

May the Lord forgive you for your neglect of our warnings which cost the death of an innocent man!

—Commission of the Council of Relatives of E.C.B.
Prisoners in the U.S.S.R

17. *May He Die of Hunger!*

The police knew very well that under their protection life was not rosy for me, but since, according to them, I was taking much too long in ridding them of myself, another plan was devised: to make me die of hunger.

For years I had not received any money from the West. The police knew this, since all the mail was meticulously censored. One day, however, my brother again sent me some money. On this occasion I went to the chief of police a dozen times. Finally, tired of straining my nerves and bowing to him, I said to him:

"Friend, I see you do not want to give me the money. I give it up. Do what you want with it."

And I went out. The matter was definitely settled. As long as I stayed in China, I heard nothing more about the money. Several years later, when after my sentence and expulsion I told my brother about it, he told me that the People's Government of China had sent it back to him.

The Communists, once more, had succeeded, but that was not enough for them. They knew I was supported by my parishioners. So they gave a warning in all the meetings that anyone who brought anything to the Catholic mission or helped it in another way would be considered guilty of hostile plotting against the state and liable to imprisonment.

My situation was becoming very serious, but God did not want me to die of hunger. A little while after the announcement was made, my maid came to me one day, very upset—as she often was at this time.

"Chennfu,"[1] she said, "Grandmother Li got in through the front gate with a big basket of soy beans."

I thought immediately: If a spy saw her, that's it, I'm caught.

"Dear Grandmother," I said. "You have been very rash. Think! A spy or a policeman may have seen you. If so, it is over for you, and I go to prison."

Firmly the old grandmother replied:

"Chennfu, prison or no prison, we Christians just cannot let you die of hunger: that is unthinkable. I pray you, take these beans."

What could I do before so much love?

[1]Priest (in Chinese)

"Come with me, dear Grandmother," I said. "Let's go to my room. We will be safer there than here in the hall."

Almost immediately the old woman began to cry.

"Chennfu, life is so hard," she said between sobs, "I don't know how much longer I can stand it."

Old Li's son carried the label of a reactionary. He had gone south with the last Nationalist troops and, since the mother had to expiate her son's serious crime, they had expropriated her, leaving only a small plot of ground that she herself had to cultivate, despite her seventy years. Who else could have done it for her anyway? No one was left. Her relatives would have nothing more to do with her, for fear that they too would be put on the black list.

"Chennfu, I don't know what will become of me. I have to leave my house, and I am so attached to it! But the Party needs it for its own end, so they are throwing me out. The Communists say that the house belongs to them, because my son, a reactionary and enemy of the state, has lost all rights to it."

Dear Gradmother Li was crying uncontrollably. I took her two hands in mine and tried to encourage her. I spoke words of comfort, well aware, of course, that that wasn't much. And yet, any comfort, even simply through words, soothes and lifts up, because behind us stands another comforter—Jesus Christ—who works much better than we do.

All of a sudden Grandmother Li pulled something from her pocket and held it out to me with both hands, according to Chinese politeness. I wondered what in the world could be in that little package. The wrapping was not very attractive: worthless straw paper.

"May I open it?" I asked.

"Of course, Chennfu, it's for you."

I opened the package. Inside the straw paper were a few pieces of candy of the kind one gives to children.

"Chennfu," said the old woman, seeing my astonished face, "I wanted to bring you a little bit of pleasure. I said to myself: times are so difficult for the chennfu! Don't we know that the Reds consider you their target? That is why I set apart enough from my meager resources to buy you a few pieces of candy and add a little sweetness to your hard life."

She went out and I was left alone. Before me were the beans, fruit of the work of her hands, and a few pieces of candy bought with the little money that, in view of her uncertain future, she could so well have used for herself: something of so little value in itself and yet more precious than gold and gems, because each bean and each piece of candy shone with that genuine Christian love that lives by sacrifice.

The Communists, in their hatred, wanted me to die of hunger, but Christian love preserved me.

—Alois Regenburger
"Tonnerre de Chine"
("Thunder of China")

The Martyrs

to Solzhenitsyn

Bears, tigers, lions
Spring from their deep den
And spectators cheer
As they appear

The Christians stand firm
Before the beasts of prey
From afar a song of joy
Surges toward the sky

Before the emperor's eyes
A dreadful hecatomb:
Women, old men, children fall
A holy harvest to their God.

—Dr. Felix Leon

4: The Cries of Silence

1. *From the Depths of Hell*

Believers in Communist countries beg for religious freedom. They extend chained hands to the Christians of the Free World; they send petitions to high authorities in the West. But alas, the majority of "brothers" in this Western world are preoccupied with their own problems and have no time to listen, to read, to discover and understand their neighbor who suffers so unjustly. "We are too busy, we have our own problems . . ." That line comes to mind, I've heard it many a time.

"Leave us alone, such things are out of date," people have said to me when I poured out my soul, telling them how countless Christians are enduring the most atrocious persecutions, simply for believing in Christ.

"What about it? . . . So the Christians send us petitions and letters. First of all, it's their problem; they accepted the system and only have to put up with it . . ."

It's apparently too complicated to understand "how" they have accepted the system. And we're tired of explaining it to people who pass so lightly over these pages of history, perhaps unparalleled anywhere.

Poor brother of the East! We no longer have time to see you, to hear you, and to understand the loneliness of your miserable life.

"You know," say Westerners, "we live moment by moment.

Life is short, we work for a comfortable existence . . . To each his own fate." Yes, that is the frank response. To each his own fate, here on earth. And then?

Our brothers who live in countries darkened by Satan appeal to you, to each one of you, who for them represent brothers from a bright and powerful world; they beseech you—though they don't know how their cries for relief affect you—to help them in this terrible battle against the powers of darkness! *"Send petitions to the embassies of our country! Ask them to give us religious freedom!"* These are the "alms" begged of you by hundreds of thousands of Christians pitilessly tortured.

They hope, by engaging your help, that the U.N., the World Council of Churches, the Vatican, and the Church in its entirety, will sense the support of the Christian populace, your support to all Christians, and will then engage in real, resolute action toward Communist authorities represented in the Western countries.

Pray for them! Your brothers count on your intercession!

Listen to the voice of the twentieth-century martyrs! Read their testimonies, their letters, their petitions!

Do not let yourselves be dragged along by the selfish mob; pause near the saints begging for love, begging for a bit of your heart . . .

—Nicole Valéry

2. Petitions of Persecuted Believers

To U.N. Secretary General Mr. U Thant, with copies to the U.N. Commission on Human Rights and to the President of the Council of Ministers of the U.S.S.R., A. N. Kosygin:

Analyzing the situation of E.C.B.[1] believers in the U.S.S.R., the Second Congress of Relatives of E.C.B. Prisoners is very concerned about the mockery of their most elementary rights, namely: (1) The free confession of faith in God; (2) The holding of prayer meetings; (3) Distribution of sacred books: Bibles, Gospels, and all other religious publications, among believers; and (4) The education of their children in the home according to their convictions and the basic laws of the country.

From a general survey of the situation from 1962 to 1970, the Con-

[1]Evangelical Christian-Baptist, the "dissidents" who do not accept compromise with the atheistic government.

gress declares that believers have not been able to exercise the above-mentioned human rights. The government has, during this time, resorted to complete oppression of believers and has replaced ideological warfare against religion with physical and administrative warfare, resulting in the condemnation of 524 E.C.B. ministers for confessing their faith. Eight ministers of the church have died in prison.

All 524 E.C.B. ministers were arrested and sentenced for the following acts:

(1) Preaching the Gospel among their fellow believers; (2) Open confession of faith in God; (3) Distribution of religious publications; (4) Participation in or attendance at E.C.B. prayer meetings; (5) Private religious education of children; (6) Opening their homes to E.C.B. fellow believers for prayer meetings; (7) Refusal to testify in court against the church and its ministers; (8) Refusal to establish a compromise with atheism and the official Baptist church which has forsaken the teaching of Christ.

During the last six months mass searches were made of believers' homes, and religious publications were confiscated: Bibles, Gospels, musical pieces, song books, albums, post cards, and religious books. This deprived believers completely of religious literature.

A new wave of persecutions breaks upon the Union of Churches.

This is the real situation of believers in the U.S.S.R.

We draw your attention once more to the iniquitous breaking up of the family of Sloboda Ivan Feodorovitch, by the Soviet government, in the Verkhnedvinsk District, Vitebsk Region, Belorussian Soviet Socialist Republic.

We demand once more that all possible measures of intervention be taken toward the Soviet government in order that all such constraints be brought to an end and that:

1. E.C.B. prisoners be set free through the abolishment of laws that go against the fundamental laws of the U.S.S.R.—Lenin's decree of January 1, 1918 on the separation of church and state and the Constitution of the U.S.S.R.—as well as the universal rights of man.

2. Children taken away because of religious training be given back to their parents;

3. Persecutions against the Council of E.C.B. Churches elected by the believers shall cease.

4. Confiscated homes be returned;

5. Religious publications be returned.

We demand that this letter be published as an official document of the U.N. and sent on for the judgment of world opinion.

This is our fifth letter. The first one was dated January 1, 1961; the second, June 5, 1967; the third, August 15, 1967; the fourth, August 11, 1968.

Respectfully yours,

Kiev   The Second Congress of Relatives of

Dec. 12, 1970   E.C.B. Prisoners in the U.S.S.R.

To Dr. Eugene Carson Blake

We were pleased to learn that on the fiftieth anniversary of the restoration of the Russian Patriarchate, our country warmly received representatives of churches of many countries in our capital. These had the opportunity to visit all the churches in Moscow—there are several dozen—and thus to verify religious worship there, which gave them the impression that believers had the same opportunities to practice their faith in all the cities. But this impression is false. Although there are many large churches, these are closed, and believers in certain cities have access only to small, hard-to-reach churches.

—Letter from the faithful in Gorki
May 1969

Rumanian Believers Address the Free World

We make known to Christians all over the world, and to world opinion, that in Rumania, a country counting hundreds of thousands of believers, even the remnant of cultural liberty is once again flagrantly violated.

Toward the latter half of 1970 a vast campaign of repression was released against religion and religious activities by the state authorities.

It began with the publication of a law forbidding any meeting of unofficial churches, any assembling of Christians, under the pretext of "laziness," "waste of time," etc. . . . Fines of fifteen hundred to two thousand lei[1] were levied upon many believers in the departments of Satu-Mare, Bistrita, T. Mures, Baia-Mare, Brasov, Bacau, Trg-Jiu, Galatz, northern Moldavia, etc.

[1]The approximate equivalent of twice the average monthly salary.

Note that, despite the official permission to function that the Baptist church of Baia-Mare possessed, it was subjected to the same penalties.

For six months after the said law was put into effect, sums of around 500,000 lei were extorted from believers. The persecutions continued and were intensified. Toward the end of 1972 Jacob Alecu of the city of Sibiu, a composer of religious music, was sentenced to eight years in prison. Everywhere in the country numerous places of worship for Christian-Baptists, Brethren, and Pentecostals were closed. In the towns of Dej, Lugoj, etc. such meeting places were demolished. Many pastors and preachers were removed from their offices. Youth activity in the church was limited. The authorities claimed to control the finances of the churches, even though the state had given nothing to the churches.

The year 1971 began with numerous searches in homes, during which many Bibles and hymn books as well as other religious works were confiscated.

The persecutions became more intense; in October 1971, the following pastors were arrested: Caraman Constantin, Rascol Victor, pastor to the gypsies, Mihai Carnel, former director of a Christian chorale, the brothers Tarnavski C. and Rascol Emmanuel,[2] etc.

We entreat believers the world over, international public opinion, and all men of good faith to unite their efforts with ours in bringing pressure upon the authorities, so that religious freedom in Rumania may be respected and all those who are imprisoned for their religious activities may be released.

—The Committee to Rescue the Persecuted and
Rumania, 1971   Inform World Opinion

A Petition

. . . There is in the Criminal Code of the S.S.R. of Lithuania an article that prescribes punishment for the persecution of believers, but this article is never carried out in practice. In 1970 the Department of People's Education of the Vilkaviskis District dismissed a teacher, O. Briliene, solely because she was a believer. For the same reason the regional government does not allow her to be hired in Vilkaviskis for any work whatsoever, not even as charwoman . . .

We entreat the Soviet government to grant us freedom of con-

[2]All these Christians have been set free. Cf. *Catacombes*, No. 6, p. 9.

science, which is guaranteed by the Constitution of the U.S.S.R., but has never really existed. We do not want fine words in the press and over the radio; we want the government to help us, the Catholics, to feel that we are fully citizens of the Soviet Union.

December 1971   —*Memorandum* signed by 17,054 representatives
January 1972   of Catholic Lithuanians

Petition of *The Christ Publications*

The document which we make public comes from *The Christ Publications*, of the Evangelical Baptist Church of Silence (E.C.B.) in the U.S.S.R. It reached the West through the underground. It was apparently printed on a machine built by the Christians of that church in their underground print shop.

To the President of the Council
of Ministers of the U.S.S.R., Mr. A. N. Kosygin:

For about ten years the Evangelical Baptist Christians (E.C.B.) have been totally deprived of religious literature. Official search has not been able to find any anywhere in our country. The state printing offices refuse to print it. The Church Council made a petition to you about this, but it was not answered. Consequently we felt obligated to carry out a printing method and to build a printing machine without the support of the state, in order to produce spititual, religious literature. Our efforts have been crowned with success.

The Christ Publications represent the cooperation of E.C.B. believers, who united to print and distribute Christian literature. The believers themselves support the work through voluntary contributions and also handle the distribution. The books are free. While we are well received by citizens, the organs of the government constantly expose us to persecutions, threats, repressions, though our activities are in no way detrimental to the interests of the state. One example from the last two years is that during a city distribution of Gospels and the book *Spiritual Songs*, representatives of the administration took from us, without a warrant, about 700 copies of these works.

We do not ask that you collaborate with us to produce this literature, which is necessary to believers, but we simply entreat you to stop hindering our work. We beg you to legalize the literature that carries the mark of *The Christ Publications*. We also ask that you clear the way for the organs of the state to return what has been confiscated. On our part we pledge to print only Christian literature of interest to the community, nothing else. We also pledge not to disclose our printing methods and the diagrams of our machines to anyone, no matter who it is.

To complete our request, we ask that you give believers the chance to enjoy the benefits of the rights guaranteed by the Constitution of the U.S.S.R. and by the Declaration of Human Rights. And we ask that you respond to the grievances of believing citizens of our homeland.
June 5, 1971

◖Ｙ◗◖Ｙ◗

Violence and Falsehood

"We shall be told: what can literature possibly do against the savage onslaught of violence? But let us not forget that violence does not live alone and is not capable of living alone: it is intimately related, by the tightest of natural bonds, to falsehood. Violence finds its only refuge in falsehood, falsehood its only support in violence. Any man who has chosen violence as his method must inexorably choose falsehood as his principle."

—A. Solzhenitsyn

◖Ｙ◗◖Ｙ◗

3. *The Story of Pavel Ritikov*

I greet you, dear friends of the Council of E.C.B. I am your brother in the Lord, Pavel T. Ritikov. I have been deprived of freedom for three years. My heart advises me to address myself to you, knowing that you are chosen by the Holy Spirit to protect the prisoners who have been condemned for loving God and trying to faithfully carry out his commandments, which flagrantly contradict the atheistic commandments of this world. As you know, I was falsely accused of capital crime. I spent seven months without trial in the prison of Voroshilograd, in a special dungeon with very dangerous prisoners— old offenders and militiamen accused of murder, whom they would stir up against me by promising premature release. I was often led from my dungeon to the chief's office where Major Anenko, member of the K.G.B. in Kiev, Major Krokin, member of the K.G.B. in Voroshilograd, and the propagandist Romashko, would press me to join them in secret work by saying: "If you consent to work, you will be freed; otherwise, we will sentence you to five years of prison, where you will rot, and if finally you are freed, we will invent such a tale as to turn all believers away from you." But I did not consent to become an apostate, a wolf in sheep's clothing. It's terrible to think of it—to be a believer and lead a traitor's life and under the order of atheists to undermine the Church. After seven months of mockeries, I was tried in private with Petchny in Krasnodon. The court was surrounded with militiamen. No one was allowed to enter; neither believers nor wives and children. We were not allowed to ask questions of the witnesses, who had been indoctrinated beforehand so that the lie invented by the examining magistrates Obramenko and Sivolopov would not be shown up. As we had no lawyer, we could not talk, and under this pretext they denied us the right of defense and wrote at the end of the protocol that we ourselves had refused to speak in our defense. The trial took place with doors open. Yes, the doors were open. But in the corridors, there was no one; the building was surrounded by militiamen, who roughly sent everyone away and kept the children from seeing their fathers for the last time. And although Petchny and I each have six children, we were sentenced to five years' loss of freedom.

After the trial they led me to the prison and once more to the chief's office, where the propagandist Romashko was. "What did I tell you," he exclaimed; "they will judge you in private and you will not be able to tell the believers what the K.G.B. is doing. During the trial I was sitting in the next room, which the judge entered from time to time to ask my advice, and it was according to my instructions that you were sentenced to five years of prison." Then Romashko pulled from his pocket a piece of paper that was not even signed by the major and began to boast that it was to him, the propagandist, that the general of the K.G.B. had given this paper promising freedom to the condemned if they agreed to collaborate with them.

To the query, "According to what laws do you act?" Romashko replied: "We act according to unwritten laws. Believers are to the Communist régime as scabies are to the body. But we will soon get rid of it."

I addressed Romashko: "From Nero to the present time there is an inerasable, sordid blot upon the persecutions, and you continue in this way." And my advice: "Stop before it is too late, before God has dropped the sword on your shoulders." After these words they took me back to my dungeon and soon afterward sent me to the camp for convicts in Petrovk. But even here Major Romashko's paper, like an annoying fly, does not leave me in peace.

One day they called me to the office of the colony chief, where again Romashko offered me conditional freedom. He would say: "We know that a foreign parcel has come for you, addressed to your wife Galina. We will arrange a meeting between you and her. You must persuade her to surrender all claims to the package and to send it back, because by accepting it she will jeopardize the prestige of our state. They will know abroad that the believers are locked up, and they will send parcels to help their families. Tell her also that she must break all contact with the Council of Relatives of Prisoners. Otherwise we will bring her to trial and deprive her of both her freedom and her children." And at the propagandist's last visit: "You must become priest in the registered prayer house and be continually in contact with us. Otherwise you will be tried again and your imprisonment extended."

Dear friends in God and members of the Council of Relatives of E.C.B. Prisoners, I tell you that I scorned all these proposals, and I beg you to pray that God will strengthen me, body and soul and grant me health. For "to suffer for a just cause is to conquer!"

May the Lord bless you and help you to follow the difficult path of his redeemed people.

With all my love, your brother in the Lord,

—Pavel Ritikov

Despair of the Children

No, the name of "Mother" is never erased from the souls of little children, and no toy of atheism can soften their grief.

Who can begin to measure the despair in the heart of a child taken from his mother?

We can declare with head raised high that our children have a solid education, that they are disciplined and not contaminated by vice, and that you will not find them among the tens of thousands of juvenile delinquents.

On the basis of the "Marriage and Family" law, Article 19, children are isolated and imprisoned because of their religious education.

Horror of horrors! The world has never known anything like it!

These methods were used by Pharaoh, murderer of children in ancient Egypt; by Herod; and by Nero, renowned for centuries for his bloodthirstiness. And all the while there exists the Declaration of Human Rights, which you have signed.

—1453 mothers of Soviet families

4. *Denunciation of the Persecutions*

Some Christians, while not wishing to ignore the tragic conditions imposed by the totalitarian states upon their brothers in the Communist world, feel that the best method to help them is by not heedlessly shouting the truth about their sufferings. According to them, it is better first to help the recognized churches, which are subjected to pressures that threaten their existence, and to maintain what remains of religious life in them. Public denunciation of the persecutions, by irritating the Marxist-Leninist authorities, would lead these leaders to limit even more the little freedom the churches have and the opportunities now open for worship.

Such a view implies a complete misunderstanding of the real situation. It reveals an ignorance of the official church, of the Communist ideology, of the concepts and methods of the Party. And it is invalidated by experience.

That some of the faithful may participate in the few services that are still held is an important consideration. But it must be emphasized that this is the limit of any manifestation of the faith; that closing places of worship, demolishing them, or transforming them into movie houses, antireligious museums, or "useful" buildings has continued ever since the Soviets came into power.

Religious freedom, according to the Constitution of the Soviet Union, consists exclusively in attending worship services where this is still possible; while any religious instruction and any catechism, considered propaganda for an ideology contrary to the system, are offenses punishable by law. The priests who take no notice of this are sent to prison or concentration camp and subjected to the worst treatments to make them deny God. Those who are set free are reinstated in ecclesiastical offices only if they agree to become "correspondents" of the K.G.B. and denunciators of those of their congregation who want to share their faith, if only with their own children. Some refuse and are doomed from then on to never finding work; others, with tortured souls, resign themselves to it; still others "adapt" and are thus ushered into a good career in the official church. Seminaries include chairs of atheism, and "theologians" or "bishops," pure militants of the Party, are charged with destroying from the inside the church they supposedly serve. When we realize these things and that the battle against "religious derangement" is the first article of the prevailing ideology—a fundamental objective that is sometimes put off, sometimes discarded by various means, but always resumed as soon as possible—we may ask what can exist of spiritual life and what can be the future of the faith within the framework of the official churches.

Let us listen to Solzhenitsyn. Let us listen to those thousands of Lithuanian Catholics who had the courage to sign a public protest. Let us refer to the biography of the "patriarchs" and the "metropolitans" whom the Party placed over the Orthodox church "of Moscow and All-Russia," who assure their colleagues in the West, naïve enough to shake hands with them (or not disgusted enough to refuse), that at home the faith is perfectly free and that there are no religious persecutions. Only then will we understand what those churches are and what message they can bring to men.

Of course things are not so simple. No one can presume to think that down to the last rung of the hierarchy to the farthest parish of the capital of the U.S.S.R. there are not priests who try at risk and peril to live and act in keeping with their calling. No fortress is so solid and well guarded that human ingenuity cannot find a crack; neither the ideological, political, and police stronghold of the Marxist state nor the spiritual prison it encloses can be impenetrable to the action of Providence or simply to that of great-hearted men. Thus, against and despite the church and the systematic efforts unfurled by a power hostile to the faith—a declared, official enmity— that upholds the ecclesiastical hierarchy at the cost of its involvement in this enterprise, some priests will act as men of God. These are heroic exceptions to an order that is imposed by force and guile and, from the inside, slowly poisons the church to death.

The authentic church, the living, victorious church, is that of the Catacombs. It is that of Orthodox, Catholic, Baptist, and Pentecostal Christians who accept no other limitations to confessing and spreading their faith than the material precautions of underground activity. In the name of truth and the truth of the faith we must make known the marvelous resurrection of the Church of Jesus Christ after fifty years of materialistic and atheistic indoctrination. We must repeat the testimony given in prisons and camps under physical and moral torture and announce the conversion of executioners subdued by the love and forgiveness of their victims. We must inform men of our time that even today an epic story, among the most admirable in the history of Christianity, is unfolding.

Is this a bad service to render to Christians under the Cross? They are the first to believe the opposite and to make it known to those they can reach. Anything proving to them that the Christians in the West understand their trials and their warfare gives them immeasurable support. They never cease to ask their brothers in the Free World to uphold them in prayer. And how can it be otherwise?

The evidence alone should tell us: we double their persecutions by adding the oppression of our ignorance and indifference. The silence of Western churches will be for future historians, as it is for the martyrs, one of the greatest scandals of all time.

How can the truth be a disservice to them? To believe this would mean total ignorance of their oppressors.

For such strategists as the Communists, the spread of truth is "objectively"—to use their term—a power, or the generating element of an alarming power, upon the chessboard of their permanent war. The more it grows, the more discreet and procrastinating they will become in their battle against the Christian faith.

That the truth embarrasses them, that nothing holds for them greater dread, is proven by their tenacity to falsehood. If they did not fear it, why the profuse assurance from their pseudobishops and their pseudotheologians to their colleagues in the West? Why the trips to the Potemkin organized for the same reasons? Why the privileged place for propaganda in the preoccupations and activity of the Soviets? Why the official denials that the Soviet ambassadors trouble themselves to send to newspapers in countries where they are authorized to controvert such scandals as the imprisonment of opponents in psychiatric asylums?

To proclaim what is true and right is not only an absolute duty; it is the best means to intimidate the torturers and mitigate the sufferings of the Christians in the underground church.

—Philippe Brissaud

5. *Admirable Russian Mothers*

Not long ago in France a letter signed by three hundred women of the wealthiest class mobilized the press. Transforming a personal drama—undergone in ignorance, though only God can judge—into an act of fame, the Woman's Liberation Movement demanded and continues to demand, using any amount of publicity, free and unconditional abortion for any woman. It ridicules marriage, extols divorce, and by its appeals for "liberation" prompts the formation of a new feminine generation: virgins ashamed of their state . . .

Nearly four years ago in the East, a letter signed by 1453 mothers of Soviet families and addressed to their government, was suppressed against world opinion. How we wish that the three hundred French signers could read, with the heart's eyes, this rending and highly instructive document by their Russian sisters! For, in the East, it is the simplest, poorest women, and those given the most children, who have best understood the sublime requirements of motherhood. It is not enough to bring children into the world; God must also be given to them.

When one knows the power of maternal instinct, the tremendous cleavage felt by any normal woman when she faces separation from the being born of her body, one may also measure the heroism of those Baptists who teach the Word of God to their children, knowing that they may—by that very fact—have them torn away by government decision in defiance of the most categorical provisions of the "Declaration of Human Rights."

Nadezhda Sloboda, Evgeniya Azarova, the Lord bows to your sufferings, because to you it has been given by reason of your faith, to live the drama of Mary, mother of God: climbing to Calvary, immobilized beneath the Cross, offering her Son to suffering and death. You share fully in the Redemption. And in the West, in our crumbling civilization, we need all the light born of your humble sacrifice.

The sufferings of your children torn from your motherly tenderness would be totally unbearable to us if we had to believe they were useless. But in the immense exchange of the Mystical Body, we think we see that threatened souls are saved by the tears of those Russian children.

That is why, in the face of so much distress, this appeal by Soviet women to the world's conscience must find an echo. We must consider it a warning at a time when too many Christians question the necessity of baptizing their children or confirming them in the faith by an active catechism. The heroic choice of Soviet mothers is a startling reply to our hesitations. It shows us what is required of God's true children.

This unbelievable courage on the part of more and more Russians, who openly sign petitions and protests when their faith in Jesus Christ is shaken, this courage must be imbued in us, for it certainly comes from God. One day, perhaps, it will be required of us. How will we respond? Where do we stand with regard to our faith, our creed, our Christian behavior in everyday life?

"We are resolved to hold close our innocent children, and if it is necessary, we will die with them."

To these Soviet mothers, so totally given in sacrifice to Christ the Redeemer, what can we say?

—Sophie Daria

Defense of the Faith

I appeal to Christians the world over to resist the Communists and refuse to trust them in any way. All their assertions are lies intended to deceive and subjugate the peoples. Every Christian must remember the words of our Lord Jesus Christ, which declare that one cannot serve two masters at once. In the same way it is impossible to compromise, even in thought, with godlessness. Everything must be put to work in defense of the truth of the Christian faith.

> —Letter to U Thant from
> the mother of a Russian monk

6. *Parents and Children*

Interrogations and Repression of Children

To the Soviet Government:

. . . A letter from Christian-Baptist mothers was sent to you, expressing great sorrow over the various repressions against Christian-Baptist children and parents. The letter was signed by 1453 mothers from 43 towns. In total disregard of this, inquisitions are becoming frequent. In Kishinev interrogations of school children by the organs of the K.G.B. and by the prosecutor focus on religious themes. The children of Dubchak, Chernykh, and Fedorenko were also questioned. A letter giving detailed descriptions was sent to you by parents. The questioning extends to other cities: Gomel, Pavlodar, Barnaul, etc.

It is certain that to continue this will result in the refusal of children to attend school and of parents to give them over to such abuse.

This problem has once again been brought before the Christians of our country.

As usual, the authorities ignore the laws of the country. In the children's school certificates are mentioned their religious denominations and membership in a Christian family. Yet Lenin's decree of January 23, 1918, confirmed by that of March 1966, clearly indicates the separation of church and state. As an example we attach a photocopy of such a reference for Maya Nikolaevna, an 8th-grade student of secondary school Number Four of Jeltyevady, Dnepropetrovsk Region (Ukraine), dated June 14, 1969.

In the present letter we have very briefly touched upon various aspects of the situation of E.C.B. believers, and only on facts. All these cases of persecutions of families, the sacking of prayer houses and print shops, etc. have a goal: arrests and consequently new orphans and deprived families . . .

By commission of the Council of Relatives of E.C.B. Prisoners, persecuted for the Word of God.

March 16, 1970   —Ritikova, G. Y.: Petaekha, I. E.;
                                  Bytkova, M. I.; Velchinskaya, Z.

A Mother's Appeal

Dear mothers, I address myself to you to ask you to pray for my son Vladimir, to support him with your prayers. He is imprisoned for preaching the Word of God, for singing hymns of praise . . . My son is in a difficult situation. That is why I entreat you, dear mothers, to unite with me in prayer and to ask the Lord to keep my son alive, as he kept Daniel in the den of lions . . .

                    —The mother of Vladimir Sinchenko

An Open Letter

I address myself to you, leaders of the nation, and entreat you to consider my case. Five years ago I was like all the other country people, not knowing God. As soon as I became a Christian, I was exposed to mockery and persecution. Stones were thrown in my windows, the doors were taken off, the room invaded. The current was cut off and . . . later, by court decision, my children Galya and Shura were taken from us. The children suffered greatly. Who can describe their sufferings? Twice they escaped from the children's home and tried to come home, but they were pursued and taken back.

On October 16, 1969 the president of the Kolkhoz, Bykov, and the secretary of the Kolkhoz, Voltan, knowing that our letter of indignation was of no effect, arrested my wife Nadezhda Stepanovna, mother of five children, who was judged and sentenced to four years of imprisonment. She was judged for her testimony of faith in Jesus Christ in that remote corner where the light of Jesus Christ has never penetrated. At the same time my brother Sloboda Vykenti and my brother-in-law Kurach Petra were judged. I was left with three children: Kolya (10 years), Lucia (7 years) and Pavlik (5 years). I did everything to replace their mother. They were under the paternal roof, in warmth and comfort, and friends helped me in my task.

But the militant atheists, having full supremacy, did not stop there. They watched us constantly and forbade any relative to visit us. Even that did not satisfy them. On January 16 of this year they drew up, in complicity with other officers, a false accusation; accordingly, justice took the rest of my children . . . .

I was left alone, in an empty house. The voices of the children and of their mother are no longer heard. The words of the Lord comfort me: "They persecuted me, they will persecute you also." Oh, you persecutors of the living God, stop, repent of your ways; the tears of the orphans form a heavy veil. The Lord receives them in his cup of passion. You have taken my wife and five children, but the Lord has not abandoned us. Whether I live or die, the Lord is always there.

Send my wife and children back home.

Nevertheless, may His will be done in everything.

March 4, 1970

—I. F. Sloboda

Village of Dubrava Vitebsk District, Belorussian S.S.R.

7. *The Hierarchy is Enslaved*

At the beginning of the persecution of the church, that is, from November 1917 on into 1927, the hierarchy of the official Russian Orthodox Church paid a heavy tribute in blood and suffering through imprisonments and deportations, bowing to the fury of a power fighting all forms of belief in God.

Servility began June 29, 1927 when the "locum tenens" (guardian) of the patriarchal throne, Metropolitan Sergey, expressed in his message "our gratitude to the Soviet government for its interest in all the religious needs of the Orthodox population," announced that "we have required of our clergy abroad a written pledge of total loyalty to the Soviet government in all its public activity," and openly recognized "the Soviet Union as our homeland, whose joys and success are our joys and success and whose failures are also our failures."

While many bishops protested against this stance, a few countersigned it. Until the end of World War II, however, the church was not recognized, and therefore its servility could not become evident, at least not in the free world.

Recognition took place when the U.S.S.R. entered the political world scene, that is, toward the end of the second World War. Stalin's satanic genius realized that an enslaved church would greatly serve his foreign politics. He understood that the Western World in its naïveté would accept with joy and without discernment the declarations of a few prelates who would affirm that the U.S.S.R. is a completely democratic and tolerant nation. Thus, Patriarch Alexei declared to the Assembly of Friends of Peace of the Soviet Union in Moscow in May 1955 that "the Russian Orthodox church completely supports our government's foreign policy, not because it is not free, as our enemies assert, but because this policy is free and just and corresponds to our Christian ideals, as taught by the church."

In this same period Metropolitan Pitirim, visiting London, declared that "the Orthodox church in the U.S.S.R. does not lack for money and leads a rich, free life."

At a press conference in Copenhagen, in 1956, Metropolitan Nikolai affirmed that "not only are there no religious persecutions, but there never have been. Certainly there are cases of clergy arrest and deportation, but these are for crimes against the state, and the church must have nothing to do with defending such criminals . . . Relations have been stable since 1918 . . ." When the reporters expressed astonishment, the metropolitan repeated: "Yes, since 1918."

In reaction to the many meetings held in Madrid, Paris, and Geneva in 1964-65 to protest the persecution of the faith in the U.S.S.R., Metropolitan Pimen, actually a patriarch declared: "Western reporters have no reason to be concerned about the state of the church and of the believers in the U.S.S.R. . . . The articles in Western newspapers interpret the situation falsely and present the life of the believers in a bad light . . . The Orthodox church is flourishing." He also wrote to a Russian emigrant, "Freedom for the believers came only after 1917, and the Russian Orthodox church is fully active . . . Its members enjoy complete freedom in exercising their religious duties and have no cause whatsoever for anxiety about the future."

This bondage manifests itself, not only abroad, but also inside the U.S.S.R. Complaints about the enslaved hierarchy reach us from the faithful in the U.S.S.R. These are numerous and often virulent: "Metropolitans Nikodim and Pimen have the gall to say in *Izvestiya* that there are no arrests among the clergy." And, in reply to Patriarch Alexis' address: "I respect your age, but truth forces me to face you squarely: you are a pitiful aristocrat, entirely lacking in any sense of honor." The Orthodox of Gorki, formerly Nijni Novgorod, complained in 1969 of not having been supported by the patriarch and the synod in their proceedings before the civil authorities to obtain the right to have a church. Professor of physics V. Chalidze who considers himself irreligious, wrote on February 26, 1971 to Metropolitan Pimen to express his indignation at the hierarchy's refusal to support the faithful in Naro-Fominsk, who for forty years have begged for the right to have a church. In fact, the metropolitan's secretary expressed the opinion that "if the government does not agree to open the church, it must not be the will of God and therefore there is no room for supporting the request of the faithful of Naro-Fominsk."

Especially noteworthy is the letter from two priests in Moscow, Nicholas Eshliman and Gleb Yakunin. In guarded but categorical terms they accused the hierarchy of conceiving the diabolical plan to corrupt the church.

As for Solzhenitsyn's letter to the patriarch, that is sufficiently shown to all. There are also bishops who protested against the servility of the church. For example, Archbishop Ermogen and, today, Archbishop Paul Golichev.

It is thus an established fact that the hierarchy of the official church of the U.S.S.R. is entirely in the hands of a power whose goal, announced many a time, is to destroy the Church. Justification was sought for this enslavement, or at least some means to ease it, in order to fulfill the hierarchy's desire to maintain a semblance of worship. But we must remember that the Church, which has known many persecutions in its two thousand years of existence, has never allowed for slavery to a secular power or for duplicity.

—Archbishop A. Troubnikoff

8. *The Church and the Atheistic Government*

All of us who actually make up the Russian Orthodox church, particularly the bishops and the priests, are responsible before God for the confusion in which it finds itself . . .

The church, faced with an antireligious government, has every interest in rigorously respecting the principle of separation of church and state; the existence of a special department to enforce this principle is thus in complete accordance with the church's point of view, as long as that department strictly carries out its functions and does not exceed its powers.

Nevertheless, during the period 1957-1964, under personal pressure from N. Khrushchev, who became guilty "of subjectivism and administrative abuses" that ultimately were condemned by the Communist party of the U.S.S.R. and the Soviet government, the Council on the Affairs of the Orthodox Church radically changed its nature from an official organ of arbitration to an unofficial and illegal organ of control over the Moscow Patriarchate.

The actual state of the Russian church is such that its entire inner life is subjected to the intrusion of the leaders and representatives of the Council. This interference aims to destroy the church . . . .

It is clear that such interference can be explained only by the tolerance of the high ecclesiastical authorities who, to satisfy the "princes of this world," have permitted the freedom of the church to be trodden underfoot . . . .

Certain bishops believe very seriously that they save the Russian church by their silence: "If we protest against the illegal acts of the council," they say to themselves, "we will be deprived of registration, and our chairs will be occupied by careerists and adversaries of religious freedom. The situation would be even worse."

But in truth, what purpose can there be in this "mission" of saving the church, taken up by these bishops who wish to defend their seats from "wicked pastors," if all they do is keep silent and tolerate the immoral violation of religious freedom carried on by council officers, permitting these "wolves" to seize and to disperse the flock? What do they save, these bishops, except themselves? Don't they bring upon their heads the terrible words of the prophet: ". . . Thus says the Lord: Ho, shepherds of Israel who have been feeding yourselves! Should not shepherds feed the sheep?" (Ezekiel 34:2).

The "pernicious tactics of silence" are contrary to everything taught us by the edifying example of the Holy Apostles and the great confessors of the faith. Saint Paul the Apostle knew well and clearly testified that after him would come into the Church "wolves that will not spare the flock"; yet he took no precautions and, despite the entreaties of his beloved flock, went courageously to his glorious destiny of martyr for the faith (Acts 20:17-38).

We must again remind the pastors who think they can save the church: it is not we, bishops, priests and laymen—weak children of our Mother the Church—who save the Church of Christ, but it is She, full of maternal tenderness, who saves us, Herself having been saved by Christ.

only Christ Can save us!

Moscow
Nov. 21, 1965

—Nicolas Eshliman & Gleb Yakunin

Corruption in the Church

Cowardice and greed govern the Russian church in the person of its episcopate, corrupting the young and creeping over religious life . . .

Such is the corruption, the greed and the cowardice that spread in the living body of the church.

Must we give examples?

. . . Today at the head of an important religious institution is a young man of thirty-three, without any knowledge or experience of life, without honor and without heart.

All his actions are guided by cowardice, by fear of losing a pleasant situation.

—A. Levitin-Krasnov

Crisis in Church Administration

The spirit of compromise, implanted by Metropolitan Sergey, has led to the fact that since 1960 the Moscow Patriarchate and the majority of bishops have knowingly taken a secret part in all the activities of the Council on the Affairs of the Russian Orthodox Church, oriented toward closing churches, limiting the propagation of the faith, and undermining it among the people . . . .

The Moscow Patriarchate refuses Christian apologetics and ideological combat against contemporary atheism. It has taken this attitude as the fundamental principle of its activity, whether at home or abroad. The religious and moral instruction actually carried on by the Russian Orthodox Church can neither interest the young nor exert a positive influence. The faith is therefore not spread among them, and the future life of the church is already threatened.

The acute lack of priests is felt in every bishopric, even for the small number of churches that are open. To spread and establish the faith, it is indispensable that the number of worthy priests, devoted to the church and capable of propagating the faith, be increased. But the bishops have absolutely discarded all selection, teaching, and formation of religious staff, and thus have decidedly crippled the faith and the church . . . .

The activity of the Moscow Patriarchate abroad is conducted in the first place to conceal with lies and shameless slander the massive and illegal closing of churches, the persecutions of believers and of their organizations, and the secret administrative measures taken to limit and undermine the faith in the U.S.S.R.

Secondly, the activity of the patriarchate is carried on through seduction, lies, and any other means possible in order to lead the world-wide Christian movement astray and thus destroy it. Such is, for example, the proposal on the part of the Moscow Patriarchate at the meeting of the Orthodox churches in Rhodes: to renounce Christian apologetics and ideological combat against contemporary atheism. The activity of the Moscow Patriarchate abroad constitutes conscious treason against the Russian Orthodox church and the Christian faith. It acts as secret agent of world-wide anti-Christianity. Metropolitan Nikodim betrays the church and the Christians, not out of fear, but conscientiously; to unmask him completely, along with the Moscow Patriarchate, means the end of his adventurous career.

—Boris V. Talantov

Petition to the Eastern Patriarchs

If the members of the Synod, Nikodim and Pimen, deny the fact that persecutions are taking place in Russia, they are guilty of lying and calumny. The Orthodox faith, the true pastors of our church, the monks, and the laity are the objects of frightful cruelty on the part of atheistic Communists. Most of our true pastors have been refused residential rights because they defended apostolic traditions and open meetings. They have been banished from the church and lead a vagrant life.

"The Orthodox Christians of all Russia"
1964

◍◍◍◍

9. A Letter to Patriarch Pimen

. . . Why must I present my passport when I go to church to have my son baptized? What canonical requirements must the Moscow Patriarchate fulfill by the registration of those being baptized?

We must admit astonishment at the strength of soul in parents, at the dimly perceived spiritual resistance inherited from olden times, with which they undergo this accusing registration procedure, exposing themselves to persecution at work and to public derision by boors. But that is the end of their perseverance, for the baptizing of infants is generally the totality of children's contact with the church. Subsequent means of instruction in the faith are completely closed to them, as is the possibility of participation in religious services, sometimes in communion, and even in attendance. We rob our children by depriving them of this unique, purely angelic perception inspired by divine worship. They will not regain it in adulthood and will never even know what they have lost. The right to perpetuate the faith of their fathers and the right of parents to teach their children according to their own conception of the world are scoffed at, and you, the heads of the church, have accepted the situation. You promote it, finding an authentic proof of freedom of belief in this fact: that we must give up our defenseless children, not into neutral hands, but into the clutches of the most primitive and unscrupulous atheistic propaganda; in the fact that for young people torn away from Christianity—so they may escape contamination—moral instruction has been confined to the narrow way between the propagandist's writing pad and the criminal code.

We have already lost half a century; I am not even talking about retrieving the present; rather, how may we save the future of our country—the future that will be made up of today's children? Will the idea of the right of power be definitely fixed in the mind of the people, or will the power of right emerge from hiding and shine once more? It is this choice that, in the end, will determine the true and profound destiny of our country? Can we restore in ourselves some Christian traits, if only a few, or will we lose them all completely and abandon ourselves to plans guided by the instinct of self-preservation and by self-interest? . . .

We are losing the last traits, the last marks of a Christian people; how can that not be the principal concern of the Russian patriarch? Concerning the least distress in faraway Asia or faraway Africa, the Russian church has its impassioned opinion, but on the pains of our own country, it never expresses one. Why are the pastoral messages that come down to us from the high ranks of the church so traditionally soothing? Why are the church documents so favorable, as though they had been published by the most Christian of peoples? From one unruffled message to the other, will not the need to write them disappear completely some fine day? There will no longer be anyone to address them to, there will be no more faithful left except those employed in the patriarchate chancellery . . .

Your Holiness! Do not completely ignore my unworthy appeal. It may be that you will not hear such things every seven years. Do not give us reason to assume, do not let us believe that, for the high clergy of the Russian church, temporal power is above the heavenly and earthly responsibility is more terrible than responsibility before God.

Neither before men nor, especially, in our prayers can we pretend to believe that exterior shackles are stronger than our spirit. It was not easier when Christianity was born, and yet Christianity stood fast and expanded. And it showed us the way: sacrifice.

Though one is deprived of all material powers, in sacrifice one always carries the victory. And we ourselves have seen numbers of our priests and cobelievers choose a martyrdom worthy of the first centuries . . .

—A. Solzhenitsyn
Lent, 1972

10. *An Appeal to Patriarch Pimen*

The faithful of Naro-Fominsk have appealed to me. For forty years the residents of this town have had no church, but the hope of having one has not left them. The authorities ignore the law, reject their requests.

Who are these people who keep on in the name of the faith? They are the Orthodox like those who for centuries saw some spiritual comfort in the Church; like those who vainly looked to spiritual masters for the blessing of living and suffering.

And now desiring to resurrect the church, these folk, seeking the blessing of the spiritual fathers, have come to their bishop, the head of the church, hoping for his blessing.

His Excellency's blessing was refused. Refused by your secretary,

Father Victor. According to your secretary, if the authorities do not agree to open the church, God does not wish it and therefore there is no place for blessing.

I am not religious, but in this I discern the fact that believers are rejected by their pastors. Yet is it possible that His Excellency has of his own will rejected those who came to him, that he refuses a father's intervention and blessing upon them?

—Prof. V. Chelidze
Feb. 28, 1971

11. *Metropolitan of the Soviets*

There is the case of Nikodim. When we speak of the Church of Silence, of the faith in the catacombs, and of the persecutions in the East, we cannot ignore the role of this Orthodox prelate.

As actual metropolitan of Leningrad, Nikodim is, in a sense, the Minister for Foreign Affairs of the Orthodox Church of Russia. As such his influence is considerable, as much on relations with the Vatican as from the perspective of ecumenism, which is an important question today. Indeed, Nikodim frequently travels to the West. The question that immediately comes to mind is this: a prelate of such importance, who has so much freedom to move about, is he not a tool of the Soviet power?

In such cases it is best to refer first of all to the biography—the "bio," as the Bolsheviks say—of Nikodim. Aiming at first for a teaching career Nikodim—his real name Boris Rotov—was born in 1929 and took holy orders in 1947. He was then 18 years old. Called to Moscow in 1959 by Patriarch Alexei, he succeeded Metropolitan Nikolai as commissioner for foreign relations in June of that year. In 1960 he became bishop and in 1963, at 34 years of age, metropolitan of Leningrad. A quick and surprising ascent.

It is no less instructive to observe certain stages in his religious career. This unique ecclesiastic was in fact trained in Yaroslavl, through correspondence courses from the seminary in Leningrad. (In the U.S.S.R. correspondence courses are excellent.) Before being called to Moscow and then to Leningrad, the young Nikodim was appointed head of the Russian Mission of Jerusalem in 1956. Under the Soviets this position has always been given to a confidential servant of the political police.

It is unreasonable and frankly stupid to believe that, ever since

the Bolsheviks took over Russia, they have not sought to place their
own men in the bosom of the Orthodox church. The biography of
Boris Rotov, the said Nikodim, comports perfectly with such practice.

—Roland Caucher

⬥⬥⬥

Statement by the Metropolitan

When the persecution of religion is mentioned, two things are
often confused. When it is said in the West that antireligious propaganda is becoming more intense, many denounce it as persecution, but it is something completely different, namely, an ideological battle . . .

It seems to me that all those who come to us without precon-
ceived ideas must become convinced that there is no antagonism
between believers and atheists in our country. Believers of the
U.S.S.R. share the same rights as other citizens.

—Nikodim
Metropolitan of Leningrad and Ladoga

⬥⬥⬥

12. *Sermon to Churches in the West*

Dear brothers and sisters in the West:

The one addressing you is a Christian sentenced to isolation in a
Communist prison cell. For two years I have been speaking by spiritual telepathy with my former parishioners, and I believe it
works. Now I have decided to take a step further and to communi-
cate with you who live in faraway countries.

In order to succeed I have kept silent for a long time. I stopped
delivering sermons to my parish community. For an even longer
time I even stopped speaking to God. I did not allow a single inner
voice to trouble the quiet. I kept silent both inwardly and outwardly.
I called to mind that, before the fall of Jericho, Joshua commanded
his people, "You shall not shout nor let your voice be heard, neither
shall any word go out of your mouth, until the day I bid you shout"
(Joshua 6:10). When the people began to shout after such a long
silence, the wall fell down flat (cf. Joshua 6:20). How far you can
reach in spirit depends on the length of your silence.

The voice of Jesus reached the whole world and continues to be heard after two thousand years because he imposed silence on himself until he was thirty years of age. Silence, although he had so much to say!

I was silent because of love for you. Now listen! He whose vision is narrow cannot think rightly. The man who knows only what goes on in his own room may be killed the next moment by someone who has already entered the next room with the intention of murdering him. If your horizon is limited to your parish, your church, your country, you are condemned. What will happen if another country has already prepared weapons to kill you? What if another religion possesses valid elements unknown to you that may prove it can assure salvation?

Only the strategist who knows what is happening on the entire front can think correctly. "The world is my parish," John Wesley said. The world—not the earth, but the cosmos—with all its inhabitants and its Creator, that is the Christian's horizon. He does not stop at anything less.

Don't tell me that so vast a horizon is reserved for the highest church leaders and does not concern the ordinary Christian. All Christians are of the highest rank, because they participate in the divine nature. The thinking of Christians is in terms of the entire cosmos and its Creator; it embraces infinity and eternity.

I in my solitary cell, prey to a tuberculosis that has invaded my whole body, I am sitting with the angels as in a theater, and I watch all that happens, that has happened, and that will happen. I remain attached to my body only by a very weak fluidic tie. My spirit has escaped from this house of madmen in which humanity with its cursed mentality is doomed to live.

Now I see reality as it is: a burden that I must carry.

If God is in me, all the responsibility of the cosmos is mine. "If a man loves me, he will keep my word, and my Father will love him, and we will come to him and make our home with him" (John 14:23). Don't tell me, Satan, that I have not kept his word. You know not our human vocabulary. Jesus did not set as a condition for his living with us that we fulfill his word, but that we keep it. I have not fulfilled his word, but I have kept it unaltered. Like David, I danced before the ark containing the tablets of the law that I have broken in my personal life. Even David did not abuse his royal power to change the commandments.

So God lives in me. And if he lives there, he brings with him all his responsibilities. They become mine. That is why Jesus said that I have the power to forgive sins or to retain them (John 20:23), to bind and to loose (Matthew 16:19). If God lives in me and in you, it depends on us whether beauty will conquer or whether humanity will increasingly degrade itself.

If God the Father and Jesus Christ live in the Christian, his task becomes that of transforming perverts and extortioners, the immoral, the obsessed, the ambitious; of transforming a neurotic world into a world full of serenity. If the Father lives in me, each time someone says Our Father he also addresses himself to the Godhead who is in me. I feel the prayers of all humanity addressed to me, as though my address—Cell No. 11, Prison of the Ministry of Interior Affairs, Bucharest—were actually God's address.

I used to ask myself why the Church repeats the Lord's prayer so often. Now I understand. Every time I say this prayer, I remember that humanity expects me and my brothers, the bearers of Godhead, to clear the way for his reign to come, for his kingdom of justice and joy. It is up to us to see that his will is done on earth. We owe the bread of life to the starving. We owe forgiveness.

Brothers and sisters in the West, you are free. Don't you know anything of Communist evil? Some may remain indifferent. But there is something worse than indifference, and that is indifference to indifference. Some of you may not even care that the Church has become indifferent to the cries of millions of men martyred by the Communists.

I see you assembled in your churches, praising God with your magnificent hymns. But why don't you leave God alone? According to the Talmud, God says: "Oh that men would forget me and start loving one another!" To rescue Christians oppressed by the Communists is a service that pleases God more than your masses and liturgies.

Jesus said that the second commandment—"Love thy neighbor"—is like the first, which is to love God. If you love us, the Christians in Red camps, you love God because he is in us, in Cells 11, 12, and 13 and in the cell with the rats and the one for tortures.

I cannot tell you what to do for us. The pastors among us have been killed and the sheep scattered. Care for these sheep, gather them together again. Our Bibles have been confiscated. Our families eat garbage. I know not what to do. But you are the dwelling place of the omnipotent and omniscient God. He must know. I talk to him. Which means I talk to you. I say a prayer. Listen, it is addressed to you: "Our Father who art in heaven." What heaven is more beautiful in his eyes than your believing soul? He is within you. Deliver us from evil. Communism is evil.

Brothers and sisters in the West, deliver us. Amen.

—Richard Wurmbrand
Sermons in Solitary Confinement

♦♦♦♦

13. *How Shall We Save the Persecuted?*

On November 11, 1971 a declaration of the Lutheran Bishops Council of Norway was promulgated throughout that kingdom, calling the people to take note of the persecutions of believers, Jews as well as Christians, Moslems, and Buddhists living in the Soviet Union and in countries subject to it. One of its passages emphasized our responsibilities in these terms: "We must consider ourselves traitors to the cause of the Gospel itself if we forget this situation, if we hesitate to talk about it, and if we neglect to do all in our means to arouse world opinion."

Most extraordinary is the fact that more such calls must be made before some Christians begin to ask themselves if there may not, after all, be persecuted believers and whether this persecution is really due to "religion" and not to the reaction of an established régime to political opposition.

♦♦♦♦

Violations of the Declaration of Human Rights

Certainly there is no lack of texts; I think of all the letters sent to the General Secretariat of the United Nations denouncing specific cases of violations of the Universal Declaration of Human Rights and more particularly of Articles 18 and 19 on the freedom of religion—including the right of religious instruction, as well as that of celebrating the rites—and on the freedom of opinion and of expression, involving the right to "search, receive, and spread . . . information and ideas by whatever means of expression there may be."

Now, as you know, the cases of violation of these rights—the reasons for these letters—are countless. It is sufficient to recall three of the most typical:

(1) That of March 1969, signed by 1453 mothers, demanding respect for their children's right to receive religious education and protesting against the separation of children from their believing parents because of religion and against various other forms of violence.

(2) That of March 1972, signed by 17,054 Lithuanian Catholics, denouncing religious persecutions suffered by the church in their country;

(3) That of the Council of Relatives of Dissident Baptist Prisoners

of the Soviet Union, revealing the conditions and kinds of torture preceding the death July 16, 1972 of Ivan Vasilievich Moiseiev, soldier in the Red Army, guilty in his zeal as novice of testifying to his faith in season and out during his military service. If the twenty-year-old martyr could literally have been "guilty of giving himself over to religious propaganda," forbidden by the Soviet law, it is no less than monstrous that he was tortured to death by officers and soldiers in violation of Article 5 of the Universal Declaration of Human Rights.

We need not justify these complaints here; the documents are there, irrefutable in the scandal of reported facts and in the proofs attached to them.

Where Silence Proves Useless

For many years now numerous petitions have been presented both to the World Council of Churches and to various religious and humanitarian groups, urging them to push for the completion of the Universal Declaration of Human Rights by means of amendments to ensure respect for the rights affirmed therein.

Many governments have been affected and, at various times in recent years, have given instructions to their representatives in the United Nations "for the occasion when the question of such an addition to the declaration should be broached." Since these instructions have been secret, it is impossible to know what concrete proposals they contained.

When the General Assembly of the World Council of Churches was held in Uppsala in 1968, the question of persecutions in Eastern Europe was posed to members of the Council who are "specialists in international questions." All of them insisted on the need for the least possible publicity because "the more that is written or spoken in public, the more difficult, or even impossible, it is to act."

This thesis has continued to be held by the World Council. The retiring General Secretary, Dr. Eugene Carson Blake, never ceased to minimize the persecutions, almost unilaterally insisting on the violations of the rights of man in other continents! At the meeting of the Central Committee of the World Council of Churches in January 1971 in Addis Ababa, he did indeed energetically oppose the the violation of the Declaration of Human Rights, but then declared that any possible intervention on his part would only make matters worse. In other words, direct action is out of the question, unless it has to do with striking South Africa or Portugal and bringing moral support, exceeding material help, to black racism and Marxist revolutionary movements under the pretext of fighting white racism. This was evident during a session of the same committee in Utrecht in 1972.

As for the United Nations, the little hope of broaching the question of a complement to the Declaration of Human Rights in the 1967 fall session was ruined by the "Six-Day War" and its effects. The Arab states and the Soviet Union and its allies wanted at all costs to avoid any topic that could possibly lead to discussions favoring Israel. Since then the situation has not changed, and several states seem firmly resolved that it so remain, fearing that debate would lead to categorical refusal and thus jeopardize the Declaration itself.

In short, up to now no possibility of improvement is in sight, and the World Council of Churches, like the Commission of Churches on International Affairs, continues to affirm that all initiative in this realm can only seriously impair any future possibilities for betterment. Thus, the conspiracy of silence has brought no improvement; if the situation of the Jews has not ceased to worsen since 1968, that of other believers is just as disastrous.

A Norwegian Initiative

On February 1, 1972 an exceptional debate took place in the Storting (Norwegian parliament) following an interpellation on human rights in the Soviet Union by Bergfrid Fjose, a member of the Christian People's Party. For the first time a parliamentary assembly was involved in such a question and exposed the persecutions of believers of all confessions. No less extraordinary was the fact that all parties represented in the Storting contributed to the debate, the extreme left reacting forthrightly against the general conspiracy of silence reigning in these matters.

In his reply the minister for foreign affairs, Andreas Cappelen, stressed the 16,800 complaints received by the General Secretariat of the United Nations concerning violations of human rights and the absence of procedural rules for their study that would enable the United Nations to follow up on them. Given the secret character of the negotiations involved, it is important, Cappelen declared, that a world climate of opinion be formed so that it becomes impossible to defer again the codification of means to legitimatize

112

the intervention of the United Nations and of the Council of Europe in complaints of this kind.

In 1969, during the meeting of the Human Rights Commission of the United Nations, a plan was adopted to establish a secretariat to study each complaint and to determine obvious violations of the Universal Declaration of Human Rights. The Economic and Social Council of the United Nations opposed the plan, arguing that it was incompatible with the sovereignty of the countries involved. Norway nevertheless persisted in its wish to see negotiations completed without too much modification in the wording of the plan.

The necessary condition for attention to complaints is that traditional ideas about U.N. relations to member states be modified. The former's power in matters heretofore considered that the province of the individual country must be widened. It is quite evident that various states are not yet ready to renounce the provisions of Article 2, Paragraph 7 of the U.N. charter, which affirms the principle of noninterference by the central organization in the internal affairs of member states. Modification can be achieved only if world public opinion brings it about.

The time has come when the Universal Declaration of Human Rights must be understood as inoperative without the recognition of the supranationality of the Human Rights Commission and the consequent power to intervene in all cases of violations of these rights in any of the member states.

From Words to Action

Our responsibility as Westerners is a double one:

(1) We cannot stop the spread of information concerning violations of human rights, but must use all possibilities offered by the mass media. The World Council aside, how can a world opinion, such as called for by the Norwegian government and bishops' council, be formed without such information repeated everywhere, always, in season and out of season? That the World Council is mistaken in claiming that silence alone permits action is clear; nothing works more effectively on the Soviet government than the fear of world reaction. Certain errors in judgment committed by religious authorities anxious to follow the Geneva directives confirm our assertion. A Presbyterian church in the U.S.A., for example, allocated $10,000 to assure the young Communist Angela Davis, charged for complicity in murder, the services of a great lawyer—

a decision provoking the withdrawal of so many members that it lost $2 *million* in revenue, as reported in Sweden by Dr. André Appel, General Secretary of the World Lutheran Federation.

(2) Spreading information means words while, as Minister Cappelen insisted, we need action. Unfortunately, the coalition of anti-European forces, powerfully and underhandedly supported by the Kremlin, succeeded in keeping Norway out of a united Europe, which brought the downfall of the government. Up to now nothing leads us to believe that the new government will be the spokesman for that complement to the Universal Declaration of Human Rights so rightly emphasized by Andreas Cappelen and his colleagues: "The United Nations must apply judicial means of intervention."

The above reveals how delicate the situation is and what problems it brings on the international scale and on the legal level. Do not hastily conclude that it does not concern you, however, and that you are powerless to act. Naturally, we cannot intervene as individuals before the United Nations! But what we can do—each of us who has read these lines—is to become personally concerned: you are voters, you have a representative in parliament. Wouldn't it already be "an act" if each one of you intervened before this representative, no matter to what party he belongs, so that he may take as his own cause the respect for the Declaration of Human Rights, the ground of such great hope when it was ratified by the Soviet Union and, since then, the source of so much bitterness?

You will be told, of course, that France has still not ratified the Declaration of Human Rights, the ground of such great hope when it was ratified by the Soviet Union and, since then, the source of so much bitterness?

You will be told, of course, that France has still not ratified the Declaration of Human Rights even though it brought about the granting of the Nobel Peace Prize to Professor Cassin. That is no excuse. On the contrary, that ratification will some day be the agenda of our assemblies: What an occasion to draw upon the resources necessary for its efficacy!

Put yourself to work today. Move from information to action. Give to our specialists in international law the certitude that they are backed by the country; to our governments the conviction that the instructions they give to their representatives in the United Nations will result in modifying both the texts and the international climate. Then the day will no longer be distant when it will be unimaginable that a twenty-year-old boy should die, like the Vanya who was tortured and drowned July 16, 1972, only because he could not help testifying to his faith!

—J. G. H. Hoffmann

14. *The Free World in the Face of Persecution*

"We are guided by the universally accepted principles of humanity, established by the Universal Declaration of Human Rights," affirms the President of the Presidium of the Supreme Soviet, N. Podgorny, in his letter of April 2, 1971 to the president of Pakistan.

In reality, the Soviet authorities scoff at one of man's most sacred rights, that of parents to rear their children according to their beliefs. "Parents . . . must have the opportunity to rear their children according to their convictions" affirms the Treaty of UNESCO concerning discrimination in teaching, a treaty ratified by the Soviet Union in 1962.

Actually, the Christian mother who insists on her right to rear her children in the Christian spirit is reprimanded by the Party press: "She does not have such a right. Soviet citizens are educated by the entire socialist society through the means, among others, of school and family. The socialist society educates them in the Communist spirit" (*Pravda de Lvov*, August 18, 1964). As for the violation of the Treaty of UNESCO on discrimination in the realm of instruction: in 1966 the legislative organs of the Soviet republics not only confirmed the discriminating measures imposed upon Christians since the first days of Soviet power but also established even harsher penalties for "the organization of special meetings for children and adolescents by officials and other members of religious groups" and "the systematic organization of catechism classes for minors" (cf. for example Edict No. 220 and Article No. 221 of the Presidium of the Supreme Soviet of the R.S.F.S.R.).

Christian believer Boris Vladimirovich Talantov, who died January 4, 1971 in a Soviet prison, testified in his complaint to the attorney general of the Soviet Union on April 26, 1968, to the fact that the authorities took the children of Mikhail and Tatyana Sloboyanina away because they were "educating them in the Christian faith."

On October 17, 1971, in the newspaper *Soviet Russia*, Moscow attorney Gussev confirmed that in the U.S.S.R. "the government authorizes no one to impose his views on children." He illustrated his declaration by referring to the affair of Nadezhda Voronova, who "assembled children . . . in an apartment, giving them religious sermons . . . It was a gross attack on legislation of worship . : . Popular judgment justly sentenced N. Voronova to loss of freedom."

In Lithuania in 1970 a Catholic priest, A. Seskevicius, who taught children the foundations of Christian faith and morality, was sentenced to one year of prison. In 1971 similar sentences were pronounced upon two priests, I. Zdebskis and P. Bubnys, and in January 1972 an elderly woman, Kleona Bichuchail, was condemned to one year of prison for "organized instructions of children." . . .

In Russia itself, church authorities do not defend the right of the church and of Christian parents to rear children and youth in the faith. The assembly of free bishops of the Russian church, which met September 24, 1971 in Montreal, "testified with sorrow" to the fact that "it is not the official representatives of the partriarchate who demand freedom of conscience for Orthodox citizens, but lowly priests, writers, scholars and men of action, among whom are some unchurched and even unbelievers."

We, the free bishops of the Russian church, call upon the United Nations, the Human Rights Commission, UNESCO, as well as the parliaments and governments of all free countries to urge the government of the Soviet Union to respect its obligations as a member of the U.N. and adhere to the Universal Declaration of Human Rights and the treaty of UNESCO concerning discrimination in the realm of instruction.

We the free bishops of the Russian Church address ourselves to the world at large, calling for support for the Christians and followers of other confessions in the Soviet Union.

Help the Christians obtain freedom for those who have been locked up in prisons, concentration camps, or "special psychiatric asylums" for declaring the Word of God.

Help the Christians of Russia secure the return of children taken away from them.

Help the Christians of Russia to defend their rights at school and in the religious communities, as well as the right to teach their children privately the truths of the Christian doctrine.

Help the Christians of Russia defend the most sacred right of man— that of rearing his children according to his own convictions.
June 18, 1972

—Appeal of Russian Orthodox
Bishops to the world community

Letter to the Clergy and the Faithful

Let us remember the method used in Russia by the plotters of the Revolution and later by the Communists, with the aim of lowering the spiritual level of our people by inciting the young to indecency and debauchery. To attain this goal, they even organized special clubs for propagating negligence of the laws of ordinary morality. This propaganda of "liberal ethics" surrounds us more than ever nowadays and is often inculcated in children from school age onward.

Today, as in the time before the Russian Revolution, such propaganda aims to corrupt contemporary society. It uses an ancient method: history is full of examples of nations that have perished from the plague of debauchery. The Lord destroyed the cities of Sodom and Gomorrah. Babylon perished. The Roman Empire collapsed. The free West may be subjected to the same corruption, and because of its weakened determination, it may as a ripe fruit fall into the hands of the Communists.

Metropolitan Philaret

The Obligation to Know

I am convinced that to speak out is today the only way to fight against the evil and arbitrariness that reign in my country . . . . Everyone must know. Those who want to know the truth, but are exposed to appeasing and lying newspaper articles that put to sleep the public conscience, must know. Those who do not want to know also know— those who close their eyes and stop their ears and hope someday to justify themselves and emerge untainted from the mire and say: "My God, and we know nothing about it!"

—Anatoli Marchenko
My Testimony

Role of the World Council of Churches

In the fall of 1970 the World Council set aside $200,000 to support groups and movements, mainly in Africa, involved in the fight against racial discrimination. The Mission Behind the Iron Curtain desires by this letter to draw the council's attention to the discrimination against Christian confessions in the Communist world.

According to the documentation, containing detailed information, attached to this letter, most of which was published in the world press, there are behind the Iron Curtain common cases of discrimination and persecution of persons because of their faith. Christian parents have been deprived of their right to educate their children according to their principles; young men of high morals are sentenced to long imprisonment solely for the "crime" of having tried to act in conformity with their faith in Christ. Young Christians are refused all professional higher education. Persecution has reigned under various forms for fifty years.

We are well aware that *officially* the church has the right to exist in Communist countries; that Christianity is not actually tolerated is obvious from the fact that all religious activity other than regularly scheduled services is prohibited. Who would be satisfied to be Christian only between the walls of the house of God? . . . .

In an interview given by you, Mr. Secretary-General Blake, to *Vaart Land* on October 13, 1970 on the subject of organizations that have been granted aid by the World Council of Churches, you said that, if there were groups entangled by the same problems in Eastern Europe, they would benefit equally from your support.

The totalitarian control of Communist countries prevents disenfranchised Christians from seeking help from you directly. This control also keeps them from establishing any organization for ending such discrimination.

In the name of those hundreds of thousands of Christian brothers and sisters, the Mission Behind the Iron Curtain assumes the authority to ask the World Council of Churches to set apart $200,000. to help and support them. As for the official churches, to give them any aid would be useless, since the atheistic authorities exert strict control over all financial means put at their disposal.

Your subsidies will be used to print Bibles and New Testaments, almost completely lacking because of atheistic governmental action. They will also serve to help the persecuted and their families . . . .

—Bishop Monrad Nordeval, President,
The Mission Behind the Iron Curtain, to
Dr. Eugene Carson Blake, General
Secretary, World Council of Churches

Appeal of Catholic Lithuanians

Since our country does not have proper representation in the United Nations, we Catholics of Lithuania, using the means dictated by the situation, address ourselves directly to you.

Our appeal stems from the fact that in our republic the believers cannot enjoy the rights stated in Article 18 of the Universal Declaration of Human Rights. Basing their case on this article, our priests, various congregations, and individual Catholics addressed themselves repeatedly to the highest authorities of the Soviet Union, demanding an end to the violation of believers' rights. Several petitions by Catholics were sent to the Soviet government:

1. In September 1971, a statement drawn up by the Catholics of Prienai, signed by 2000 people.

2. In October 1971, a statement formulated by the faithful of the Santaika parish in the Alytus District, signed by 1900 persons.

3. In December 1971, a petition drawn up by 1344 parishioners from Girkalnis in the Raseiniai District.

All of the petitions were sent to the ruling authorities in the U.S.S.R., but none of these gave an official answer, even though it is legally required that government offices reply to petitions from citizens during the month they receive them. There was an unofficial answer: the repression of believers was intensified.

The appointment of priests is also decided by government officials.

Even though the Criminal Code of the Lithuanian Socialist Republic prescribes penalties for the persecution of believers, in practice these laws are never applied. In 1970 the Department of People's Education for the District of Vilkaviskis dismissed a teacher, O. Briliene, because of her faith. The Vilkaviskis regional administration did not permit her to work even as a maid in her own town. No one punishes these officials, and therefore intellectuals are afraid to profess their faith openly.

Government officials do not allow the faithful to restore burnt-out churches, even at their own expense, such as those of Sangruda, Batakiai, and Gaure. With enormous difficulty permission may be obtained to hold services in private homes, but never are believers allowed to equip a chapel, not even where a church once stood.

We could cite many cases of persecution that cause distrust of the Soviet Constitution and its laws. That is why we beseech the Soviet government to grant us freedom of conscience, which is guaranteed by the Constitution of the U.S.S.R. but has up to now not been put into practice. We do not want fine phrases over the radio and in the press, but rather efforts on the part of the government to help us, the Catholics, to feel that we are fully citizens of the Soviet Union.
December 1971

—Appeal of 17,054 signatories
to Kurt Waldheim, Secretary
General, the United Nations

On the United Nations

A quarter of a century ago the United Nations was born, bearing the hopes of humanity. Alas! in an immoral world, it has become immoral. It is not an organization of united nations, but an organization of united governments, where all governments are equal: those that have been freely elected, those that have been imposed by force, and those that have taken power with weapons . . .

The United Nations has shown no effort to make the adoption of the Declaration of Human Rights—its best text in twenty-five years— the condition to enter its midst. Thus it has betrayed those lowly people placed at the mercy of governments they have not chosen.

—A. Solzhenitsyn

15. *The W.C.C. and Communist Subversion*

We live in an age and in a world that considers freedom to mean the right to buy on credit and to be able to protest verbally and safely. And yet this world has for several decades now decided to acquiesce in what is called "the course of history." We regard as martyrs agitators and terrorists from our university departments and high-income districts, even when they enjoy newspapers, the radio, and television in their prison cells. But we do not wish to believe in the continuing existence of a hell where millions of human beings—not just intellectuals or the religious, but factory workers, clerks, and peasants—are beaten, tortured, drugged, locked up with the insane, or doomed to a slow death in labor camps for endless winters.

If there are those who do not want to hear what is really happening in the East, there are also those who do not want it to be heard, even though their position among the civil, moral, and religious elite would make it their duty to enlighten rather than poison opinion. Among these hierarchs are most of the leaders of the World Council of Churches who, like a number of the "intellectuals" high in the Roman Catholic hierarchy, have only one fear: not to be found to-morrow in the camp they are firmly convinced will gain the Victory, the camp called Socialist.

It is clear that, among these religious leaders, the issue of serving, propagating, and sustaining the faith—and thus perhaps dying for it and for the salvation of men—no longer exists. Rather, the faith must be "arranged" and "adapted" to secular criteria, particularly to those established by the totalitarian régimes with which they want to maintain a dialogue without offending them. Ecumenism becomes a pretext. The church becomes just another instrument for the building together, with its avowed adversaries, of a New World, divided into great economic, cultural, social, and political spheres. The church stoops to the level of the masses suppressed by tyrants instead of helping those masses raise themselves toward God by resisting their tyrants.

These men forget that across the centuries the churches that have stood their ground—as well as all religions that seek to raise men to God—succeeded only by refusing to serve those carriers of a New Order built on force. Naïveté, belief in a utopia, and cowardice, therefore, are not the only explanations for the attitude of W.C.C. leaders and other representatives of the faith who transform themselves into servants of the secular. Betrayed from the inside, the churches have also been infiltrated with people systematically trained to penetrate them and then to turn them away from their spiritual goal.

In the summer of 1969 the Central Committee of the W.C.C. campaigned for the renewal of diplomatic relations between the United States and Cuba. Only two delegates of the American Lutheran Church dared to vote against it. That was only the beginning of an evolution toward viewpoints that exactly duplicate those of the World Peace Council, the FSM, and other organizations with headquarters in Prague and Moscow. Beginning in 1970, in the name of the fight against racism, the W.C.C. decided to subsidize terrorism. Two hundred thousand dollars were distributed to nineteen so-called Liberation Movements by the twenty-seven unanimous members of the Executive Committee, representing 239 Protestant, Anglican, and Orthodox churches. Eleven of these movements are notoriously and strictly Communist. To cover itself, the W.C.C. claimed to have the promise of these organizations that the funds would not be used for military purposes. How will the W.C.C. control this? Pastor Richard Molard admitted that it could not do so. However, he added, "the ecclesiastical institutions thus show that they are aware of the position that Christ would have them hold" (*Le Figaro*, November 23, 1970). They hold to that position so well that at that very same time the W.C.C. decided to open a $252,000 credit to the Polish government as "social aid" and $210,000 to help the thousands of deserters of the United States army all over the world.

They continue the same course in 1971: condemnation of South Vietnamese aid to Laotians who resist Communism; condemnation of agreements among South Africa, Portugal, Rhodesia, and Malawi, which decided to fight together against subversion; support by Dr. Blake for the 600,000 Algerian workers (his figure is inaccurate) in France who are "victims of injustice and racial discrimination." That is, no doubt, why so many Algerians prefer working in France rather than in their own country.

And yet, not a word on the persecution of Christians in the southern Sudan; not a word of support for the 17,000 Lithuanian Catholics who have just made known their suffering and despair in a public appeal. Not a word of encouragement for the millions of Protestants, Baptists, Unitarians, Orthodox, Moslems, and Jews from suffering, secret, persecuted churches and religions. By contrast, from January 13, to 16, 1972, Dr. Blake and his friends organized an ecumenical conference in Kansas City, bringing together 600 officials in order to perfect a "strategy against the continuation of the war in Indochina." As Antoine Casanova, a Communist, wrote in *L'Humanité* in April 1968: "The dialogue between Christians and Communists finds its origin and basis in one essential tenet: the absolute primacy of all real, terrestrial, secular problems . . ." The W.C.C. agrees completely, since it has aligned itself for eleven years now with this "essential tenet."

Of the spiritual, of God, they will speak later! Msgr. Nikodim and his friends now have more important business.

—Pierre de Villemarest

To Speak the Truth . . .

Only "The truth makes free" (John 8:32).

For Christians of all confessions, truth is neither a system nor an ideology nor a philosophy.

Truth is someone: Jesus Christ (John 14:6.) To betray the truth is not only a moral transgression. It is in the fullest sense of the word an act of treason, if not apostasy. And always it is a denial.

There are different ways of denying the truth. The most common, treated with the greatest indulgence by those who call themselves Christians, is the gesture of Pilate washing his hands.

Basically, *"What is truth?"* (John 18:38)

The one who is truth stood before him, beaten, scorned, crowned with thorns. He said nothing.

The liturgical reform of Vatican II reminded us of the sins of omission. We accuse ourselves of these, but are we aware of their extreme seriousness?

St. John of the Cross says that "we will be judged by love." Our sins of omission mean, in the first place a love lost, betrayed, refused under all sorts of plausible pretexts.

I have in hand a letter, signed by a Catholic monk who plays an important role in the ecumenical movement initiated by Vatican II, who states with reference to the persecution of our Christian brothers in the Soviet bloc: "All that is true, but it would be better not to speak of it . . ."

Between the lines the answer becomes obvious. It could upset the Moscow Patriarchate, therefore the Soviet Council of Religious Affairs, therefore atheistic Communism. "Above all, stay out of trouble!" The summit meetings can well afford to keep quiet. Freedom to travel in the U.S.S.R. is certainly worth the freedom of these millions confined, tortured, and humiliated.

To this, the retort: "But what can we do? A protest from the Vatican or the World Council of Churches could only aggravate the situation. It is better therefore to keep silent!" Better, they assume, to ignore such cries as those of Solzhenitsyn, directed to Pimen, Patriarch of Moscow—unless, of course, it is given the cosmetic treatment, as was done recently in a magazine controlled by the state secretariat, thanks to Father Jeludkov's letter. We await with curiosity the reaction to the answer given by Felix Karelyne to Father Jeludkov. Cosmetic treatments take time!

The tragedy is that for most Christians truth is an abstraction and not the one who dared to say: I am the truth—the truth that sets you free.

There is no such thing as freedom outside of truth!

Hence they prefer to pass over in silence the one whom scripture calls the father of lies, the adversary defeated by Jesus-the-Truth in a single battle in the desert—such victories always take place in the solitude of the desert—as a prelude to the cross.

By his holy passion Jesus Christ conquered falsehood forever, of whatever kind, wherever it comes from, even though it drape itself modestly in diplomatic reasoning.

"Let your yea be yea and your nay be nay." No diplomatic loophole will overcome this sharp command that has meant death to millions of martyrs.

But here shines the paradox of the Gospel: Those who suffer for their faith in prisons of the godless are much freer than we who compromise the truth or hide it under a bushel: free with that inward liberty that alone counts in the end since no one can take it away!

A very serious question remains that we must all ask ourselves:

Free on the outside, gorged with the goods of the consumer

society, is it not we who are the true slaves of falsehood, whether explicit or implicit? It is so convenient to bury one's head in the sand and to say with Pilate: "Basically, what is truth?"

—André Martin

16. *Miracle in the "Devil's Cell"*

I lack words to describe accurately the sufferings I underwent through the enusing eternity of hours.

Only the brothers Vassily Zhapkov, Nicola Naumov, Yoncho Dryanov, and Yanko Ivanov who endured this trial with me know, for they had to go through the same martyrdom. Pastor Zhapkov told me afterwards: "Mitko, it was the worst of what I had to endure over there."

"Lord Jesus, Savior and Redeemer of my soul, my life is also in your hands. Your will be done," I prayed while trying to evade the heavy drops of water that fell incessantly. I began to sing in order not to hear them, and I prayed harder than ever so that my body would no longer feel the pain. While my physical strength continued to decline, the Holy Spirit gave my soul the power needed to support my suffering body. What was mortal in me seemed to be groveling in a Dantesque hell, although the glory of God shone in me like a light in the darkness of the night.

"Father, forgive them for they know not what they do," I cried. And the word came back to me, "Love your enemies, bless those who curse you, pray for those who abuse you and persecute you." Once more the Lord's words were living bread to me and a source of refreshment. I regained my self-control and walked up and down my cell. Was the biblical miracle of the three young men about to repeat itself? Thrown into the furnace by their king because they would not disobey God, they were protected by an angel, and the fire did not touch them.

To me also, the Lord sent his angel during those difficult hours. He was suddenly at my door, opened it, and I heard the murmur of a voice. It was the voice of Gavulov, who was replacing Bogdanov, the one who had for the last months closely supervised the development of the torture program.

"Mr. Mateev, I listen to your singing and praying even for me. Tell, me, how can you do it? Where does such strength come from? The other pastors have it, too."

I listened solemnly, as though I were receiving a confession. The

124

voice continued: "Mr. Mateev, I want to become a Christian. I want to believe and become as strong as you and the others. What must I do to become a Christian?"

The voice of Saul of Tarsus must have sounded like that when a flash of divine light had thrown him to the ground on the Damascus road and he had asked, "Lord, who are you?"

The voice behind the door had stopped, waiting. I answered: "Outside, in my jacket, there is a New Testament. Take it and read the words of God."

"Can't you tell me now?" the voice pleaded.

"That is impossible, because what is happening to you is not my work, but God's. To accomplish it, you must be born again. I am praying for you. You must also try to pray."

An invisible hand shut the door. A man had discovered a crack between hell and eternal life and had passed through. The death cell had become a baptistery, and the drops of water, destined to wipe out a human life, had given divine life. On the threshold of hell, in the main prison of Sofia, a miracle had taken place.

I never saw Gavrilov again. I learned later from a nurse that he had repented and found the faith. In 1949 he was condemned for "collaboration with incarcerated pastors" and executed in the secret police building of Löwenbrücke. His soul is with God . . .

I woke up in a room of the prison hospital. A nurse told me it was January 11, 1949, my fortieth birthday. I had been shut up in the "Devil's Cell" on January 1. What had happened to me? To this day I do not know. But the supervisory committee must have feared that I could not endure preparations for the trial. I was carefully watched by Penka, the nurse, who collaborated closely with Bogdanov and was always present, syringe in hand, the moment our tormentors went too far. She had orders to keep the supervisory committee informed of the state of my health every hour of the day. The whole process would have collapsed like a house of cards if one of the 15 "actors" had failed.

But it is Penka the nurse who deserted her role. Impressed by the behavior of the Protestant pastors, she became a convinced Christian. She transferred to the Alexandrov hospital and worked for ten years in our underground church. She is the one who told me about Gavrilov's wonderful conversion and of his martyrdom.

—Mitko Mateev
"Mit Jesus Durch Die Teufelstelle"
("With Jesus in the Devil's Department")
1972

Sweepings

To the Saints considered sweepings,
By harsh treatments driven insane,
To Christ's beloved, trapped by torture's reapings
—Satan would crush them while his hours remain—

For empty prayers I ask forgiveness,
For keeping silent in our fear.
Our tears before Him would be bitterness,
If torment crossed the borders and drew near.

I love the thought that in your cell
You gaze from darkness to the Master;
His promised peace fills like a well,
In Him you love your executioner.

Sweepings of the world: jewels of the Son:
Such is the condition your choice brings
To the Prince of Life is joy in what you've done
And sweetness to the King of Kings.

—Andrée Dufour

5: Communism and Religion

1. *From Anti-Christianity to Anti-Communism*

Many think that Communism is only an economic or political doctrine or a scientific theory. The fact that must be grasped is that, first and essentially, Communism is a universal religious system, a general view of the world, of history, and of man, inspired by faith in Man as God.

It is quite clear that Communism (systematic humanism) and Christianity (systematic theism) are rigorously antithetical. Their opposition is systematic: any true Communist is systematically anti-Christian; any faithful Christian is systematically anti-Communist.

But the methods of Communism's anti-Christianity and those of Christianity's anti-Communism must be radically different, precisely because of the Communist system and its basic motives on the one hand and the Christian system and its basic motives on the other.

Communist anti-Christianity will use revolutionary methods, closing upon the Christians the doors of an historic hell. Any device is approved, in particular the use of falsehood and continual violence.

Christian anti-Communism will use reforming methods, completely in line with the Word of God, serving the Gospel Truth and the love of neighbor within the realm of the Church and serving the law in the political and social realm. Christians, far from hating the Communists, must love them as God's creatures, as neighbors, even as enemies. But loving the Communists and calling them to turn from the religion of autonomous and deified man to the religion of a revealed God also means not to give in to Communism, not to compromise with it, but to resist it systematically, for the good of all, including the Communists themselves.

Because Communism wears a mask whenever circumstances and tactics demand it, some do not realize the fact that it is a universal and anti-Christian religious system.

As long as it is not in power, Communism more or less conceals its true character and seems to defend in the name of peace and justice—those two natural goals of many men—only political, social, or economic views.

When it is in power, communism takes off its mask, suddenly or slowly, completely or in part, and seeks to impose the anti-Christian system, up to then more or less camouflaged, in spirit and in fact.

Only systematic anti-Communism on the part of Christians, only systematic Christianity (which is far more than an anti-Communism!) can prevail over Communism.

Between the religion of man (the religion of the revolution) and the religion of the triune God (the religion of creation and redemption) the final battle, a struggle of systems, is being waged. The outcome of this battle, of this struggle, is life eternal and temporal for men.

Faithful Christians can and must oppose Communism in every sphere of human existence—(conjugal, family, professional, political, and cultural)—not with conservatism in the face of situations that need to be changed and reformed, but with a persevering quest toward transformation and progress in the light of what God reveals, teaches, and commands in his Word.

First and foremost, however, faithful Christians must regain, in a non-Christian or de-Christianized world, a continually renewed spirit of evangelization and dedication.

It is not from men but from God, from his Word, from his Spirit that salvation for men, eternal and temporal, comes.

Only a systematic Christianity can victoriously oppose a systematic Communism. Only the Word of God and the Spirit of God can conquer—first of all and every day in ourselves—the spirit of death and inhumanity that belong to humanism, to the religion where autonomous and sovereign man is substituted for the living God.

—Pierre Courthial

2. *The Objectives of Communism*

It is often said that Chinese Communism is not as pernicious as the Russian variety. That is a serious mistake. Anyone who knows the principles of Marx and Lenin and sees Chinese Communism at work discovers the same basic principles; it pursues the same goals as its elder Russian prototype and uses the same methods.

In the long run, Communism has two objectives, one within the borders of its own country, the other extending to the whole world. To attain these goals and all their ramifications, the Communists use cruelty and stop at nothing. I became convinced, through many experiences, that this is true in China.

Inside the country, the Communists seek by all possible means to extend and subsequently maintain dominion over the whole nation. But they cannot pursue this goal openly: they know very well that men would not want such a system and so they give the impression of seeking something else; they proclaim great goals to catch the imagination and win the people over, goals that apparently will be of great benefit to the masses. They know that in all countries the people are generally poor and that man naturally aspires to wealth and well-being, and so they promise heaven on earth. And since they also know that the well-to-do will not voluntarily share their goods with the proletariat, they present the rich classes as enemies of the poor and preach class struggle, which takes place under the leadership of the Party; that is, they urge the poor to take with force the goods of the rich, whom they call capitalists. But the aim is fictitious; the real purpose lies elsewhere. In the final analysis what Communism wants at all costs is not the well-being of man, but solely the rule of the Party.

According to Marxist thought, man has no spiritual soul, he has no free will, he has no worthwhile personal rights. The Communists consider man a mere animal, only more developed and endowed with dangerous qualities. That is why they train him by means of brainwashing.

The Marxist leader holds absolute power over man and treats him like a beast of burden. Whether he sends him to prison or labor camp or fires a bullet in his neck, he is only exercising his right, as he also does when he assigns to the beast of burden his portion of food.

The Communists operate on the principle of contempt for man. The day they begin to consider him a person would be their ruin, and they are fully aware of this.

Party doctrine gives to the Communist leader the right to exploit all work capacities of everyone under his rule and to make him serve the Communist ends. If millions of families are thus sacrificed, that is of no importance; what counts is the power of the Party.

Communism recognizes the existence only of matter. If, then, nothing besides matter exists, there is no God, no heaven, no hell, no eternity. Since God does not exist, all religion establishing a relationship with what does not exist, must be absurd. Since there is no heaven and no eternity, there can be no happiness for man anywhere but on this earth; since there is no God, there is no moral law involving absolute, eternally valid standards.

With sound logic the Marxist dictators call good that which serves Communism and evil that which does not. Lying, pretense, breaking promises, murder, reducing man to slavery for Communism's benefit—that is good. And good must be done and evil prevented. What, then, is evil? Any form of non-Communist government is evil, any religion is evil, any man who rejects Communism is evil. The Reds are convinced that their form of government is the only good one; none other has the right to exist; all must be replaced by Communism. The same reasoning holds for religions and for all those who do not believe in Communism. If all unbelievers are not immediately liquidated, it is for tactical reasons. They will catch up later, when the whole world will have become Communist.

The Communist system and its ramifications are so far from the natural behavior of man that we can clearly recognize extrahuman influences, that is, Satanic ones. Of themselves, men are incapable of inventing something so inhuman and imposing it upon their fellow-creatures. The Communists share with Satan the hatred of God and the desire to abolish all religion; they share with him the hatred of men, for whom they have an unprecedented lack of respect and whom they treat with savage cruelty; they share with him the uncompromising execution of their plan.

The external objective of the Communists is to impose their system on all nations, so that it may extend its rule to the ends of the world. They have openly declared this; they do not hide their ambition to reach this result by world revolution.

The leaders of the Chinese Communists have always kept this double goal in sight. They have seized power by every means: good, evil, even dreadful. Now that they have solidly established their position, they seek to strengthen it; at the same time they work relentlessly for the triumph of Communism in all the countries of the free world.

—Alois Regensburger
"Tonnerre de Chine"
("Thunder in China")

◊◊◊

The Nature of Communism

Communism is all-comprehensive, and as such enacts as completely as possible a Satanic offensive. It sets up against the Creator-God a self-creating humanity. It opposes the Trinity, the mystery of love, with the dialectic, the mystery of hate. It counters human brotherhood with class struggle. It counters the spirit of prayer, penitence, and sacrifice with the passions of envy, jealousy, and vengeance. It counters the hierarchy of the Church and the Sacrament with the machinery of the Communist party. It counters the Redemption consummated on Calvary by Christ our Lord with the persecution of the members of his Mystical Body and the destruction of the image of God in man. It counters the freedom of the children of God with the slavery of a multitude of collectivized robots. It counters devotion to the heritage of the past with the rebellion of the young against all that defines, enriches, and forms them. It counters Christian civilization with the doctrine of totalitarian slavery and the techniques of barbarism.

—Marcel Clement

◊◊◊

Freedom Under Dictatorship

I maintain that religious freedom not only does not exist under Communist dictatorship, but that it cannot exist. I mean that, even if there are—as there may be—men of good will who are sincerely scandalized by certain excesses like those I denounce in my articles, they do not realize that there is a "logic," in order not to repeat "dialectic," a logic that is stronger than the individual will.

—Gabriel Marcel

◊◊◊

3. *Dialogue and Its Dangers*

Dialogue means that one takes the other seriously and approaches him with respect and love; in no way does it imply the changing of divine revelation in order to suit the views of a partner in dialogue and thus reach an agreement more easily. Dialogue does not mean that even an iota of the essential doctrine of the Church may be modified or interpreted in such a way that one versed in another religion or an atheist can accept that doctrine without renouncing his former position . . .

It is extremely doubtful that any real dialogue can take place between Catholics and atheistic Communists. We say "real" because, unfortunately, false dialogues are mushrooming everywhere, causing great confusion among the faithful.

As long as atheism is only a theoretical conviction, dialogue with men who hold to it remains possible. But when, as in national Socialism or Communism, it becomes an essential element in the doctrine of a militant and highly organized party, especially if words have become an instrument of propaganda for the party, then the indispensable basis of dialogue is missing—namely, that the shared acceptance that the exchange of words constitutes a theoretical discussion. If for either of the participants dialogue is only one among other means of political propaganda, any real discussion becomes impossible. This is clearly the case when one speaks with a member of a Communist party or with an official agent of a Communist state . . .

The desire for dialogue must never keep us from seeing that common interest for the future by no means defines common concerns between Catholics and Communists. Analogously, an artificial basis for dialogue between Catholics and Marxists is made by playing on the meaning of the word "humanism" . . .

First, the materialism of the Communist creed is incompatible with any kind of humanist ideal. If man is nothing but matter that has reached an advanced stage of evolution, it is impossible to speak properly of humanism, since any humanism essentially presupposes that man is conceived a spiritual being. The humanist ideal carries with it intellectual and moral values and their development. These have no place in the materialist conception of man, even if in practice the Communists obviously cannot avoid taking intellectual values and achievements into account in one way or another.

Second, the idea of a determinism according to the imminent laws of economic development—and the historical relativism that goes along with it—is equally incompatible with a consistent humanism.

Finally, the totalitarian nature of Communism, which considers the individual man as a simple means and measures his value strictly by his usefulness to the collective, excludes all possibility of conciliating Communism with humanism. Communism goes beyond and above all other ideologies in its profound and consistent depersonalization, which deprives the person of all his rights . . .

For the Communists, it is perfectly logical not to tolerate Christianity; they know very well that what Christians call humanism has no place in Communist ideology and very definitely constitutes an obstacle to the fulfillment of their plans. The equivocal use of certain terms by Catholics, therefore, only serves Communist propaganda, while sowing confusion among Catholics themselves . . .

—Dietrich von Hildebrand
The Trojan Horse in the City of God

4. *Peaceful Coexistence?*

It is not the Communists who most hinder our help to the persecuted. It is rather the Catholics who, with each smile and each tactical concession from the Red leaders, believe that the end of persecution is in sight. They are contaminated by the slogan of peaceful coexistence. Since the day it was launched by the sly Khrushchev, they underestimate the mortal danger of Communism and flirt with dubious peace movements, progressivist ideas, and wolves clothed in sheepskins who enter the fold of the Church.

It does not seem impossible to us that this so-called progressivism originates in part from fear and from concern for comfort. A practical materialism that loathes sacrifice is spreading more and more in the Church. There is an increasing lack of a fighting spirit and especially boldness to turn against ourselves and take on voluntarily the hardships that this turning point in world history demands of us. Many apostles of peaceful coexistence are the very image of fashionable Communists who try to preserve their security and well-being by compromising with tomorrow's leaders. And so they must appease their conscience. That is why the pernicious character of Communism is minimized and why news of the moral domination of the Communists is considered exaggerated and partisan. That is why, in the name of coexistence and in the interest of a peace that is no real peace, they try to make the Church in the Free World another Church of Silence. And they do all they can to make people believe that Communism has grown up and modified itself.

Well, it is not true. One does not see convinced Communists make peace with God and give freedom to the Church. Those who claim that the situation of the persecuted Church has profoundly improved in Communist-dominated countries are mistaken. . . .

In Communist countries under Russian authority nothing has changed. Freedom of religious instruction is still limited there.

Control of religious practice and measures of constraint against practicing Catholics are not abolished. Separation between church and state is a farce. No stop has been put to party and governmental meddling in the administration and jurisdiction of what is clearly the domain of the Church. Education of future priests is reduced to a minimum or completely thwarted. The right of religious instruction is taken away from parents; merciless pressure is exerted on them to give their children an atheistic education. The scandal of puppet pastors and Quisling prelates continues.

This persecution is not a matter of profuse bloodshed, but rather the systematic strangling of all essential organs of the Church and the total extermination of all religious life. And this is done so efficiently, with so much imperturbable logic, that we must attribute such extraordinary rebellion against God to an unnatural cause. As one priest, a council member from Eastern Europe, put it: "Communism is collective demon-possession . . ."

It is certainly possible that Communism now has good reasons for advocating more moderate policies toward the Church. It would be irrational to exclude this possibility, but it would be no less unrealistic to forget a half century of treachery on the part of Communists and to negotiate with them as with normal conferees. Let us judge them no longer by their words but by their actions, since so far they have been able to deceive all the churchmen who have negotiated with them. Their actions continue to aim for the total destruction of the Church; so long as this is not radically changed, the Church cannot make a pact with Moscow without losing the trust of the oppressed . . .

Let us not be deceived. All the apparent concessions and all the rumors about Communism's more liberal attitude toward the Church are actually only refined means to break the latter's resistance, lead it to progressive capitulation, ravish the confidence of the poor, and reestablish the authority of the Communist leaders.

In reality, the state of the persecuted Church is becoming more and more serious. With sadness and anger we are forced to acknowledge that the Communist oppressors strive with increasing success to transform into a desert even the last bits of the terrestrial paradise where God could walk about in peace. Since they have never succeeded in completely winning over those of mature mind and normal judgment, they make gigantic efforts to corrupt by force and guile millions of defenseless children in order to enslave them to their system . . .

—Werenfried van Straaten
"Où Dieu pleure"
("Where God Cries")

◢◥◣◤◢◥◣

5. *Strategy and Tactics*

It seems nowadays that Communism has become acceptable in certain circles. They say that Communism is becoming middle-class; that it is growing old; that the Communism of Brezhnev is not that of Lenin; that government practice has softened the rigorous line of the early Communists; that it no longer persecutes; and that it extols peaceful coexistence.

How do we know if what they say is true or false? If false, then Communism is still that of Lenin, and nothing has changed. One may ask why periodically there are reports that Communism has changed its attitude. We reply: for two reasons. The first is that the Communists themselves are interested in spreading this rumor as a psychological disguise. The second, more serious one is that this slogan of change launched by Moscow is propagated and amplified by men completely ignorant of the real nature of the doctrine.

What, then, is the real nature of Communism? Atheistic Communism is based on the theory of matter only. Matter, by an internal process, has passed from a nonthinking to a thinking and finally to a rational state, or living matter, which is society. This theory is called dialectical materialism, and the process, which is extended into living matter, or society, becomes historical materialism. The goal now is to bring together the necessary conditions for passage to a new state of living matter, of society. This new state, qualitatively superior, the Communists call the classless society, and the historical passageway to this society, which is the keystone of the whole system, is called the world dictatorship of the proletariat. Excepting this theory, nothing exists—no God, no morality, no being. It is in fact the negation of the real, that is, subversion.

But, since those who are to be persuaded to cooperate toward this result would in no way be enchanted by such a cold and empty view, the ultimate truth must be disguised, must be hidden by making acceptable propositions to the masses. What is kept secret is generally called strategy; what is revealed is called tactics. Communism by its propaganda gives the impression of change when actually its final goal, its real strategy, remains unaltered. The role of tactics, as Lenin used to say, is to conceal the strategic movement until the last moment.

For the Communists, then, there exist two languages: one for the initiates, who are called *apparachicks* and the other, a deceiving tongue, for the plain people. Therefore any policy, any propaganda, any proposal made in broad daylight by the Communist party constitutes the famous ancient approach of the Trojan Horse.

It must be emphasized that the victims of these tactics are generally the believers, especially the Christians. That is understandable. Christ's disciples learned from their master that God is creator of all things, that man is a creature who must respect the laws of God in the order of the universe (both nature and society) as revealed in history through his Son Jesus Christ, who died and gloriously arose. To believe in the resurrection: that is the faith, that is what makes one a Christian. But it is also that which draws the world's hatred, and in our times the resurrection is the protest against the anti-resurrection that is the foolishness of the dictatorship of the proletariat. This dictatorship, claiming to inaugurate heaven on earth, sets itself up as substitute for Christ's promise to return.

To reach their goals in the countries where they do not have control, the Communists will not directly attack believers; they will not publicly cast doubt on their beliefs and argue about the redemption. On the contrary, the Communists will tell the Christians that they respect their religion, that they consider religion to be a private matter, a matter of conscience. And they will practice the special tactic known as the policy of the extended hand, which means that not only will they not attack the Christians with respect to their faith, but will above all urge them to the common task of bettering the lot of the working class.

It must be admitted that these tactics of concealment have too often succeeded. They have opened the way for divisions among the Christians, caused the greater mass of workers to forget the abuses of Communism wherever its tyranny has been exerted, and brought to Communism the cooperation of deceived men. At the same time and despite censorship, the free nations have learned the dreadful effects of Communism in those countries where its subversive power has taken over and abolished freedom; there it is no longer a matter of an extended hand, but rather a savage and systematic liquidation of everything that recognizes the divine, even civilized culture itself. What is true for the religious realm is also true for the domains of politics and trade unions. Those who believed the promises of the Communists were their first victims.

Despite the reassuring articles of the Soviet Constitution (Article 124 on religious legislation, Article 126 on work and trade unionist legislation), the commissars of the people descended upon their former friends as heavily as upon their reputed enemies. Monks, jurists, writers, ministers, generals, peasants—all categories, sexes, and age groups—were struck with persecution and death, which continue to this day.

A strange epidemic of blindness has struck the Free World. While a free man is assassinated in China, a cardinal tortured in Hungary, a talented and free-spirited writer imprisoned, it is whispered in timorous and ignorant ears that Communism is liberation; it is bread and also roses.

Finally, by virtue of the same tactics of camouflage, the Communists use the precious and principal human blessing, which is peace, to serve in the preparation for the most infernal of dictatorships. Make no mistake. Despite the dramatic exactions made as much in the U.S.S.R. as in all the countries colonized by the Communists, those countries are not yet completely communized. Let us not forget that in the mind of Lenin and his successors the countries improperly called Communist are but provisional and preparatory stepping stones to the real Communism of the classless society. The persecutions are but an introduction to the realization of the subversive plan itself. The persecutions are only the prelude to a much vaster, indeed, Satanic enterprise. Awaiting the realization of this plan, they need peace. And only God knows all the efforts and capital used in this world venture of seduction. This blackmail with peace is the grossest moral swindle of the century.

Communism very plainly urges disarmament when it is dealing with so-called bourgeois nations. In its own affairs, wherever it has succeeded in imposing its régime, armaments as well as war industry receive priority. May 1, a day for universal celebration of work, sees the peaceful parades in all the warmongering nations, while in Moscow the lines consist of armored forces and vehicles, rockets, and war banners.

The essence of Communism is its aggressive plot against civilization, that is, against the fruits of the religion of Christ.

Under such conditions can we believe the words of a Communist? Can we believe that there exists a sincere Communist? And are strategy and tactics always at work in the person of the militant Communist?

To answer these questions properly is to set down the marvelous mystery of man. Though he be a consistent Communist, man nonetheless possesses an immortal soul, and that soul in large measure remains free and escapes the implacable logic of the totalitatian system. For this reason we may say that it is God who sets us free. Man cannot play at tactics with God. The subversive theory of Communism must then be dissociated from those whom it has deceived: mere professional militants.

Communist man, finally, is characterized by expectation, a sense of history. He is the one who, in his deepest self, awaits the great evening. It is up to the fervent followers of Christ to tell him that he is not the only one who waits. The first page of human history, says Pope Pius XI, shines with the promise of a Redeemer. In the last day, this word can deliver the Communists from both dialectic and tactics. Our message to them is that the Lord is coming back.

—Georges Sauge

6. *Enemy Stratagems*

Following the directives of party leaders, our comrades must find the means to penetrate the very heart of each church, to put themselves in the service of the new secret police organization, unfurl extensive activity in the very midst of all the church activities, launch a large-scale attack, become thoroughly involved, even appeal to the help of God, and, to succeed in forming a unique front, use the great charm and seductive power of the feminine sex. Consequently, to attain this end, to divide the churches from the inside and set various religious organizations against each other, the organ of the Party has set down the following nine rules:

1. Comrades must introduce themselves into schools established by the churches and poisoned by their doctrines. They must spy upon reactionaries to become aware of their activities; they must mix with the students and adapt themselves to their opinions; acquaint themselves with regional activities, keep an eye on these, and, methodically wedge themselves into all sectors of ecclesiastical action.

2. Every comrade must find the means to become, by baptism, a member of the church and thus *deceptively clothed.* Register with the Legion of Mary or, in the case of Protestants, join the Crusaders. Once there, everyone must go into full action, using fine words to move and attract the faithful; they must go even further and try to divide radically the various groups of the faithful, even while appealing to the love of God and pleading for the cause of peace. In this way they will destroy the venomous propaganda of oppressive imperialism.

3. Our comrades must attend all religious services and kindly, graciously, and intelligently using the most varied methods, join the clergy and spy upon their actions.

4. Schools founded and directed by the churches are an ideal field for penetration. All the while feigning the most refined benevolence, the activities of our organization must apply this double rule:

Stick to the enemy to destroy the enemy. They must mingle joyously among directors, professors, and students in order to gain dominance over them, applying the principle: To divide is to govern. Moreover, they must seek to establish contacts with the heads of the families of students to reinforce the basic work of the revolution and carry out all our secret activities.

5. They must take the initiative in all activities, penetrate all institutions of the church, win the sympathy of the faithful, and thus become capable of assuming control of the church itself.

6. By aligning itself with Party directives, the commanding cell will attain the goal set for it, that is to penetrate all ecclesiastical organizations, promote action for peace, and thus exert our influence upon all sectors.

7. On the iron principle of "crush the enemy by using the enemy itself," we must seek to induce some high-placed member of the church to come to China and procure for him the documents and necessary authorizations. By this false and secret action we will be helped to attain our goal, because that person will reveal to us the true face and the true situation of the church.

8. Activist comrades must have the spirit of initiative, discover the weak points of the ecclesiastical organization, exploit the divisions, neutralize the religious and ecclesiastical venom by instilling our counterpoison, and put everything to work to deploy our combat lines.

9. Any comrade occupying a post of command must have thoroughly understood that the Catholic church, enslaved by imperialism, must be cut down and wholly destroyed. Protestantism, which makes the mistake of following a policy of coexistence, must be hindered from making new conquests, but we can let it die a natural death.

Feb. 12, 1957

—Secret order from Office No. 106,
Chinese Communist Party

The 13 Commandments of Sun Tsu (500 A.D.)

1. Corrupt everything good in the country of your enemies.
2. Embroil the members of the leading class in criminal enterprises.
3. Undermine their reputation and give them up at the right time to the disgrace of their fellow citizens.

4. Secure also the collaboration of the most vile and abject men.
5. Disturb by every possible means the efficiency of governments.
6. Spread strife and discord among the citizens of the enemy country.
7. Set the young against their elders.
8. Undermine the traditions of your adversaries.
9. Disturb by every possible means the arming, provisioning, and order of enemy troops.
10. Destroy the enemy's will to fight by means of music and sensual songs.
11. Call upon prostitutes to complete the work of corruption.
12. Be generous with promises and gifts to obtain information. Especially do not regret the money that thus used brings in good profit.
13. Place informers and secret agents everywhere. Only the man using these means and knowing how to apply the methods that provoke corruption and strife is worthy of ruling and commanding. Such a man is a treasure to his sovereign and a pillar of the state.

7. Communist Methods of Penetrating the Church

In the early 'fifties NATO Secret Services discovered that, within the usual network of espionage and counter-espionage, the Soviets had set up a department especially for the penetration of churches. In satellite countries the goal had been set in 1945: infiltrate the churches in order to control, if not dissolve, them. In 1949 a second objective was grafted to the first: penetrate the Western, Catholic, and Orthodox churches exactly as other specialists penetrate Moslem, Protestant, and other groups; then on the one hand look for fellow travelers, on the other hand recruit agents.

This slow penetration of the churches in order to dissolve them from the inside and lead them to revise the foundations of their dogma is a doubly subversive task and depends exclusively on espionage. Agents are, of course, selected with extreme care . . .

At the beginning of the 'fifties, a Jesuit priest and professor of theology at the Gregorian University was caught in the act of stealing documents from the vault where the secret records of the Vatican are kept. His name is Alighiero Tondi. He was the secretary of Msgr. Montini, who was then a direct collaborator of Pius XII and is today no less a figure than Pope Paul VI.

140

An investigation has been going on for some time under the direction of a French priest associated with the Vatican who had been an officer of the Second French Bureau in Algiers during the war. For two years each time priests were secretly sent to Eastern countries to replace those confined, deported, or shot by the régimes, a Communist welcome committee was immediately on the spot to arrest them too, even before they could take office. In addition, certain secret resolutions were obviously leaked once in a while to the Italian Communist Party in matters of managing the assets of the church.

When Alighiero Tondi was caught, he admitted that he became a priest in 1936 under orders of a special division of the Italian Communist Party and that during his training he even took a course at the Lenin University of Moscow, where the chief spies are trained. Since 1944 he had been sending his information directly to Palmiro Togliatti, general secretary of the Italian Communist Party.

The Vatican has its laws. Tondi was simply expelled from the order and the sacred confines. The following year he married Carmen Zanti, a Communist militant. Since then he travels all over Europe: in March 1965 he stayed in East Germany to advise Walter Ulbricht in matters of religious policy. Since Msgr. Montini became Pope, Alighiero Tondi declares, rightly or wrongly, that he has been pardoned because "those in high places" were able to understand that he has always had one goal: to work for peace and the reconciliation of souls.

—Pierre de Villemarest
"L'espionnage soviétique en France"
("Soviet Espionage in France")

The Struggle Against Religion

We must fight against religion; that is the ABC of all materialism and consequently of Marxism. But Marxism goes further. It says: We must know how to approach the masses with particular discretion .... We must know how to comply with every sacrifice, use (whenever needed) all stratagems, use guile, adopt illegal procedures, keep silent sometimes, conceal the truth sometimes—to the sole end of penetrating the trade unions, of staying there and accomplishing, in the face of all odds, the Communist task."

—V. I. Lenin

Communism vs. Religion

It is necessary to work out an integral system of scientific-atheistic education capable of reaching all layers and groups of the population and to impede the dissemination of religious ideas, particularly among children and adolescents. The duty of all party organizations and ideological institutions is to develop systematically and coherently scientific-atheistic propaganda, to explain patiently and convincingly the inconsistency of religious beliefs. It is especially important to improve the substance of atheistic activities. By means of the press, radio broadcasts and conferences, the hypocritical morality of religion and the attempts of churchmen to adapt themselves to the demands of the moment must be unmasked; the incompatibility of Communism with religion must be demonstrated . . .

—N. Khrushchev

The Uses of Atheism

A true propagandist of atheism cannot and must not remain the man who speaks only of the wrongs of religion. Seen from a higher level, the real propagandist of atheism is an educator profoundly interested in the lot of those who have become victims of religious ideology; he is a fighter who aims to get rid of the causes of religious inclinations.

—Leonid Ilichev

8. A Papal View of Communism

In the beginning Communism showed itself for what it was in all its perversity, but very soon it realized that it was thus alienating the people. It has therefore changed its tactics and strives to entice the multitudes by trickery of various forms, hiding its real designs behind ideas that in themselves are good and attractive. Thus, aware of the universal desire for peace, the leaders of Communism pretend to be the most zealous promoters and propagandists in the movement for world amity. Yet at the same time they stir up a class warfare that causes rivers of blood to flow and, realizing that their system offers no internal guarantee of peace, they have recourse to unlimited armaments. Under various names that do not suggest Communism, they establish organizations and periodicals with the sole purpose of carrying their ideas into quarters otherwise inaccessible. They try perfidiously to worm their way even into professedly Catholic and other religious organizations. Again, without receding an inch from their subversive principles, they invite Catholics to collaborate with them in the realm of so-called humanitarianism and charity; at times they even make proposals that are in perfect harmony with the Christian spirit and the doctrine of the Church. Elsewhere they carry their hypocrisy so far as to encourage the belief that Communism, in countries where faith and culture are more strongly entrenched, will assume another and much milder form. It will not interfere with the practice of religion. It will respect liberty of conscience . . .

See to it, Venerable Brethren, that the faithful do not allow themselves to be deceived! Communism is intrinsically wrong, and no one who would save Christian civilization may collaborate with it in any undertaking whatsoever. Those who permit themselves to be deceived into lending their aid toward the triumph of Communism in their own country will be the first to fall victims of their error. And the greater the antiquity and grandeur of the Christian civilization in the regions where Communism successfully penetrates, so much more devastating will be the hatred displayed by the godless.

—Pius XI
"Divini Redemptoris"

Memento

All those in Christendom who have preserved good sense, a clear mind, a tender heart, and a noble conscience must unite to raise an unshakable barrier against the hosts of impiety and immorality. To the cunning and too often victorious tactics of the enemy, who shun neither lying nor flattery, treason of hospitality nor crime, we must oppose certain and complete information, precise knowledge of the facts, clear understanding of ideas and principles, uprightness of conscience, and an ardent, stubborn will. We must not confuse error and truth, good and evil, Christianity and Bolshevism . . . With clear perception of what separates them in other areas and in mutual respect for their distinct individualities, all spiritual groups must unite to decry doctrines and practices that, under the names of Communism, Bolshevism, and Red Experience, consist of confusion of thought, corruption of the soul, negation of conscience, and destruction of the highest and most noble forms of human sensibility. In the face of this denial of the spirit, the union of all those who labor for the spirit is imperative . . .

Communism has declared all-out war against Christendom. Christendom will wage war against it—or perish.

> —Fr. Durrlemann
> ("Le Communisme contre la Chrétienté")
> ("Communism Against Christianity")

9. *The Religious Politics of Ravishing Wolves*

The hypocritical Communist policy of the extended hand was launched by Maurice Thorez in 1937 and taken up much later in the roundabout verbiage of Georges Marchais in his interview with the newspaper *La Croix* in November 1970. Revived, of course, by the recent program of the French Communist Party and again by the "week of Marxist thought" at the end of January 1972, the intrinsically perverse strategy of Communist subversion follows its deceitful course in order to confuse the leaders of the churches and the disoriented Christians of the free world.

Communism seeks a "common willingness to act in the contemporary world," and every Christian worker, Guy Bess warns us, who "believes that the atheism of his fellow-worker is sufficient reason not to fight with him against exploitation" becomes nothing but the "prisoner of an ideology that shields him from the reality of social relations."

Almost the same view imbues the document by some fifteen French bishops entitled "First Observations by the Bishops Council of the Working World in its Dialogue with Militant Christians Who Have Chosen Socialism," a document that asserts that "the working world as a whole is attracted to Socialism, whether to Communism or to other forms" and that this "essential trait of the working class" constitutes "a strong challenge for our pastors." Moreover, "there are important elements of Marxism that have been assimilated by Christian workers. They do not seem to them to be incompatible with their faith."

We do not wish to use legions of logical arguments to oppose the

144

seductive display of falsehood and to denounce the tactics of the
Trojan horse that Mr. Marchais and his disciples in cassock have
taken pains to roll into the Christian church. For then we would have
to say that, under the dictatorship of the one and only Party (the
inevitable expression of "the dictatorship of the proletariat"), political freedom is refused to any possible form of opposition. This includes the freedom to live and freely manifest a faith that always opposes atheism, even though spokesmen for the French Communist Party promise the Christians in France that "freedom of
belief, freedom of worship, freedom of religious education, and the
public expression of the churches will be guaranteed by law and in
practice." We would have to say, too, that in the countries that head
the international Communist movement thousands of believers are
condemned to hard labor in Soviet reeducation camps because of
their religious convictions and their Christian activity, even though
Mr. Marchais assures doubters that "the socialist law will guarantee
religious freedoms against all persecution and all administrative repression." We would have to repeat, even shout from the housetops,
those revealing words of Lenin: "Let us make the commitments asked
of us; but when the time comes, let us remember that Communist
honor will consist in not fulfilling these commitments, if such is the
interest of the proletariat"—even if the Marxist-Leninist who is being
interviewed, pretending those commitments have been forgotten,
tries to lull the vigilance of Christians by his roundabout phrases.

In one of the broadcasts of *La Chaine* for the Church of Silence,
we tried to compare the falsehood of the words, ideas, formulas, and
promises of Mr. Marchais and his company with the truth of God;
for the light of his Word implacably condemns all that contravenes
the perfect law, which is the law of liberty in Jesus Christ:

1. How can we conceive that "new possibilities are consequently
opening for common action" between Communists and Christians;
that "we can work perfectly well together for the building of Socialism despite our philosophical differences" when that "socialist society," already realized in the East, is founded on injustice and the
violation of human dignity? When it does not seek "the Kingdom of
God and his righteousness" (Matt. 6:33)? We obey only one instruction in what concerns common action, participation, cooperation,
and collaboration with the Communists—the instruction of the Gospel:
"Be not unequally yoked together with unbelievers. For what part-
nership have righteousness and iniquity? And what fellowship has
light with darkness? What accord has Christ with Belial? . . ."
(II Cor. 6:14, 15).

2. How can one be *both* Christian "and" Communist? On the one

hand we hear: "Yes, there are in our ranks Christians who are 'at ease' . . . They are full members of the Party." Does a spring, asks the apostle James, "pour forth from the same opening fresh water and brackish?" How can a Christian serve two masters at the same time? *"For,"* Jesus teaches us, *"either he will hate the one and love the other, or he will be devoted to the one and despise the other.* You cannot serve God and Mammon" (Matt. 6:24).

3. How can we accept the Marxist formula of the class struggle within Christianity itself when Jesus Christ does not ask of us hatred, vengeance, and revolt against the established order, but love for all social classes, the fervent obedience to his divine commandment: "Love your enemies, bless them that curse you, do good to them that hate you, and pray for them which despitefully use you, and persecute you . . ." (Matt. 5:44)?

4. How can we believe with all evidence to the contrary that, "tomorrow as today," the French Communists, established firmly at the helm, will exclude "any recourse to whatever method of constraint there may be to bring about the triumph" of their ideas when Jesus reveals the future conduct of his foes: "You will be delivered up even by parents and brothers and kinsmen and friends, and some of you they will put to death; You will be hated by all for my name's sake" (Luke 21:16, 17)?

5. How can we let ourselves be duped by the illusion of religious freedom when Communism has for ages crucified Christ and released the Barabbases of history, and that freedom is in reality "a cloak for maliciousness," since the people who "live in [the] error" of their atheistic politics, who "are themselves slaves of corruption" (II Peter 2:18, 19), can never guarantee a true and total freedom for the Church of Christ?

6. How can we understand "the realistic commitment" of those who boast that their aim is not "to build a society against the Christian working masses, but with them" when the French Communist Party is not with God, but against God, against Jesus Christ, against the evangelical doctrine of those "Christian working masses"? Our Lord and Savior put us on our guard once and for all: "He who is not with me is against me" (Matt. 12:30).

7. How can we acknowledge the Communist policy of the extended hand? It has even contaminated the World Council of Churches, which does not cease to extend its hand to the atheistic revolutionaries of the third world and to the church hierarchy that has compromised with atheism in Soviet-dominated countries.

But the believers of the Church of Silence refuse this strangling hand because, according to the Bible, it is "a slack hand" (Prov. 10:4), "the hand of our enemies" (Luke 1:74) raised "against God." They recognize only one extended hand: "the mighty hand of God" (I Peter 5:6), the hand of his endless love, of his promises of protection and faithfulness, of his pardon and mercy.

These witnesses from the catacombs know very well that in the last days false prophets will slip in among unsuspecting Christians, as well as ravenous wolves and ungodly persons who hasten to make void the grace of God. To every promise constitutionally guaranteed, to every temptation, this is their sole response: *"Begone, Satan! for it is written, 'You shall worship the Lord your God and him only shall you serve'"* (Matt. 4:10).

—Guy Serveux

10. *Sing Unto the Lord*

In prison or in freedom the Christians in Communist countries take the trouble to rejoice always. Despite the great difficulty in fulfilling this Gospel command, it is still accomplished, thanks to the power of prayer and the revival of the religious hymn.

At the beginning of my imprisonment, I would pace up and down the ten square feet of my solitary cell, singing for the Lord and praying; certainly not out loud, as that was forbidden, but silently, inside myself. The well-known psalms and hymns came to me and resounded in my head and in my heart.

One day the guard—who saw, through the peephole, the movement of my lips—opened the door slightly and whispered:

"What are you doing, talking to yourself?"

"I am singing," I answered.

Since then, as I learned several years later, he spoke of me always as "Madwoman 24."

Indeed, that "Madwoman 24" and so many other "madmen" who filled the various political prisons continually praised and prayed to the Lord; that is how they could be strong and rejoice, though mistreated, tortured, and mocked.

Before my arrest I had composed some music to Psalm 1, versified by a dear brother in our circle. What great joy was ours when the music had been completed and we were able to meet secretly and sing it together "in the same mind and the same judgment."

While I whispered it later in my cell, loneliness disappeared, and I found myself once more, carried on the wings of the melody and its words, with my brothers and sisters, reliving the wonderful moments spent together with the Lord in our midst.

Thus, through faith in God and peace from on high, human suffering was accepted as testing or chastening, as instruction or strengthening of the spiritual person.

Viewed from this angle, tribulations did not overcome us; on the contrary, they made us happy, they plunged us into a happiness inexpressible in words. And it was this that materialized in poems and hymns.

Almost every Christian who went through prison felt this need to create verses or songs of praise to the Lord. It was a means to discharge a happiness too great for the soul. Most of these works *sui generis* did not pretend to be perfect. Their immortality is not of this world; it belongs to the beyond. It is the angels who award them according to the standards of heaven.

Below is an example, a song composed in a labor camp while marching to the barracks, about four miles from work. The sunset and semidarkness allowed the first stars to be seen . . .

—Nicole Valéry

Near to Jesus

Listen then to what my heart
one fair evening told me,
my gaze fixed upon a star
upon a shining star:
   "What could I, tell me, what could I have done
   in a life that without Him has no meaning?
   With the weight of heavy sins and bitter pains,
   every day a burden greater than before,
   exhausted by great struggle and frustration,
   alone, with no one else, alone, confused,
   what could I have done amidst my cruel concerns
   far from Him?"
The star that shone above
gave me answer,
sending by its rays
a song into my heart:
   "You must ever cleave to Him!
   Recall His firm support

and all He represents in what befalls you.
Make to Him your gift of fervent love, unending love,
let yourself be guided by Him, without hesitation,
be faithful in His service, ever faithful,
happy every moment, and forever,
near to Him!"

6: Miscellany

1. *Unity in Suffering*

The daily suffering, the prisons, and the lack of political and religious freedom taught us to agree and to have no dissensions among us, but to be—as the Apostle Paul exhorts—"united in the same mind and the same judgment" (I Cor. 1:10). We knew that, through our sufferings, we were stripped of the old man, of the conformist and carnal man, which is always the seed of discord, of fierce disputes, of quarrels, enmity, animosity, and divisions of belief. We knew, we felt, in being one in Jesus Christ, that we had put on the new man, which always completes itself through knowledge and the unity of brotherly fellowship, according to the image of the One who created it, in order to form one body by means of the bond of perfection which is love.

Over there, in the darkness of prisons or Communist labor camps, there was "neither Greek nor Jew, circumcision nor uncircumcision, barbarian, Scythian . . ." (Col. 3:11). In the bolted dungeons there was neither Orthodox nor Protestant, priest nor pastor, Sunday as day of rest nor Adventist Sabbath, icons nor open sky for everyday prayers, Gospel nor dogma of such and such a church, the pomp of the mass nor the simplicity of the Lord's Supper, the seven Orthodox sacraments nor the two Protestant ones. Yes, over there in the prisons Christ was really all in all, and through Christ we reenacted the unity of the early Church when "the company of those who believed were of one heart and soul" (Acts 4:32). Yes, in Communist prisons and in the midst of a society disfigured by tyranny and lack of freedom, the Church of Silence has realized spiritual unification of all believers under the crushing law of sufferings. This church, I affirm, turns out to be the root of the only valid ecumenicity: the Christocentric ecumenicity according to the tolerance and nondenominational character of the Gospel of Christ.

Why not speak the truth? That ecumenicity, so fervently desired by us in the world of prisons, is alas! unrealizable up to now in the Free World, which I accuse before men and especially before God. It is a corrupt and confused world that boasts of forsaking God, rebels against divine commands, and always resists the Holy Spirit; it hates Jesus Christ and denies him by warring against the Lord with political lawlessness, foolish atheistic doctrines, and spiritual insensitivity.

It was in prison, in the intense fellowship of Christians in chains, that we untiringly experienced the Gospel harmony of brotherly friendship and discovered the underlying causes of church division.

> —Sergiu Grossu
> "Nous attendons une nouvelle terre".
> ("We Await a New World")

2. *Ecumenicity of the Catacombs*

One could also speak of the incarnation in Russian life of another problem, which is the topic of theoretical discussions in the West: ecumenicity.

I still remember the time when the sects, which had acquired considerable freedom after the revolution, caused a great upheaval in the Orthodox church. In the 1920s these sects made great progress, and the vast majority of their adherents were deserters of the Orthodox church. Propaganda against Orthodoxy was the ground of activity for Baptists, Evangelical Christians, Adventists, Dukhobors, and other groups. Orthodox propaganda, which at that time was still inspired by the official traditions of the old régime, responded to the sects with bitterness and irritation, even hatred. There seemed to be no way to appease such unforgivable antagonism. But what happened? For years Orthodox and sectarians peopled together the convict prisons of Berea, slept side by side on prison pallets, ate the same prison soup from the same rusty tins.

At the present time the Orthodox church and the sects hardly ever compete . . . One can see a new spirit in relations between Orthodox and sectarians. The old mistrust and mutual hatred have completely disappeared and given place to respect and sympathy. Facing the same problems favors still closer relationships . . . Thus, an ecumenicity in living religious practice is taking place in Russia. It does not consist in conferences, official meetings, and pompous banquets, as in the case of Amsterdam ecumenicity. It is obvious which of the two is the more authentic.

—A. Krasnov-Levitin
Letter to Pope Paul VI

"That They May Be One . . ."

. . . Referring to the words, "that they all may be one," many Christians aim for unification and not unity. Now unification and unity are different. The great statue seen in Nebuchadnezzar's dream was "mighty and of exceeding brightness," but in one blow it was broken and carried away by the wind "like the chaff of the summer threshing floors" because it was made of gold, silver, bronze, iron, and clay. In it there was unification, but not unity (Daniel 2:31, 35). In contrast, unity is pure despite its many members who, though many, yet form one body; thus unity is complete and without division (I Corinthians 12:12, 25-27; Romans 12:4, 5). If Christians, referring to Christ's prayer concerning unity, actually seek only unification, they show by that very fact that they ask according to their desire and not what pleases the Lord. That is why the goal of unity has never yet been reached in our brotherhood.

"That they all may be one; as thou, Father, art in me, and I in thee, that they also may be one in us" (John 17:21).

After serious study, we see that the prayer of Jesus Christ lays a double foundation, because it includes first of all the unity of the redeemed with God, then their unity among themselves in God. Consequently, our unity with Christ as the head of his Church is the basic condition without which there can be no real unity among Christians, for we are members of his body.

—Appeal of the "Initiators," E.C.B.

3. Solzhenitsyn: Christian Writer

Not being a specialist in literature, I would never have let myself speak of Solzhenitsyn if I had not been struck by what I cannot call other than the Christian inspiration of his work. What fills me with joy in the presence of the Solzhenitsyn "miracle" is that this first national writer of the Soviet period of Russian literature is also a Christian writer.

When I speak of Christian writer in general, and of Solzhenitsyn in particular, I refer especially to a profound and total, although perhaps unconscious, understanding of the world, of man, and of life; an understanding that, in history and human culture, was born and developed from the Biblical and Christian revelation. Human culture as a whole had, and certainly will have, other origins, other sources. But only Christianity, only the Old and New Testament revelation, contains a conception of the world that, infusing human culture, reveals to it, not only the possibility of a Christian culture, but also its reality. Unable to delineate this conception, I can only describe it as a triunitarian perception of creation, fall, and rebirth. I am convinced that the work of Solzhenitsyn is founded precisely on this perception and that thereby it is Christian.

As a whole, the work of Solzhenitsyn deals only with atrocities and sufferings; it treats only evil. Truly, the world he created "rests in evil," not only in a more or less symbolic or metaphysical sense, but literally: in the nightmarish reality of concentration camps, of Mavrino's *sharashka*, and of the cancer ward. Yet nowhere in his work—and the reader may judge for himself—do we find, do we even suspect that ontological denigration of the world, of man, and of life that for a long time has gushed aggressively from numerous works of art. For lack of space I cannot and do not wish to marshal quotes because, and this goes without saying, it is not in them that everything consists, but in the general tone of the work, in its inward music that does not lend itself to purely formal analysis. In that music, seemingly entirely woven with cries of suffering, the ultimate depth of reality slips in mysteriously and readily reveals itself—the Biblical and evangelical "praise" of the world's creation. In all of Solzhenitsyn's work that "morning of creation" shines invisibly, yet perceptibly. Thus Kostoglotov, having just left the cancer ward, rejoices: "It was the morning of creation. The world had been created anew for one reason only, to be given back to Oleg. 'Go out and live!' it seemed to say . . . His face radiated happiness. He smiled at no man, only at the sky and the trees, but it was with that early-morning springtime joy that touches even the old and the sick. He walked down the well-known pathways . . . The first morning of creation—who can act rationally on such a day? Oleg discarded all his plans. Instead he conceived the mad scheme of going to the Old Town immediately, while it was still early morning, to look at a flowering apricot tree . . ."

It is unnecessary, of course, to demonstrate that evil and suffering occupy a central place in Solzhenitsyn's work. But we may notice that evil for him is placed within a Christian context and a vivid experience of the "mystery of evil." And nothing distinguishes the Christian religion from a non-Christian one and from a philosophy or ideology more than its attitude to evil. All other religions and philosophies tend, really, to explain evil and thereby even to make it inoffensive, because the explanation legitimizes and finally justifies it: *phenomenon bene fundatum*. Only Christianity, whatever scholastics of all times may have dogmatically affirmed, does not explain evil. Rather, it is the only one that shows it clearly. For the whole problem lies in this, that for Christianity evil is not a reality grounded in itself or evil in itself, as may appear to those—even Christians—who denounce the forces of evil. Nor is evil simply a negative sign, the mere absence of good, as utopian rationalists of all leanings seem to think. For Christianity, evil is always and above all the Fall.

Only that which is uplifted can fall, and the more exalted, splendid, and precious it is, the greater the horror, the pain, and the suffering of its fall. Evil is the fall of what was once exalted, of the precious and splendid, and that is what constitutes suffering, horror, and pain. To live the evil and to feel it as fall amounts precisely to showing evil as evil. And it is this we find in Solzhenitsyn: real, unique, concrete evil; not some general ethereal essence, but rather that horrible, painful, irreversible point. Mavrino's *sharashka* and the cancer ward are reflections, not of this world, but of the fallen world that by its "fall" testifies to freedom, wholeness, and life . . . Evil for Solzhenitsyn is real because it is always personal. It is not contained in impersonal systems, nor does it emanate from structures of the same kind, but it is always in man and by man. Even in the *sharashka*, even in the cancer ward, evil does not manifest itself as man's imprisonment by forces and fates beyond his control, to be stoically endured after explaining and accepting them. Evil is always and above all evil men—men who have chosen and always choose evil, men who have really chosen to serve it. That is why it is a fall every time, a choice every time.

But faith in the possibility of man to be reborn, the refusal to pronounce death upon whoever or whatever it may be, can no more be eradicated from Solzhenitsyn than from Christianity. Everything is possible on condition that man discovers his conscience, just as the effeminate and spoiled State Counselor Second Rank Innokenty Volodin discovered it, as the inhabitants of the *sharashka* discovered it in their "immortal soul of zeks." What caused Volodin, what compelled him on that festal evening to phone the condemned doctor? What compelled several men to prefer the despair of concentration camps to Mavrino's relative well-being? There is an answer to this question in the work of Solzhenitsyn, and it springs finally from the conscience of the writer himself. In this horrible, apish, evil, and fallen world, conscience secretly begins its rule. It triumphs and illumines man.

One last point: we live undoubtedly in the decadence of Christian culture, due above all to the loss of its source and sustenance: the "triunitarian" perception. All around us men passionately seek other roots, other foundations, other grounds for culture: culture that rejects God! For the Christian, clearly, the worst thing is to see that there is no longer opposition on the part of other Christians. Some are ready to withdraw to the catacombs, abandoning all responsibility with regard to culture. Others are ready, almost with joy, to join the enemy, convinced that they act as Christians. Alas, it is mainly the Christians themselves who write about the death of God and the Christian justification for the secularization of culture. Thus, culture is abandoned to the devil, who is a murderer from the beginning of the world, of man, and of life.

But now in this night, in a country that has for more than half a century officially denied Christianity, its name, and its calling, there arises a solitary figure, who with all his work proclaims an alternative to lying and sin, and thus delivers us. A writer, a Russian writer, a Christian writer. For this deliverance, for this testimony declared in Russia, through which that nation is returning to itself and to the world, for the fact that "the image of eternity hidden therein—clear, peaceful, intact" has been preserved, we offer to Aleksandr Solzhenitsyn all our thanks and our hearts overflowing with joy.

—"Le messager orthodoxe"
("The Orthodox Messenger")
No. 53, 1971

A Prayer of Thanksgiving

How easy it is for me to live with you, oh Lord my God! How easy it is for me to believe in you! When my thoughts waver, assailed by doubt, and my spirit fails, when the most intelligent see no further than this evening and do not know what they should do tomorrow, then, Lord, you send me the clear certitude that you exist and that you yourself will ensure that not all the paths of goodness are barred!

At the height of world renown I contemplate in wonder the path of hopelessness that led me to this point, from which even I have been able from afar to transmit among men the reflection of your glory!

As long as it is needful, you will give me the means for this. And when I can no longer do it, you will have entrusted the task to others . . .

Aleksandr Solzhenitsyn

4. *The Gospel by Radio*

The Communist customs officials cannot prevent the infiltration of Christian literature into Communist countries, but they manage to make the work difficult and dangerous. Sometimes underground printing presses are discovered, and this leads to arrests.

The Communists do not have customs officials in the air. Radio waves reach their destination. In Red China some have been condemned to death for listening to foreign Gospel broadcasts. Despite everything, however, they listen. In the Soviet Union jamming stations exist, but these are very costly. The U.S.S.R. territory is huge. There are vast regions in that country where the radio is listened to. In European satellite countries, the messages are clearly received.

A young Chinese smuggled out a letter in which he said he had been an atheist. Then one time he saw in a film a woman carrying a cross. He asked what this meant: they told him that it was the symbol of Christianity. But he could not learn what Christianity was. There were no Christians in that region. By chance he tuned in to a Gospel broadcast. He listened to the broadcasts one after the other and began to love Christ. He asked: "Does God accept someone from Red China? Several times you have mentioned the church in your sermons. But here God lives in heaven and there is no church between us and him—we are in Red China here. All the churches have been closed. How can we get to heaven?" The poor boy did not know that he had many churches. The entire universal Church is his. He poses a second question: "How should I pray? You always close with prayer. I don't know how to pray." But then he explains what he understands by prayer and gives what seems to me the most beautiful definition I've ever heard: "Prayer consists of speaking all day in such a way that an amen can be said after each conversation." You cannot say amen after quarreling with your wife.

We have letters written by Russians converted through radio broadcasts, even though they have never in their lives seen a Bible.

New congregations are created in this way. I quote a letter from Rumania: "We want you to know that during the last three months more than fifty souls have been converted in our village, merely by

156

listening to the radio, among them the wife of the chief of police. In this village, there were no believers before. Now they all listen to the Word of God. Work as much as you can, and God will reward you."
—Richard Wurmbrand
If That Were Christ, Would You Give Him Your Blanket?

◭◭◭

Radio Broadcasts for the Church of Silence

"The heavens are telling the glory of God; and the firmament proclaims his handiwork.

"Day to day pours forth speech, and night to night declares knowledge.

"There is no speech, nor are there words; their voice is not heard; yet their voice goes out through all the earth, and their words to the end of the world."

—Psalm 19:1-4

◭◭◭

The Chain Radio Broadcasts

(by Trans-Europe Lisbon, every
Sunday and Thursday, *from 9:45 to 10:00 P.M.,*
on short wave, 31.06 m.)

"La Chaine" broadcasts began May 6, 1971 to transmit messages and news by which Christians in the Free World can better realize and understand the deplorable situation of prosecuted believers under atheistic régimes.

Since most of the Western churches, the newspapers, radio and television, and even the World Council keep silent; bearing in mind Communist propaganda which strives to subvert "the weak and ignorant," as Bossuet used to say; to counteract the horrible persecutions committed in the East against the children of God—it is imperative to plead, by means of the air waves, for our martyred brothers, to denounce the lack of religious freedom in countries where religion is incompatible with the Marxist-Leninist ideology, to participate in the suffering of this church of the catacombs.

Unfortunately, "La Chaine" broadcasts still have an inferior technical quality; its messages are very often jammed. And yet, excepting a few persons who have never been able to "catch" them even once, the letters that reach us speak of the joy and happiness of our dear friends who take the trouble to listen, despite all difficulties and hindrances, to the programs devoted to the Church of Silence, that is, to the fact of persecutions in countries with atheistic totalitarian régimes. A Swiss brother, for example, writes that he was able to "follow almost everything despite the jamming . . . toward the end of the message." For a sister in Belgium "the broadcasts of Thursday, October 28 were perfect in every way." Other friends, who also follow our radio broadcasts, thank the Lord "that his help is always the same for our brothers 'in chains' for the cause of the Gospel."

Completely aware that there are enemy forces fiercely opposed to our achieving broadcasts of a technical and spiritual excellence, we will continue to fight in the name of the Lord against the ideological and practical atheism of our day, the source of hatred and religious persecution. Despite all the difficulties, hindrances, and uncertainties that still threaten us, we count on the brotherly intercession of all who love the Church of Silence and expecially the gracious hand of the Lord our God.

In preaching, Jesus must be living and real in us, since he alone has the words of eternal life and the power to restore the most fallen creatures in the most unjust society. Thus we can confess him before men and repeat, even under threat of torture and prison, the words of Gregory Boruchko before his judges at the trial of the Odessa believers in 1967: "You prepare torments, but actually it is God who decides, because not a hair can fall from our heads without God's permission. Suffering is the vital nerve of Christianity. The Church lives as long as it suffers because the Lord Christ suffered martyrdom and he has asked us to follow him."

—Sergiu Grossu

5. Danger in Asia

President Nixon's doctrine had a disastrous result, which I predicted last summer (1971) when he announced his trip to Communist China. That summer I visited the Philippines, Vietnam, Hong Kong, Taiwan, and South Korea, and I wish to give you a glimpse of the great storm that the President's policy of appeasement provoked in Asia.

In July I saw the Philippines at its worst, because a month of continual typhoons had discharged 360 cm of rain upon this beautiful island country. The political situation was bad. The Communist Huks planned to ally themselves with corrupt politicians, incite to revolution, and stir up anti-Americanism in order to create a Red Republic of the Philippines. Through martial law and a series of rapid actions, President Marcos was able to win the confidence of the Philippine people; he is cleaning up politics and the army, placing new men of integrity in charge, and reshaping a clean, honest republic, modeled after Taiwan.

I spent only two weeks in Vietnam, because I had to follow a close schedule in the other Far Eastern countries, but I was able to see a Vietnam trusting its armed forces, which had been able to stop and conquer the twelve divisions of the North that had crossed the 17th parallel to occupy the Hue region and establish there a South Vietnamese provisional government, completely Communist and without freedom.

General Giap wanted to destroy the South Vietnamese government and show the world that, upon the withdrawal of American troops, Vietnamization would be a failure. South Vietnam, despite terrible losses in its armed forces, defeated the North and proved that Vietnamization was a success. I was able to visit the combat zones and see the success of this great defensive victory. The opposition comes from their own allies, the United States, which would like to compromise with the North and bring about a cease-fire under conditions unacceptable to the South.

The destiny of 350 million inhabitants of Southeast Asia depends upon the present turning point in Vietnam. This is especially important for the Christians of Southeast Asia, who would lose their freedom if Vietnam were to fall to Communist influence through a coalition government.

During my stay in Vietnam, I talked with eight South Vietnamese bishops. All are against war as war, but they recognize that in the face of Communist aggression one must fight to keep his freedom.

I was also able to visit all the political leaders of Vietnam, the religious leaders, Chinese and other different minority groups, many Vietnamese businessmen, priests, and students and refugees. All had confidence in their army if the United States continued to support them with arms, planes, and naval air support.

I spent several days in Hong Kong and talked with a large number of both Chinese and foreign friends in the British colony. Hong Kong's prosperity continues despite the forecasts that one day it will be taken over by Red China.

Hong Kong represents a platform for news from Red China. More than one thousand young men and girls from mainland China made the seven-hour swim to Hong Kong despite great danger from Chinese Communists and sharks . . . How many perished on the way, we will never know. More arrived by other means, and that year saw the largest number of Chinese refugees, despite the Communist effort to stop the exodus. Churches, private organizations, and others provided aid to these people, who swelled Hong Kong's population to nearly six million. I obtained much religious news from the Continent that unfortunately cannot be published.

Taiwan, which I visited for several weeks, is economically prosperous; the Republic of China with its 17 million inhabitants exports more than the People's Republic of China with its 750 million. Despite the great political defeats of the Republic of China—the illegal recognition of Red China and its admission to the United Nations in 1971; President Nixon's visit to Red China; and Japan's recognition of Red China and the effort of the Chinese Communists to isolate Free China—the people continue to hope that the country will surmount the obstacles and remain free and economically prosperous. A government well organized against corruption is in charge. The leaders and the people of Taiwan have confidence that, because of their strong army, air force, and marine corps, the Chinese Communists will not attack Taiwan, since that would induce the Soviets to attack Red China, and the Chinese Communist army, constantly purged, would be in no condition to fight effectively.

The church in Taiwan is growing. There is an excellent Catholic university with seven thousand students, forty-eight secondary schools, six dioceses and one archdiocese, and many such social and humanitarian projects as hospitals and dispensaries. The 300,000 Catholics and 300,000 Protestants are more influential than their number would indicate; they hope to play a decisive role when mainland China will once again be free.

In South Korea, where I went for an important meeting, the situation is much less optimistic, I believe, because the dialogue that it has broached with North Korea is very dangerous. What brought the leaders of South Korea to begin this dialogue is the fact that the country is surrounded by enemies: the Soviet Union, Red China, North Korea, and even Japan, a power that formerly dominated Korea and is not liked. The United States, allied with South Korea for years, having decided to open relations with Red China and the Soviet Union, indirectly forces South Korea to find its own way to remain free. South Korea has 31 million people, the North has only 13 million. But North Korea is almost as strong militarily as the South, and if the United States should decide to withdraw its last division from Korea, the military balance would be alarming. This is the direct result of Nixon's policies, which force the peoples of the Far East to make unfortunate decisions in order to remain free.

I met with President Park Chung Hee and Premier Kim Jong-Pil, whom I had contacted several times in my six trips to Korea following the Korean War. On August 21, 1972, at the Blue House, I expressed my concern over these dangerous rapprochements, and I pointed out the latest disastrous floods of August 1972 that caused the death of 423 in South Korea. The Korean president assured me that he was not becoming more involved with the Communists, but that, like mighty waters, communism is a difficult tide to check.

Despite these painful circumstances, the Korean churches are thriving. A new higher seminary was recently opened in Seoul.

I also made a brief visit to Japan, which on September 29, 1972 took a tremendous step toward dropping Taiwan and recognizing Red China; Japan denounced the treaties made with the Republic of China. That action by Prime Minister Tanaka astonished the world, because Japan had been allied with Free China and the United States.

The fact that the United States did not advise Japan of President Nixon's planned visit to mainland China forced Japan into recognizing Red China before the United States, even if temporarily this official recognition was of no special advantage; on the contrary, it could do much harm to Japan through Communist infiltration and the imperceptible destruction of the Japanese imperial system by the Communists.

President Nixon's new Asiatic policies weakened the bond of Asian countries against Communism and divided the various nations of the Far East by forcing them to find hasty and often very dangerous solutions and causing them to lose their confidence in the United States.

The Christian churches in Asia look with amazement upon the growing Communist danger, still ready, just as it was several years ago, to destroy all Far Eastern religions: Buddhism, Taoism, Confucianism, and Catholic, Protestant, and Orthodox Christianity. For Communist materialists, despite their smiles and diplomatic advances in today's world, want above all the communization of the whole world and the slow but sure destruction of any form of religion.

—The Rev. Raym... J. De Jaegher

6. Chinese Kaleidoscope

Casualties to Communism in China

	Range of Estimates	
1. First Civil War (1927-36)	250,000	500,000[1]
2. Fighting during Sino-Japanese War (1937-45)	50,000	50,000[2]
3. Second Civil War (1945-49)	1,250,000	1,250,000[1]
4. Land reform prior to "Liberation"	500,000	1,000,000[3]
5. Political Liquidation Campaigns (1949-58)	15,000,000[4]	30,000,000[5]
6. Korean War	500,000[1]	1,234,000[6]
7. The "Great Leap Forward" and the Communes	1,000,000	2,000,000[7]
8. Struggles with minority nationalities, including Tibet	500,000	1,000,000[8]
9. The "Great Proletarian Cultural Revolution" and its aftermath	250,000	500,000[9]
10. Deaths in forced labor camps and frontier development	15,000,000	25,000,000[10]
Totals	34,300,000	63,784,000

[1]John S. Aird, "Population Growth" in Eckstein and Galenson (Eds.), *Economic trends in Communist China* (Chicago: Aldine, 1968), p. 265. There are wide-ranging figures regarding the "Long March" (1934-1935). Hugo Portisch, *Red China Today* (Chicago: Quadrangle, 1966), p. 131 offers the usual estimate of 100,000.

[2]This figure would include, for example, the New Fourth Army incident of January 1941 and numerous minor skirmishes during the war. See Peter S. H. Tang and Joan M. Maloney, *Communist China: The Domestic Scene, 1949-1967* (South Orange, N. J.: Seton Hall, 1967), pp. 60-69.

[3]One official statement lists half a million "feudal bullies" eliminated in the north by June 1949; this would not include Manchuria or other areas under Communist control. The figure of one million is probably closer, given the intensity of the early part of the "land reform" in this early period. Cf. *Problems of Communism*, No. 2, 1952, p. 2.

[4]This figure is taken from a Department of State estimate and is given in several places. Franz H. Michael and George E. Taylor, *The Far East in the Modern World* (New York: Holt, 1956), p. 457 use the figure for the first four years of Communist rule. George M. Beckmann, *The Modernization of China and Japan* (New York: Harper & Row, 1962), p. 520 cites the same figure from a later government estimate. As noted above, the Soviets give a figure of 25 plus million for the period 1949 to 1965.

[5]*The New York Times*, June 2, 1959.

[6]The larger figure is the official U.N. command estimate of Chinese Communist casualties. Aird prefers a more modest assessment of U.N. performance against the Chinese "People's Volunteers." The Chinese Nationalist guess is 1,540,000.

[7]On some of the background for the range of estimates, based on discussions in Hong Kong and subsequent studies, see two special supplements which the author did for *The New Leader*: "Letters from the Communes," June 15, 1959 and "Hunger in

China," May 30, 1960. Valentin Chu, in another *New Leader* supplement entitled "The Famine Makers," June 11, 1962, places the deaths of peasants during the "leap" at a minimum of one million.

[8]The figures on Tibet are also uncertain, but the International Commission of Jurists found clear evidence of genocide. Stanley Ghosh, *Embers in Cathay* (New York: Doubleday, 1961), p. 190, notes that the number of people immediately killed in the revolt of 1959 was 65,000, according to reliable sources. Troubles with other minority groupings have also led to casualty figures. See, for example, the interview by Hugo Portisch with the former Sinkiang "Culture Minister" in the *Vienna Kurier* of May 8, 1967. The Uighur leader, probably with very little urging from his Soviet hosts, discussed Chinese policies that had resulted in the deaths of thousands of Uighurs. He cited, for example, the case of the village of Kutcha, where he claimed that 10,000 people died in 1959 alone, all Uighurs.

[9]These figures are certainly conservative estimates. As noted in the text, more than 50,000 are reported to have perished in Wuchow, Kwangsi alone. On May 30, 1967, Radio Moscow (obviously not the most reliable of sources) estimated that more than 100,000 had already been executed in the course of the Cultural Revolution. These figures would also include the casualties of the Hsia-Fang or "rustication" movement which sent Red Guards to the countryside and frontiers when the army started to put the lid on the Cultural Revolution and bring it to a halt. They also include the wave of public executions that were part of the move to restore order and started in 1969 and continued through 1970. James Yeh, writing in the *Mainichi Daily News* in Tokyo on September 4, 1969, reported on the executions in some detail and also quoted the official Peking figure that by that time more than 25 million young people had been sent to the countryside.

[10]Robert Conquest in *The Great Terror* (New York: Macmillan, 1968), p. 533, estimates an annual casualty rate of 10 per cent in Soviet slave labor camps. It can be doubted whether conditions in China are any more humane; stories heard from former inmates in Hong Kong can be hair-raising, indeed. Granting a 10 percent annual death rate in Chinese Communist labor reform camps over the 20 years of their formal existence, the figures given are obviously conservative.

Mao's Paradise

What sort of rule is this which occasions the execution of untold numbers of young people, such as those whose bodies floated into Hong Kong in 1968 and again in 1970? Where is the consistency of apologists who maintain that the rule of Mao has brought new spirit into China, and then argue about the disfigured, tortured and bound bodies floating into Hong Kong, that the Chinese have always been that way?

It is worth remembering that at the very moment in June 1971 when reporters were commenting on Mao Tse-tung's creation of the new Chinese man (see, for example, Seymour Topping's dispatches in *The New York Times*) troops of the People's Liberation Army were machine-gunning scores of their fellow Chinese who were attempting to escape to Hong Kong from Mao's new paradise. Many of the youths drowned in the attempt, and others—the

few—who made it told stories which were reported in the Hong Kong press, but were omitted in the euphoria that surrounded the first American direct access to Communist China for journalists and a few specialists in more than two decades. The number of casualties occasioned by attempts to flee China, though not included in the preceding table, cannot be considered insignificant.
—"The Human Cost of Communism in China"[1]

Militant Atheism

Materialism, with all its negative consequences, is only the outward symptom of a deeper trouble that actually affects large sectors of the human family: a weakening of faith in God, even its total loss. And when atheism becomes militant and aggressive, as it has already been, it becomes an even greater peril to individuals and to nations. All peoples of our continent who fear God, and their religious leaders, must confront this common danger. Asia, which saw the birth of great world religions, must not succumb to godlessness.
—Pope Paul VI

[1]Washington: U. S. Government Printing Office (1971)

7: The Persecuted Churches

1. *Churches and Christians Under Atheistic Communism*

The Communist tree can be judged by its fruit: hatred of God, passion to destroy all religion, merciless battle against Christ and his Church, persecution of Christ's disciples, contempt for man, and the crushing of his dignity and freedom—in all domains, totalitarianism and sectarianism coupled with an incapacity to solve even the problem of daily bread for the peoples under its yoke . . .

All these thorns and thistles, presented as fruit delightful to the eyes and good for food, these theatrical figs and grapes, testify by their very display that they are the work of the father of lies. For not only has Communism never lost sight of its ultimate goal, it has always known how to make the best of situations, go around obstacles, hold out its hand when necessary, flatter, smile, change masks. Sometimes it persecutes by iron, fire, torment, chains; sometimes it turns sly and tries to seduce and win over the believers. Behind all these various tactics is a unique strategy: the death of God, the fresh crucifixion of Christ.

The age-old battle between two cities is before our eyes, in our time, for our salvation or personal damnation according to the side we take: the city of men according to the Spirit against the city of men according to the flesh, the Body of Christ against the regiment of Satan.

In the U.S.S.R. Christians have been oppressed for more than fifty years by a Communist power that has never swerved from its course, even during brief periods when relief tactics became necessary.

Since the beginnings of Communism the official religious authorities have been broken or subjugated. What has survived is a hierarchy totally subjected to the party through the agency of its commissars of religious affairs, a hierarchy fulfilling party orders that aim to destroy the church or to exploit it for the Communist cause.

But always there has been heroic resistance from bishops, priests, and congregations. And always it has been put down with implacable fury, by torture, prison, deportation and—the ultimate monstrosity—confinement in psychiatric hospitals controlled by the K.G.B. Betrayed by leaders who continue to cloak the régime's atrocities with their authority (they encourage the systematic destruction of churches), Soviet believers have taken refuge in churches not recognized by the state. They are like the first Christians and worthy of great admiration. They sacrifice everything for Jesus Christ: their situation, their lives, their security, everything a human being can legitimately desire of peace, happiness, and family joys. They proclaim their faith in law courts, and by their lives, their example, and their words they win conversions even in labor camps and prisons.

From the sacrifices of these generations of believers will come an officially Christian Russia, the starting point, if God wills, for a worldwide Christendom.

In the other great Communist country, China (perhaps having a different brand of Communism, but one as intrinsically perverse and anti-God), tens of thousands of Christians died or suffered in the torment of a revolution that massacred millions of men who, treated like insects, were the subjects of a monstrous experiment. The government tried to reduce the church to slavery by eliminating uncooperative pastors and replacing them with its own creations.

There, too, the Christians are cut off from the outside world; that is the import of the "Three-Self Church." A Bureau of Religious Affairs is the real head of the official religious authorities. Bishops, supposedly elected by the people, are actually appointed by the government.

Today all is night and silence for the Christians of China. There no longer exists a publicly visible religious life. The Christians lead an unseen existence, as do those of other religions.

The conciliating efforts by the Catholic church—validation of episcopal ordinations, favorable words to the U.N. concerning China's admission to the U.N., diplomatic contacts—do not seem to have any immediate power to ease the vice and bring even slight alleviation to the plight of believers.

Among the nations colonized by the Soviet empire, Czechoslovakia offers the most complete and unchanging example of what happens to the faith of a people subjected to the Communist régime.

The official attitude is the same as in all the Communist countries. The Constitution solemnly proclaims freedom of worship, but the state suppresses all freedom to propagate the faith and reap the social results. At the same time it does everything in its power to spread antireligious propaganda, concentrating its efforts in the realm of teaching. The same destructive measures, long and persistently used against religion in the U.S.S.R., are also used in Czechoslovakia, especially against the Orthodox church.

Communism is patient, stubborn, systematic. As in the U.S.S.R., believers shun pastors openly sold to the party. The hope of renewal resides in this underground resistance of the faith, which cuts across all social classes and includes both common people and intellectuals.

Too often today we forget to talk about Hungary, another country that also had a brief, quickly smothered "Spring." And yet the Budapest Spring has as much significance as the Prague Spring. Tanks crushing the Hungarians' move for freedom are as criminal as those of Czechoslovakia. The sixteen years since then do not justify our neglect.

After his sacrifice Cardinal Mindzenty must remain a symbol for all believers, a sign for all those who wish to follow the royal way of the cross, an example of Christian courage in confessing our faith and emulating Christ.

The Cardinal gave in, he accepted "the heaviest cross of my life," much heavier than all those imposed by his persecutors, in order to make possible a policy of appeasement. Confronted from the very start with Communism's thorough hostility to religion, the action of the Holy See was to mitigate the gravest hardships and safeguard the essential, that is, the practice of worship and the indispensable aspects of propagating the faith. The reestablishment of normal relations between the Vatican and the Hungarian government presupposes a return to a minimum of freedom for religious orders, the press, and religious instruction. At the same time thousands of priests and nuns live apart from the official life of the church because the state authorization required for pastoral work is often refused or withdrawn.

If from a human point of view Msgr. Wynchinski of Poland seems to have obtained more positive results than Cardinal Mindzenty, both their countries being unanimously faithful to Rome, that is not so much attributable to differences in attitude as to different historic events and circumstances. It must not be forgotten that Poland went through the same period of open persecutions as the other satellite countries until Gomulka took over. Its Spring would also have been smothered by tanks, but for the hesitation of a furious Khrushchev, Thanks to the restraint of the Polish Communist leaders and the wisdom of Msgr. Wynchinski, the disaster was avoided.

Today, after many ups and downs, church and state observe a *modus vivendi*. But we must not think that everything in Poland is for the best in the best of all possible worlds. Fighting is the law of life, and the Mystical Body of Christ is subjected to this law, a fact expecially evident when it is confronted with an enemy that may compromise, but never disarm. The struggle, then, certainly continues.

As in Poland, conditions in Yugoslavia have been more favorable than in other Communist countries. But since the end of last year [1971] the climate, unfortunately, has begun to change. In December 1971 Tito condemned Croatian nationalism and declared it to be symptomatic of class hostility. A campaign against this nationalism could not leave the Croatian church unattacked. Certain militant atheists publicly proclaim that the time is come to have done with liberal policy toward the church. Police and militia actions reflect this resurgence of fanaticism.

The situation is more disquieting in Rumania; the pressures and maneuvers for destruction or enslavement vary in method or degree, depending on the church. The real Orthodox church is despised and persecuted; practically all members of the clergy have gone through prison and often torture. By contrast, the official Orthodox church, as in the U.S.S.R., is subjected to the régime and is strictly controlled.

The United Church of Rumania is not tolerated; it is the only church completely suppressed in Rumania. Not even a chapel is legally granted. Two million believers and a thousand priests do not have the right to live according to their faith. When a priest and several believers are discovered during a feast or underground celebration, they are arrested and may be confined for several years.

The Christians in Bulgaria and Albania suffer the same open and violent persecution. In those little countries claiming a pure and hard Communism, the fight against believers remains brutal, without any diplomatic or tactical relief.

This is a constant of Communism: when the Christians in a country are organized and united, Marxist realism demands a compromise; on the other hand, if believers are few or divided, or if they belong to a little country, they are mercilessly crushed. The latter is the case in the Baltic countries. The "thaw" following Stalin's death brought a little relief, but only for a short time.

More and more often, Christians—whether from the Baltic countries, the Ukraine, or Cuba—are raising courageous protests against new and refined methods of persecution of the faith and repression of human rights. These cries, alas! while reaching us, do not succeed in shaking our apathy as indifferent and satiated Westerners.

And yet the believers of the Church of Silence ask for nothing other than what the Soviet Union demands for Africa or Vietnam: the end of colonial domination and the realization in practice of basic human rights in private and religious life.

—Henri Carton

2. Thirteen Countries of Religious Persecution

The U.S.S.R

It is not astonishing that the official authorities look upon the growing attendance at services and especially the attraction of young Communists to the solemn rites of the church and even to dialogue with the church with as much displeasure as is provoked by the courageous resistance of the underground church. In the face of manifestations that resemble a far-reaching religious renewal—even the most radical atheists must admit to this—party leaders have understood that henceforth prohibitions and penalties would have little effect; the last sociological reports have shown that, despite very energetic activity on the part of atheistic movements over the past decades, "a certain segment of the population believes in God." In view of this state of affairs, which is impossible to hide from the public at large, *Pravda*, organ of the Communist Party in Moscow, in an August 18, 1971 editorial invited all advertisers, teachers, writers, and artists, as well as the mass media, to devote themselves actively to the instruction and reconquest of the faithful. At the same time, the usual tactics of persecution and harassment would be exchanged for the spread of antimissionary information.

According to an article by a correspondent for the journal *Die Welt* (No. 191), the citizen to be reconquered will no longer be demoted or transferred to another region, as was done in the past. It is better to approach the believer on an individual basis and try to win his confidence. He must also be given a great sense of worth; it is only in trying to penetrate his intimate thought that the atheist can help the believer to grasp the meaning of Communist life and to realize the inconsistency of his religious opinions.

The Soviet analyses of new "advances" of religion among Soviet citizens remark that in the movies "the churches often appear as symbolic of the great, eternal Russia," that (as in *Anna Karenia*, for example) religious ceremonies are mixed in and apparently fascinate the spectators. The same films are televised, and the effect is multiplied. The mass media must, then, avoid idealizing church life; programs must, according to present orders, be made more interesting to all those who have broken with the church.

The active fight against religious nostalgia requires—as reported by the correspondent mentioned earlier—"the introduction into actual life of solemn but nonreligious rites. Care will be taken to give to marriages, births, and the granting of corresponding civil documents a character of celebration and an emotional quality."

Pravda considers it perfectly proper for workers to ask for more solemnity in civil offices and halls reserved for marriages, since marriages and births should be festive occasions for all those involved. New socialist traditions corresponding to Communist world and life views must be introduced into daily life.

More stress than ever before must be laid upon atheistic instruction in the schools and universities and on educating the necessary staff. What is really needed, and apparently more or less missing, is that the instructors themselves be versed in the subject. And *Pravda* must call upon all party committees and ideological organizations to introduce Leninist principles into life.

Control of respect for legislation in matters of worship and religious functions will be reinforced. Atheistic education will be accompanied by criticism of "bourgeois religious propaganda" in order to disclose the "reactionary character of clericalism in capitalist countries" and to unmask attempts to curb the vigor of socialist ideology.

But what did Berdyaev say? "You will win, but after all your successes, it is Christ who will triumph."

—Wilfried Kroll
"Commandos Jésus"

China

When I arrived in China, I was struck by the widespread traumatism that seems to have seized the church in China. It was obvious that the Chinese Catholics and their priests lived as though after a violent shock: bewildered, fearful, reduced to silence in order not to risk being beaten again.

This state of things consequently prohibits passing judgment on the attitude of Chinese Catholics and their priests. In Rome itself the example is set: a single Chinese priest, Msgr. Liwei-Kuang, was expressly condemned by the Vatican for collaboration with the Communist authorities. But no other excommunication has been pronounced, not even against the so-called bishops whom the party elected between 1958 and 1962 without Papal authorization.

The Chinese Catholic church in mainland China is in the trough of the wave. It is said here and there that its silence does not mean death; on the contrary, like the primitive church of the catacombs, there is preparing in China a magnificent spiritual renewal, forged in silence and suffering. Despite all my faith, I am more pessimistic. The Chinese Communist persecutor is nothing like that of ancient Rome. As one young Frenchman put it, Communist ideology "robs us of our souls.

Chinese Communist persecution—no other word can depict the policy of Communist leaders in religious matters—not only affects the physical freedom of individuals; in a thousand ways closely related to those described at the beginning of this book, the Communist party seeks to turn man every day more and more into the docile instrument of its policies. I am frightened to see the ignorance and naïveté of many of my fellow-believers at this point. Let them ask other Catholics who have recently visited mainland China; any honest one among them will confirm what I say. Even for the transitory visitor, the facts are clear.

You do not by chance meet a Chinese believer or clergyman in mainland China; even if that were to happen, the man would certainly refuse to talk. The walls have eyes and ears, and you the questioner may be an aggressor.

The Chinese Catholic Church is Chinese, and that means that it prays for the victory of the party, instrument of victory for the Chinese people. The Chinese Catholic Church is Chinese, and that means that it lives enclosed within itself, xenophobic, suspecting everything non-Chinese. It professes Christian love and Communist hatred, forgiveness of sins and class struggle. Above all, it makes itself very small, very tiny in a dark corner of the empire; it wants to be forgotten, and we cannot tell whether this is to preserve hope or whether hope no longer exists.

—Jacques & Thérèse Marsouin
"Nous avons enseigné en Chine populaire"
"We taught in Mainland China"

In its fight against the Church of Christ, the Chinese Communist state launched the dissident movement of "Three Autonomies" (1951-1955) demanding:

1. Self government: a total break of the Chinese church, whether Catholic or Protestant with its wordly ties, first of all with the "imperialist" Vatican.

2. Self-support: the church must receive no foreign subsidy, so that it will die out for lack of means of subsistence, since the Christians will be unable to support it with their meager personal contributions.

3. Self-propagation: the church of China must become a Chinese church, with its own language, liturgy, and theology, because Western theology has "for centuries suffocated Chinese thinking."

The goal of the Chungking Reform Committee—these reform committees are the controlling organs of the Chinese National church—is to "unite priests and Christians in love for their country and their religion; to support the "Common Program"; to conform to government policies . . ." (Article 2 of the statutes).

Committee members are obligated to "study hard, improve their statecraft . . . participate in all constructive work for the new republic, become good citizens . . ."

North Korea

The real fight against religion began with the withdrawal of the occupation forces in October 1948. The Soviets chose to leave this task to the North Korean Communist leaders, after having carefully indoctrinated them and taken pains to see that the constitution of the People's Democratic Republic of Korea proclaimed freedom of worship. With the departure of Soviet troops, however, hostile activity by the provisional People's Government of Kim Il Sung began immediately.

This was initiated with the dissolution of Catholic associations, which were transformed into Communist societies. Catholics were forbidden to attend public functions and to teach in the schools. In the latter the study of Marxism was made a requirement, and particular care was taken to see that seminary students also took the courses. Missionaries and nuns were deprived of food tokens on the grounds that their activity was not work. Since meetings of more than three persons were prohibited, the priests were forced to ask permission every Sunday to celebrate the Mass . . .

The Christians were forced to join Communist associations, while for the young antireligious films were planned, even on the premises of the Tok-Won Seminary. A whole network of espionage was wrapped around believers and Catholic institutions, while the protests of missionaries and Christians, even Protestants, were in vain . . .

Many examples of the specious freedom established by the Communists in North Korea are reported in *Schicksal in Korea* (p. 22 ff.): "In the schools they began to teach a base materialism and to revile religion, while they did everything possible to drive Catholic pupils further and further away from the church. In offices and factories Christians were subjected to a régime of supervision and pressure in order to make the profession of Christian faith more difficult . . . The intense propaganda against religion started to arouse the interest of many pagans . . . Every day the situation became more critical. We began to realize that measures against the church were building up, awaiting only the moment of swift release . . . The Communist system had its fixed, immutable program. Agrarian reform was the first objective; religion was the sixth, whose turn we knew would come. The difference was only in that the first five reforms had been put into effect overnight, while the fight against religion was developing slowly, though persistently . . ."

—Albert Galter
"Le communisme et l'Église catholique"
("Communism and the Catholic Church")

North Vietnam

What has happened to the Christians of North Vietnam?

Several testimonies that have leaked out despite the stone rolled on their tomb speak of their strength, their self-denial, their exemplary courage in the face of adversity, outrage, and persecution; they are admired by many other Vietnamese, who openly look to them as the only hope of someday overcoming Communism.

The usual methods have been used against them: exorbitant taxes, the closing of Catholic schools and functions, Marxist indoctrination, systematic disparagement of the clergy; arrests, arraignments, condemnations, prison, hard labor, tortures, deportation, and death.

Imprisoned bishops, cut off from their congregations, call themselves witnesses for Christ; dishonored or suspected priests cannot maintain an active church; a few renegades masked as a committee of patriotic priests collaborate with the régime; the parishes are dead; people pray in secret; the sacraments are administered underground. Only the young, though they have not known freedom, dare to defy the government, but they complain that they have been abandoned by all of Christendom, which has no thought of or prayer for them.

Those who have fled to the South have, in the primitive faith of the first centuries and by their courage, emboldened a whole country in its struggle against the ideological subversion and military activity of Communism. Despite persecutions and executions, they were the first to fight the Communist offensive of Tet Mau Than in 1968; they were also the first victims. Churches, communities, priests, and believers were attacked, and as many as possible were tortured or executed. Still they resisted.

The blood of martyrs has made Christianity the greatest force against Communism in Vietnam. It has also been the greatest hope of the Church of Silence in the North, of the struggling church in the South, and of the whole church of Vietnam, which a pope declared to be the eldest daughter of the Far Eastern church.

What would happen if, God forbid! those in the South suddenly also succumbed? Could they flee again as they did in 1954? Who would take them in? They always think of France, but would that nation, so hesitant in the face of the Algerians, open its doors to several million Vietnamese? Fortunately, to appease our consciences, they would lack the boats. As Father Quynh says, "There would be only one solution: throw them to the sharks in the China Sea."

The Vietnamese, in their struggle today for peace and justice, are also soldiers for the freedom of their religion, true soldiers of Christ.

—General Vanuxem

Poland

In Poland Christianity is alive and the Christian faith a certainty at every moment. The reason for this religious vitality must not be sought in the policy of rapprochement between the Holy See and the East, manifested most recently by the important diplomatic talks that Msgr. Casaroli had with Alexander Skarzynski in Rome and in Warsaw. This religious vitality must also not be credited to the secretary of state and director of the Office of Polish Religions,

174

who thinks of two fundamental conditions for a "lasting normalization" of church-state relations:

1. That the Polish church and episcopate clearly recognize the socialist character of the Polish state and the political orientation of the People's Republic of Poland.

2. That the state respect the enduring character of the church's religious activity and make allowance for its educational function among believers: "The People's Church," he said explicitly, "will see that the religious needs of believers are fully satisfied and that the church can pursue, under favorable conditions, its pastoral and educational mission, including religious instruction of children and youth."

Father M. Maura, in his report on Poland (*Essor*, September 1, 1971), emphasizes the exceptional strength of the church, which remains "the only organized power capable of opposing the Marxist régime. Marxism has unquestionably deeply disappointed the Polish people . . . In order to show political opposition, they participate in religious demonstrations . . . To what extent, then, are political and social feelings mixed in with the faith? This is hard to say. It is a risk that has always existed for all Christian communities forced to live within the historical conditions of the moment . . .

"No doubt there are shadows, concerns for the future . . . Yet Poland today deserves the label, 'Elder daughter of the church,' so long applied to France. Poland is an example of religious vitality, of deeply rooted faith despite political take-over. This is a lesson to Western nations, which continue to become more materialistic, engulfed by the love of comfort and ease and by the absence of risk and finally of ideals."

An article published in an atheistic Soviet review reached a similar conclusion: "In the last World War Poland lost six million sons and daughters. It is a country that has suffered immeasurable torment, yet it blooms today by working for the construction of the socialist state. Life there is bursting from men who, for the most part, are believers . . . For many more years Poland will remain at once a socialist and Catholic country, a unique phenomenon not only for Europe but for the whole world."

Czechoslovakia

The Central Committee of the Communist Party of Czechoslovakia published a 140-page document on the place of religious communities in the socialist society. Beginning with a thorough analysis of religious life in Czechoslovakia, the document specified very clearly the policy that the government means to carry out in this realm, a policy related to the one effective during the hardest years of the Stalinist period.

Thus the following judgment, revealing the ease with which the leaders of the Czechoslovakian Communist party pass from what is to what ought to be: "Despite the positive stance taken by almost all the religious communities during the elections at the beginning of the year," the document asserts, "and despite the consolidation of the religious sector, we cannot affirm that religion has played any kind of progressive role in the conditions of socialist society. Such an idea would be a serious offense against the ideological principles of Marxism-Leninism . . ."

It is true that neither the Czech nor the Slovakian church has played a great role in the country's evolution over the past century. As has been observed, the Christians, whether Catholic or Protestant, show little curiosity about the world and modern history. Yet the country's period of liberalization (1968-1969) was a time of true renewal for the church. A group of priests and laymen even launched the "Action for Council Renewal," a movement that was dissolved after several months by the civil authorities.

During the years that followed the publication of the document, religious life developed greatly. Religious instruction made considerable progress. Numerous churches were built. Seminaries were full once more. The church, a dying vestige of another age, showed enough life to cause concern to the authorities whose mission had been that of restoring the socialist order.

Since then the government has not ceased to multiply restrictive measures, launching an army of more than forty thousand propagandists who give themselves full-time to their task and use effective police methods to divide the clergy and the faithful. Repression became official with the return, in July 1969, of the former leader Karel Hruza as head of the Office of Religious Affairs; he was a notorious Stalinist who had left his post the year before. After several hesitations because of popular resistance, he restored the old Peace Movement of Catholic Clergy, condemned by Rome in 1950.

Priests and monks are the principal victims of the present repression. In a single diocese twenty-seven priests were dismissed last February. Many others were sent to rural parishes. Seminary life is strictly supervised by priests under police orders, and students can be sent away by civil authorities. Since 1968 most monks and nuns have left the convents to devote themselves to parish activities. Actually, they are either sent back to the only institutions that they are allowed to manage—asylums and psychiatric hospitals —or kept in old convents, living under conditions resembling those of concentration camps.

As for the hierarchy, it is almost completely decimated. For twelve dioceses there is only one resident bishop. It cannot, therefore, put up any real resistance, especially since it could not choose between the reforming wing, begun in 1968 and inspired by Vatican II, and the old Peace Movement of Catholic Clergy, made up of former ecclesiastical officials who have sided with the régime since 1948 under the direction of ex-abbot Plojhar. The latter sees its attitude as the only one that can give the church a chance to survive. Actually its leaders, who often act without any scruples whatsoever, are only government representatives with primarily political ambitions . . .

Oct. 9, 1972

—Robert Blanc
("Midi-Libre")

Hungary

The spectacular exile accepted by Cardinal Mindszenty at the formal request of Paul VI reminds the Free World of the precarious position of the Hungarian church, which is deprived of its legitimate rights to a free existence and to activity exempt from supervision by the Council of Religious Affairs.

In an account of "supervised freedom" in Hungary, published in *The Cross* (October 2, 1971), Father Boszoki points out several facets of the state of Hungary's Christians, who recently celebrated the millenium of their country's Christianity:

1. The great pilgrimages inside and outside the country "are still prohibited."

2. Religious education is free and possible only in theory, since in reality "there is no regular religious instruction in many regions."

3. Contact between priests and youth "is impossible, even prohibited . . . between First Communion and military service."

4. "Any kind of religious assembly . . . as well as any religious instruction outside the framework of the catechism" also remain formally prohibited.

5. "Religious orders are still dissolved, excepting those for instruction in the eight Catholic colleges."

6. The Hungarian clergy is plunged in intellectual isolation. The

one existing theological review appears only four times a year. Western periodicals certainly come to the large seminaries, but their diffusion seems to be restrained."

A letter received directly from Hungary and published by Father Werenfried van Straaten ("Ou Dieu pleure") reads as follows:

"The Hungarian church has become the servant of the Communist state. It is not led by what remains of the church hierarchy, but by commissars and government inspectors, appointed by the Ministry of Public Instruction, who are practically members of the secret police. The episcopal administrative machinery, under their control, is in reality an executive organ of the atheistic state and a servant of Communist politics.

"Communist officers dictate appointments, transfers, promotions, and authorizations of clergy. 'In order to limit confusion,' these decisions are carried out by the diocesan authority. The diocesan offices in Hungary have become the organs of the state. Pious and zealous priests are unjustly turned aside from any ministry. Of course in private conversations, ecclesiastical administrators mention this constraint, but those who are unjustly punished ask themselves bitterly what good the church can possibly reap from this servile submission.

"Using constraint, blackmail, bribery, or treason, the atheists have succeeded over the years in controlling the entire ecclesiastical administrative structure, to the point where the bishops who have been able to keep their episcopal sees by government favor have not a single power left . . ."

Yugoslavia

Increasingly, signs indicate that Tito, Yugoslavia's president, is no longer master of the situation in his country. Neo-Stalinist leanings are being felt more and more distinctly, showing that Yugoslavia follows again and ever more deeply in the wake of the Soviet Union. In his own sphere Tito can no longer bring about the triumph of the policy of neutralism vis-à-vis the two blocs. This change of orientation in foreign policy is accompanied by a stiffening of policy at home. And it is the church that feels this most deeply. J. F. Balvany, correspondent of the S.K.P., writes: "The last plenary assembly of Brioni gave proof of the general plan, and the ideological organ *Kommunist* now moves to open attack. Franc Popit, political secretary of Slovenia, first accuses the clergy of having, between the two wars, exploited the misery of men and blackmailed the working class into absolute obedience, strengthening its own political influence and luxurious way of life. In addition, he reproaches the church for having collaborated with the Hitlerite occupation forces because, in Popit's words, 'these questions do not belong to the past at all. . . . Clericalism tries to enter the schools, found social and charity organizations, and abolish the separation between church and state . . . From now on the Communists of Yugoslavia will make war against whoever uses religion for political ends.' "

Such accusations were only the beginning. In Tuzla, for example, the priests S. Pavic and P. Skopljac were arrested for having begun "an activity contrary to the interests of the state and of the people during their pastorate among the workers sent to Austria." The declaration of war upon the church has two goals:

1. The church must be silenced in Yugoslavia. Its power to settle religious questions must be taken away; these must from now on be discussed only within Communist commissions. This means that the church must align itself with the ideological plan.

2. The church's influence among the many Yugoslavians working abroad must be impeded. The workers will thus be more strictly subjected to the Yugoslavian régime and the Communist party. It is obvious that what is desired is a recuperation of the flock when they return to the Soviet paradise. Doubtless that is also why a propaganda campaign was launched for their return to the fold. And yet economic concerns may also accompany ideological motives; indeed, the leaders count on money earned abroad being deposited in Yugoslavian banks.

The wave of purges in Croatia and the repressions against the church go hand in hand. Both measures are aimed to strengthen the leading position of the Communist party and to nip in the bud any deviation from the Party line. As we mentioned at the beginning, President Tito is no longer able to handle the situation. Old and sick, he cannot work more than four hours a day. All those who have tried to enlighten him as to the real situation in Yugoslavia have disappeared from his entourage and from the leadership of the party. The real leaders of the country are those neo-Stalinists, Tito's intimate advisers, who are responsible both for the lawsuits against the Croatians and for the measures against the church. Their intransigent line of conduct leads Yugoslavia into greater and greater dependence on Russia because the economic development of the country is stagnating. The Soviets have included Yugoslavia as an integral part of their Mediterranean strategy, and it matters to them that it also be an ideological certainty.

—"Menschenrecht," No. 6
September 1972, Zürich

Bulgaria

Despite all the measures taken against the church and religion, it is unanimously admitted that we are witnessing renewal inside every religious community. Atheistic propaganda has been a complete failure. A cry of alarm has just been sent out by the Central Committee of the Bulgarian Communist Party in the daily *Rabotnitchesko Delo*, which in its editorial reminds the Communists "that they have the freedom to actively develop scientific-atheistic propaganda." The newspaper demands the intensifying of the battle, especially in the universities and schools.

"The priests are more and more active, the influence of religion is spreading," comments the *Narovda Prosveta*. "The priests take advantage of religious functions (especially baptisms, marriages, burials, and other ceremonies) to explain religion, and they attempt to give a scientific aspect to their sermons."

At the same time Konstantin Kotzeff, anxious about the spread of the faith among youth, wrote in his article "Fight Against the Spread of Faith Among Bulgarian Youth": "On August 28, I saw 23 students in the Sveti Sedmotchislenizi church, 9 boys and 14 girls. On September 16, in the Sveta Petka church[1] I noticed 23 girls and 11 boys, school-age children. All of them were making the sign of the cross and lighting candles, and their faces showed that they were absorbed in their prayers." The author expressed indignation over what the priest had said in his sermon: "Believe in God, he will give you strength and knowledge."

A clear and persuasive picture of the way the antireligious battle is carried on today, as well as its fundamental failure, comes from the Communists themselves; for example, the report of Ivan Natcheff, president of the Commission for Atheism in the mostly Catholic village of Sekirovo, Plovdiv Division. Entitled "On Attacking Religion" and published in the July 10, 1964 issue of the *Ucitelsko Delo*, journal of the Bulgarian Teachers' Union, it exposes the working plan of a commission for the spread of atheism. It asserts that such commissions must exist in each town and village to fight religious zeal and lead an active atheistic propaganda, especially among the young, through schools, movies, radio, books, newspapers, meetings, excursions, amusements, and other means.

But religious zeal can be seen among Communist party members

[1] An Orthodox church situated under a house in the center of Sophia and always crowded.

themselves. Many young Communists have been punished, even to exclusion from the Party or the Komsomol for attending religious functions. These facts reveal the profound attachment of the people to their beliefs, traditions, and religion.

Following methods of violent persecution and attempts at persuasion, the Communists now use corruption. In January 1965 the first issue of the daily *Septemvriska Pobeda* of the Pleven Region announced the creation of "premiums for secularization." Thus, the young who renounce the religious marriage ceremony would receive a premium of 60 Bulgarian levas (about $30 U.S.); parents who do not have their children baptized would receive 20 levas, equivalent to $10 U.S.; and relatives renouncing the religious burial of their dead 10 levas, or $5 U.S.

—Kyril G. Drenikoff
"L'Église catholique en Bulgarie"
("The Catholic Church in Bulgaria")

Albania

During the three years after the Communists took over, the religious leaders of the various churches were deposed, imprisoned, or executed and replaced by men who had either been won over to Marxism-Leninism or were simply subjected to the régime. The pressures were so great that today neither Muslim nor Christian communities follow the usual rules of their faith. Constitutionally, religious institutions exist, but their rights are interpreted in such a way as to implement the transformation of these communities into instruments of state policy.

Officially, everything functions very well. According to the effective decrees and laws of Albania, the Muslim religious community (70 per cent of the population) is divided into two main groups: the Sunnites and the Bektash, an important sect broken off from Muslim orthodoxy. The first group is supposedly directed by four muftis of the first rank and two of the second, assisted by twenty-two mufti delegates. The second group is divided into six districts, each directed by a "grandfather" who recognizes the supreme authority of the "chief grandfather." As for the Albanian Orthodox church (18 per cent of the population), it is supposedly headed by an archbishop and four bishops; the Catholic church (12 per cent) by two archbishops and four bishops.

The actual situation is completely different. The Orthodox certainly have an archbishop, Paissi, an unfrocked priest and notorious militant Communist whose son is one of the most important members of the party's central committee. The heads of the Muslim community are also active members of the party. Both participate very actively in various "peace conferences."

As for the Catholics, the only surviving bishop is Msgr. Bernadin Schlaku, over eighty years old, placed in 1951 at the head of the Catholic church by simple governmental decision and without notice. This "Head of the Church" is confined to a supervised residence and thus subjected to permanent police control. Of the 62 deacons at work in 1945, 4 have been executed, 14 sentenced to hard labor, and the others taken into the army. Of the 364 active laymen arraigned in court, 13 were executed, 18 imprisoned, 184 evicted. No one knows what happened to the other 149. By 1953, only 10 of the 93 Albanian Catholic priests active in 1945 remained; 24 were killed, 11 were dismissed, 10 had disappeared, and 3 had managed to flee; of 60 seminary students, 2 had been killed, 4 imprisoned, the others driven away; the convents had been closed, and 3 Jesuits and 13 Franciscans executed. Following the liquidation of both hierarchy and clergy, the government decided on August 3, 1951 to establish a National Catholic Church of Albania, unrelated to Rome and under its own immediate control . . .

—J. G. H. Hoffman
"Églises du Silence"
("Churches of Silence")

"The Little China of Europe," Albania remains a closed, impenetrable country, where the only free religion is Marxism-Leninism, interpreted according to Mao's little red book.

Claude Azoulay's report, published in the No. 1163 issue of *Paris Match,* tells us about that socialist world founded on "the Chinese principle of the letter of public denunciation," that corner of the world where "ever since school age, the child is reared in the political doctrine of the country" by reciting and singing "in praise of the Savior: Uncle Enver and Chinese friends." How many Christians are there now in Albania? Only God knows, because Albania, "counting (before the war) about eight-hundred thousand Muslims, three-hundred thousand Orthodox, and two-hundred thousand Catholics, is the only country in the world," the reporter for the *Paris Match* asserts, "where all places of worship are closed."

Mr. Maurice Duverger tells the same story in *Le Monde* of September 5-6, 1971: "All the mosques and churches are closed, and the traveler cannot even visit those that are works of art, even though the government has in general restored them with the utmost care and official brochures boast of their architecture and frescoes."

Rumania

Many people ask: Well! If the Communists boast of the freedom granted to the church, who then hears the confessions of our soldiers and administers the sacraments to them? How many religious leaders and chaplains actually are there? What are the methods used in Rumania for religious education of youth and for the teaching of religion in schools? And has the Rumanian Communist party in its publicity taken a stand against the one thousand books (Communist party editions) that contain disrespectful references to the Virgin and the saints? Those who write such things should admit that they have been forced to do it; as for the bishops who, coming to the West, proclaim the existence of religious freedom guaranteed by the Constitution, they should unanimously revolt, with a holy rebellion, against all those who mock Jesus.

It is also asked: How are the organizations of Orthodox youth and those of the society of Orthodox women progressing? And the confessional schools and monastic seminaries? The seminaries should open their doors to all young people as soon as they decide to come, but we hear that those actually admitted are, by government orders, at least fifty years old! . . . Here, then is a civil measure that seeks to destroy monastery life and places devoted to pilgrimages and masses, in short, to the practice of our traditions.

Sometimes it is asked, Are there still in our country missionary teams that go from place to place, showing films and talking about God in the markets and railway stations and selling little crosses and icons? Or else, perhaps, now that the church "exults" in a new "freedom," it is the patriarchate itself that organizes caravans for the same purpose?

Someone saw, in my house, a collection of the Holy Synod reviews, printed in Bucharest. He wanted to know whether the peasants and factory workers read such advanced theological works, difficult to understand even by the priests, and whether this collection could contribute to the development of religious thought among the Rumanian masses . . .

Recently I read a speech delivered by our friend Father Anthony

Plamadeala on the occasion of his "appointment" (one cannot say "election") to the vicarship. How can it be that such an intelligent man becomes dull the moment he receives the bishop's miter?

The Communists use a Satanic method. They raise to the high positions of bishop and archbishop those who might protest at a given moment against the use of the church for government propaganda. These persons, despite their intelligence, then become tamed lambs that meekly follow the government. After expressions of thanks to the patriarchate, they flatter the commissioner of religious affairs and place themselves at his service. Together with him and his team they praise the accomplishments of the régime that has helped bring about the theoretically total freedom now enjoyed by the Rumanian church. Then begin the criticisms of the capitalist world, where family and other institutions rot and where only a Communist régime can resurrect the world.

—Archim. Roman Braga
Drum, January-March 1972
Mankato, U.S.A.

Outside of school, the high school and university students frequent literary clubs each week where they are compelled to speak against religion, even if the subject of the day is completely different. As for the parents, they are forced to read or to make their children read atheistic passages or books, so that a common front can be created against doctrine, against religion. Besides that, the Department of Religions has withdrawn all exact sciences from the seminary curriculum so that the future priest would lack rational arguments for the existence of God and be incapable of demonstrating to people that between religion and science there is no contradiction.

—*Solia*, monthly journal of the
Rumanian Orthodox Episcopate of America

East Germany

. . . I sought further information on the Federation of Pastors in the German Democratic Republic, which, even assembled, must feel outside "the system."

After recounting my former conversations, I asked:

"How does this federation insert itself into the closed system of a Communist country, where propaganda seems to leave no room for Christianity?"

"The church cannot be destroyed in one blow. They divide it. The Protestant church, having no head, is easier to fragment than the Catholic church. Besides, certain pastors preach submission to the Communist state."

"That's not Dibelius. A pastor in East Berlin . . ."

"No, the Lutheran bishop Dibelius, whose diocese extends across part of the German Democratic Republic, has serious difficulties with the government of Pankow."

"Did the Catholic priests form a group analogous to the federation?"

"No, I think that two or three of them have gone over to the enemy. But they don't interest the Communist state very much. The Catholic Church is in the minority. Being unable to destroy the Protestant Church with a single stroke, the government seeks to create an antonomous church, separate not from Rome (since it is a question of Protestants), but from the West and carrying the seeds of destruction."

I leaf through the documents they gave me, and I stop at a text to which I had not given enough attention. It has to do with a decalogue, the ten commandments declared by Walter Ulbricht in June 1958:

"Thus the baby learns to say a Godless prayer, lives in a Godless kindergarden, learns a Godless Christmas carol; the child joins a Godless scout group, the fourteen-year-old is sworn into the atheist state and is admitted to secondary school if he claims, in writing, to adhere to Marxism. The adult cannot lead a normal career unless he is married without God, and even his home will not be undisturbed unless he avoids practicing his religion. He will not feel at ease in a gang of workers unless he has renounced his faith. Even in order to rent an apartment and live in peace he must please the property committee, which is necessarily Communist. The doctrine that propaganda constantly inculcates, the doctrine seen on walls and in the press, is the one Ulbricht summarizes in ten commandments . . ."

—Henri Duquaire
"Les chrétiens en Allemagne de l'est"
("The Christians in East Germany")

Cuba

In an interview published by the Mexican journal *Excelsior*, Msgr. Francisco Obis, the young archbishop from Havana, presented a completely different picture of the church in Cuba. According to him, there was "a climate of deep spirituality" under Fidel Castro's dictatorial régime. "In a régime where work and austerity reign, men have the chance to reflect, to think about values and the meaning of life . . . The exile has removed our complicated people. Those who remain are common folk, simple yet profound."

Msgr. Obis ventures to say—in imitation of the Soviet Metropolitan Mikodim, another churchman who defends the atheistic régime—that the state considers the church "either with indifference or with sympathy."

The mawkish statements of the Cuban archbishop in no way reflect the real state of Christianity and the church in Cuba. How can Christians ponder or think "about values and the meaning of life" when superhuman work and the austerity of an oppressive régime enslave and demand blind obedience to the Communist party? When Fidel Castro has moved Christmas and Epiphany to the summer? "Because," he explains, "if Christmas, January 2 and Epiphany came in July, when heat and rain hinder work and incline men to vacation, I would not be against holidays. I do not wish to be a killjoy, but it must be said that, fine and respectable though our traditions may be, we cannot allow ourselves vacations at the best time of year for work."

Even the Chilian bishops Aritztia and Gonzales (who think that "the Christians must bring their efforts to the revolutionary process"), after being in Cuba for two weeks, had to admit that "the atmosphere was suffocating." Christians are considered second-class citizens. Baptisms occur half as often as they did before the revolution. Religious books are almost impossible to find. Christian meetings are permitted only in the church or presbytery.

In order to enlighten our readers concerning the sympathy of the Communist state toward the church, we quote from a letter by the Belgian abbot Lucien Dewulf to Don Camara in 1970: "I went there the great illusion of accomplishing the great 'dialogue' with a régime that deeply attracted me . . . I believed in the possibility of open cooperation for the common goal of progress . . . But during those six years the situation deteriorated in every realm . . . As for my efforts toward a good understanding with the régime, I feel frankly disappointed . . . Slander against the church is daily bread. During Holy Week and on Sundays, games are organized, expecially near churches. The catechists who, with their parents' permission, once taught the children their catechism, have been taken to police headquarters."

3. *Aida's Confidences*

In many parts of the world, people are interested in what is happening to a young Soviet Christian, Aida Mikailovna Skrypnykova. She went into prison twice for having confessed the name of Jesus. The first time she was sentenced to one year of imprisonment in 1965-1966. The second punishment was for three years, from 1968 to 1971.

Now Aida is free once again. The heavy doors of the labor camp opened April 12, 1971. The long days are over, at least for the present.

What is Aida like? She is young, about thirty-one years old. She has brown eyes and a slender build. Her eyes reflect joy and peace. Her prison companions trusted and loved her. Aida does not discuss her difficulties and troubles; she talks instead of the joy, the peace, and the wonderful protection of God.

"I was set free from labor camp on April 12. We were not freed at the camp site, but were first taken to another place where we spent two weeks. There I was told that I hadn't learned anything from my sentence. That's why I wasn't given a passport as the other prisoners were. I received only a paper stating that I had left prison after completing my prison term. The place where I must live is a fairly large city east of Moscow. I am prohibited from staying out after 9 o'clock. Twice a week I must report to the local police to prove that I am still in town. This rule applies for six months. If I don't change after that, the rule can be extended for another six months. I don't know what will happen after that. If I don't obey these rules, I may again be arrested and imprisoned at any time. Usually only criminals, murderers, and hooligans are subjected to such strict regulations. I seem to be classed as one of them.

When Aida left camp, they told her she hadn't reexamined and changed her ideas.

"I asked them what kind of improvement they wanted," she said. "A man then read the thoughts I had written in a notebook they had confiscated. He said, 'Don't you understand that those who bring Bibles into the Soviet Union try to harm us and nothing else?' I answered that if we had Bibles in Russia and there weren't any in Sweden, I would be the first one to supply that country."

When I asked Aida what was most painful about prison, she hesitated a moment. It was hard to answer that question, you could tell by her expression. Finally she answered, smiling.

"It was very hard to be separated from your friends. Besides that, isolation from the world was difficult to take; we couldn't go anywhere. Yet it was living without the Gospel that was the most difficult. Having been in prison for some time, I asked for a Bible, but wasn't given one. A sister brought me the Gospel of Mark. When the guards found out I had a Gospel, they were frightened. They searched the camp. Twice they set out on a search for that Gospel, and the second time they found it. For that I was locked up for ten days and ten nights in solitary confinement, in the cold detention cell of the prison.

"A few weeks after this incident, I managed to get hold of a complete New Testament and to keep the book almost to the day I was set free. The guards organized numerous searches. The Lord helped me every time, and I was able to learn in advance when a search would take place, so that I could hide that precious book. Many fellow-prisoners helped me hide it, even though they weren't Christians. Just before my release, they took away all the notes I had made during my stay. Everything I wrote during those three years was lost . . ."

"Although prison conditions were very trying," Aida said, "hope also was with me. I wasn't sad, and my spirit was fearless. For three years I was able to live with the words from St. Matthew, chapter 11, verse 30, before me: 'For my yoke is easy and my burden is light.' Even though these Biblical words were very familiar to me before my arrest, I couldn't have understood before their precise meaning and depth. Christ's burden is indeed light to carry. I experienced it many times in prison. During my confinement I had a wonderful friend, the risen Lord Jesus Christ. I had the same experience as that sister who wrote in prison that Christ gives his grace and his presence to those who are confined so that they can endure what awaits them. We are neither alone nor despised, even in prison."

Aida is not the only one to have suffered for Christ's sake. She is known all over the world. When Aida found out that her picture had been printed on a postcard and that thousands of copies had been distributed in various parts of the world, she felt confused. She said she was very happy that people hadn't forgotten her.

"Yet I understand that people see me only as a representative of all Christians who suffer, and when they think of me, they think of all the Lord's witnesses who suffer in different parts of the world for the sake of their Lord.

"In prison I received many greetings and packages. One time I was told that I had received ten packages from Norway, but that they couldn't give them to me because I hadn't renounced my opinions. I don't know who sent the packages, but I wish to express my gratitude to those who prayed for me and my brothers and sisters who share a fate similar to mine. Once I was shown a package and was told that it contained chocolate and other good things, but I decided I didn't need the contents. Just knowing that my friends cared for me was a much greater blessing. I remember taking this concern as not having been sent to me alone but to all of us. The most wonderful thing is that nothing can separate believers from one another. All those who belong to the Lord form one body wherever they are and no matter what their life conditions are. Some people think that in closed countries Christians are cut off from all contact with the rest of the Lord's family. That's why it's a great joy for us to experience a visible and concrete spiritual communion with Christians living in other parts of the world. This gives us hope in prison. For all of us I would like to express our love to those who have cared and prayed for us . . .

"Prayer must not stop with a person's release. I hope that all Christians will unite to pray for one another. We must pray that our faith be not destroyed by outside circumstances."

Why So Many Cries?

Dead leaves!
Birds fallen from the sun
All aflame before our doors,
Screams made in sleep
Long screams the devil takes
To prison . . .
Hatred is an ember
In my throat and my throat a wound:
I long to scream, but night sweeps
Too many leaves, dried,
Too many souls and dead birds,
My hardened tongue obstructs
Words of remorse.
Now in turn I lick
High bloody walls,
I whose eyes once blazed
With God's lamps, in his temple,
I who am nothing now but fraud.

Untie
Your shoes!
Run barefoot in the stone-pile,
Rip off your skin!
Hope died blindly groping,
Not far from here, behind the wall,
I tell you hope died in confusion
. . . and still you play your pipe!
—Why so many cries in the city?
It's all so simple, be still;
The tree has blossomed in prison,
Cry not without reason:
My heart is as an evangel.

                                        —Jacques Richard

8: Events of the Year 1972

In Communist Countries

JANUARY

1. Trial in Moscow of the young Soviet dissenter Vladimir
Bukovski, sentenced to two years of prison, five years of hard labor,
and five years of local banishment for "agitation and anti-Soviet
propaganda," as well as for "spread of calumnies aimed to tear
down the state and the Soviet regime."

In his last statements to the Communist judges, Bukovski accuses Soviet society in a surprising manner:

"Our society is still sick, sick with the fear that has come from
Stalinism, but it has begun to open its eyes, and the process cannot
be stopped . . . And however long my imprisonment, I will never
renounce my convictions; I will express them, because this is my
right, granted by Article 125 of the Soviet constitution. I will never
stop fighting for law and justice."

2. From *Pravda*, January 14:

"To overcome religious belief is an important condition to the
success of our advance toward Communism . . .

"V. I. Lenin wrote that we must 'give the masses the most di-
verse kinds of atheist propaganda, instruct them in the most varied
realms of life, approach them from all sides, interest them, wake
them from their religious sleep, shake them in every way, by every
means!'"

3. After a superficial trial and in total contradiction of declared religious freedom in the U.S.S.R., the Russian Baptist believers G. D. Zheltonozhko, accused of spreading Christian literature, and N. T. Troshchenko, accused of agitation for religious education of children, are sentenced as follows:

G. D. Zheltonozhko, indicted under Articles 138/2 and 187, is sentenced to three years of hard labor. N. T. Troshchenko, indicted under Article 138/2, is sentenced to eighteen months of imprisonment. Legal expenses to be paid by Zheltonozhko, 30 rubles; by Troshchenko, 20 rubles.

FEBRUARY

1. The Soviet press becomes more and more aggressive toward religion:

On November 12, 1972 the newspaper *Bakchinsky Rabochy* expresses discontent because religious traditions and rites are still very strong in the U.S.S.R. and sees no solution to the situation other than to create Soviet rites.

On November 15, 1972 the newspaper *Molodezh Gruzii* published the article, "The Fight Against Religion Must Be Scientifically Carried Out." It eulogizes the activity begun in courses for scientific and ethnic atheism at the University of Tiflis, capital of Georgia.

The November 19, 1972 issue of the periodical *Sovetskaya Latvia* complains that, because of the influence of the church and religious sects, citizens refuse to participate in atheistic meetings. That is why believers must be individually enlightened.

The November 20, 1972 issue of *Sovetskaya Moldavia* mentions the Christian Sokolov, fifty-years old, who spent half his life in prison.

2. The Polish government issues an ordinance reversing a law dating back to the Stalinist period that required clergy to write up inventories of church property. The obligation to write these up and to pay the corresponding taxes had been a constant worry to the parish priests whose time was taken up with this mechanical work. It was also a cause of friction between the state authorities and the church.

3. On February 22 Msgr. Karel Skoupy, Bishop of Brno, dies at the age of eighty-six. The Requiem Mass was celebrated by Msgr. Trochta, bishop of Litomerice, and at the cemetery the last prayers were recited by Msgr. Hlouch, bishop of Ceske Budejovice. Cardinal Koenig, archbishop of Vienna, attended the funeral but, according to the Austrian Catholic agency *Kath Press,* he was informed that the Czechoslovakian authorities considered him a "private" witness to the funeral ceremony.

4. Soviet poet Natalja Gorbanevskaya was freed from the Moscow psychiatric asylum after two years of treatment. Member of the Russian Orthodox Church of Silence, she had taken part in the small reform movement before her arrest in 1969 on Christmas Eve. Specifically, she had participated in the brief protest on the Red Square against the Soviet invasion of Czechoslovakia in August 1968.

In an open letter to Soviet psychiatrists, written in November 1970, two of Gorbanevskayas's friends wrote: "We are deeply convinced that the decision taken against Natasha constitutes a gross act of repression. We are her close friends, we have known her for a long time and have known her well, and we know her way of thinking and acting, her character. And we declare that the conclusions of the report are false."

MARCH

1. In the Soviet journal *Naukai Religiya* of March 1972, historian and militant atheist Klibanov presents a statistical study of the religious situation in the Tambov Region. Concerning the true Orthodox Christians, the author's census reveals, of course, only the visible part of that church: for the number of believers in the province under study, Klibanov gives a figure of four hundred, and in addition states that "the sphere of true Orthodox Christians is distinguished by its little communication, even in comparison with the most fanatic of other religious leanings."

2. A letter from Alexander Solzhenitsyn, Nobel Prize winner in literature, to Patriarch Pimen accuses the Russian Orthodox hierarchy of complacency in the face of the atheistic policy of the Soviet government:

"We are losing the last traits, the last signs of a Christian people, and how can that not be the principal concern of the Russian patriarch? You, the church hierarchy, you have accepted the situation, and you promote it, finding an authentic mark of freedom of belief in this fact: that we must give up our defenseless children, not into neutral hands, but into the clutches of the most primitive and unscrupulous atheistic propaganda . . .

"Many of our priests and cobelievers within living memory accepted martyrdom worthy of the first centuries. But then they were thrown to lions, while today all one can lose is his well-being," the writer added severely.

"Do not let us believe that for the high clergy of the Russian church the temporal power is above the heavenly, and that earthly responsibility is more terrible than responsibility before God."

3. Several days after Solzhenitsyn's letter, a terrible document is sent to Western correspondents in Moscow: the memorandum signed by 17,054 Catholic Lithuanians, addressed to Mr. Brezhnev. A copy of this complaint was sent to Mr. Kurt Waldheim, asking the Secretary General of the U.S. to transmit it himself to the Soviet Communist party chief.

What is the reason for the memorandum? Bishops exiled and priests condemned "to the loss of freedom because they taught the basics of the faith to children, at the request of the parents"; brutal measures carried out against those involved in the religious education of children, even though atheism is "taught under compulsion in Soviet schools"; churches burned and the faithful illegally hindered from worshipping at home; and other facts.

Conclusion: "For the believers of our people, freedom of conscience is still absent, and the church is subjected to persecutions."

4. Cardinal Stefan Wyszynski, primate of Poland, protested against a desecration committed on March 22 in Zbroza-Duza by 150 militiamen and auxiliaries who took away the tabernacle and Eucharist from the provisional village chapel.

"Our first idea was to keep silent about these events," the cardinal said, "and not to disturb the Easter celebration. We thought, however, that such a silence could be interpreted as a proof of weakness in the face of such inconsiderate acts. Such desecrations are without precedent in Poland. We regret these actions all the more in that they are contrary to recent official declarations."

5. "On March 29, 1972," we read in the underground publication *Chronicle of Events in Court*, "the Jews who had assembled in front of the Moscow Synagogue were dispersed by the police and the people's militia.

"That evening, the day before Easter, several buses and cars filled with policemen parked around the synagogue. Before noon they had erected a stockade in front of the building and blocked all the entrances to the houses facing the street.

"The assembled people were chased off the street to the sidewalk, although earlier they had been prohibited from walking on the sidewalk.

"Toward seven o'clock in the evening, the police started to clear the sidewalks and to push everybody toward the synagogue steps. People were arrested at random and taken away . . ."

APRIL

1. Alexander Solzhenitsyn, in an interview with *The Washington Post*, denounces the campaign of aspersion led against him by

194

the Soviet authorities: "Times have changed, people are no longer so easily duped . . . This defamation campaign reflects the stupidity and lack of vision on the part of those responsible for it. They refuse to recognize the complexity and richness of history in all its diversity. Nothing interests them except to muffle voices they consider unpleasant and disturbing. They do not care about the future."

2. The fortnightly *Glass Koncila* signals arrests of Catholic students in Croatia, expropriation of ecclesiastical buildings, and administrative measures against Catholic publications. All of this has created "a profound disturbance in Croatia."

3. On April 7, 1972, just before the Orthodox Easter celebration, *Pravda* wrote: "Paschal ideas are destructive and reactionary, they are not based upon any historic event . . . . Christ never died and never arose. He never existed . . .

"We know that man's exploitation of man cannot be stopped through mercy. Christianity has existed for two thousand years. The poor have called upon God innumerable times, but he has changed nothing. Only the October revolution has radically altered the worker's lot in our country."

4. A postoral letter dated April 11, 1972 was sent to priests and congregations in the name of the bishops and administrators of the Lithuanian dioceses concerning the Memorandum of the 17,054. It contains a warning against "overly massive" protests for religious freedom, in order not to "endanger" relations between church and state. Its authors, "new men" placed in office after the disappearance and elimination of most of the former bishops— two of whom are still living: Msgr. V. Sladkevicius in prison, and Msgr. J. Steponavicius, who lives under constant supervision—are directly under the minister of religious affairs, who watches and strictly controls their actions.

5. The Austrian agency *Kathpress* announces that "the students of the Bratislava seminary (in Slovakia), observed a twenty-four-hour hunger strike following the dismissal by civil authorities of seven seminary students (four of these were to be ordained in June). "Only a few [who worked for the state police] did not take part in the strike."

Two or three of the seven students were dismissed for "their activities in 1968"; the others, for activities on the part of their parents at that time, the period of the "Prague Spring".

6. A pastoral Lenten letter from Msgr. Franjo Kuharic, Archbishop of Zagreb, on the right of parents to give their children a Christian

education is very severely criticized by the Croatian journal *Vjes-nilk*.

The journal judges the archbishop to have violated the 1966 protocol between Yugoslavia and the Holy See and declares it a flagrant untruth that Yugoslavian schools impose atheism as a policy.

MAY

1. From May 2 to May 5 the ninth meeting of the Church Commission on International Affairs was held in Hungary to discuss questions of faith. The group was invited by the Hungarian Ecumenical Council. The forty-three delegates represented Lutheran and Reformed churches as well as free churches from the Federal Republic of Germany, Austria, Belgium, France, Hungary, the Netherlands, East Germany, Rumania, Sweden, Switzerland, and Czechoslovakia.

2. On May 14, in one of the public squares of Kaunas, Romas Kalanta, a student in his last year of high school, set himself on fire under the slogan "Freedom for Lithuania." Born in 1953, he was the son of a professor of higher education.

The *Chronicle of Events in Court* (No. 26) gives the following report: "Three of his comrades had surrounded him and kept anyone from coming near. They were arrested and charged with 'premeditated murder with aggravating circumstances' (Article 2 of the R.S.F.S.R. Criminal Code). Their names are unknown to the *Chronicle*.

"R. Kalanta died after several hours in the hospital. His burial was to take place May 18. A few hours before the set time, his body was secretly taken from the morgue and buried. Those who came for the funeral went to the place of his suicide. There was a very large crowd. The police started to scatter the people, but they resisted. One militiaman was almost killed before the army was called and the demonstrators were dispersed. The 'disorders' continued on the nineteenth. There were many arrests. Some persons were sentenced to ten to fifteen days of prison for 'minor hooliganism,' while inquiry was raised against several others."

3. Violent riots broke out in Kaunas after the suicide of the young Catholic, Romas Kalanta. The Associated Press writes:

"The riots started on Thursday, the day of the boy's burial, and continued Friday. The young demonstrators poured into the streets of Kaunas, shouting, 'Freedom, freedom, freedom' and 'Freedom for Lithuania.' They attacked the police with cudgels and stones and started several fires in the city . . . The place in the park where Kalanta immolated himself was encircled by the police and barred from the public. The spot had been strewn with demonstrators' flowers, but the police had them all removed."

4. At the end of May Louis Boitel, former Catholic-student leader, who in the fifties favored the Castro revolution against Batista, dies from police tortures in the Castillo Del Principe prison.

Arrested in 1960 because he refused to join the Communist Party, he was sentenced to ten years of prison but was not released when his term expired in 1970.

Tortured with bayonets, his back broken, and left without care, he weighed no more than seventy-seven pounds when he died. Despite Red Cross intervention and the appeals of Boitel's mother, Fidel Castro turned a deaf ear. The family was not even permitted to attend the funeral on May 24.

5. In the Chronicle of Events in Court we read:

"President Nixon's visit to the U.S.S.R. [May 23-30, 1972] caused strong measures to be taken by the authorities. Starting May 11, departments of the militia from various districts in Moscow convened, including the Action Group for the Defense of Human Rights in the U.S.S.R., represented by T. S. Khodorovich; the Committee of the Rights of Man, represented by expert advisor A. S. Volpin; and fifteen active participants for the emigration of Jews to Israel. They were asked to refrain from 'anti-social action' during Nixon's visit to the U.S.S.R. All those convened affirmed they had never intended to engage in illegal actions, either in the past or in the future . . .

"On May 19 they began to disconnect telephones in apartment buildings. In Moscow this happened in the homes of P. Yakir, member of the Action Group, A. Sakharov, and Chalidze, members of the Committee of the Rights of Man, as well as R. A. Medvedev and thirteen participants in the Movement for the Emigration of Jews. For nine of these thirteen persons the telephone is out of order to this day! In reply to V. Chalidze's inquiries, the Office of Disorders said that there was 'complicated damage to the cable, which would be repaired by May 29.'

"Those same days certain telephones were disconnected in Kiev. Professor Branover's telephone (in Riga) was also left disconnected at least into June.

"In Moscow and in Leningrad, those living along the roads where Nixon would be traveling were prohibited from looking out the windows."

JUNE

1. On June first of this year, after twenty years of confinement in the Shanghai municipal prison and later in a hard labor camp,

Watchman Nee, the great combatant for the Church of Silence in China, dies in the Anhwei Province. He suffered from chronic heart disease.

Born in 1902 at Swatow, where his father was a customs official, Watchman Nee was the grandson of a Congregationalist pastor of the "American Board" in Foochow, who was the first Chinese to be ordained in the province of Fukien.

Finding the Western churches to be ill-suited to the Chinese situation, Watchman Nee always sought for a more simple and more flexible expression of Christian fellowship in the church. As organizer of The Little Flock movement, he fought energetically for the evangelization of his country.

After 1948, the People's Government, claiming perhaps with deliberate exaggeration that he was head of the country's largest Christian denomination, decided upon his arrest and sentence and thus his death. His wife Charity visited him regularly until her death in October of last year. They had no children.

One last message, from Watchman Nee himself after the death of his wife, mentions his heart trouble but adds, typically: "My joy inside surpasses everything."

2. Following the Kaunas riots in Soviet Lithuania, the June 3, 1972 meeting of the Central Committee of the Lithuanian Communist Party devoted itself to ideological work.

The next day the journal *Sovetskaya Litva* reported that particular attention was given "to bourgeois and religious propaganda." It must be noted that for the first time it is recognized that in our country "religious ideology is the only ideological form opposed to Marxism-Leninism."

3. Msgr. Nikodim, metropolitan of Leningrad, resigned from his post as head of External Affairs of the Moscow Patriarchate, which he had assumed along with his duties as metropolitan. Reason: his state of health. Although only forty-one years old, it is said that he suffers from diabetes and has just had a heart attack.

Msgr. Juvenal, thirty-six-year-old bishop of Tula and right hand of Msgr. Nikodim, succeeds him as head of External Affairs.

JULY

"Moiseiev died hard, he fought death, but he died as a Christian," a Soviet officer testified, speaking of the tragic death of the young Baptist believer, which took place July 16, 1972.

Ivan Moiseiev was born in 1952 in Volontirovka, Suvorov Region, Moldavian S.S.R., to a family of believing parents. He completed the eighth grade and that same year, in the Slobodzeisk E.C.B. church, repented before God and received salvation through Christ.

From the moment of his spiritual rebirth he had a profound desire to witness for Christ. Several months before his call into the army, he took a chauffeur course and worked in this profession, which he continued in the army. At the same time he preached the Gospel with great joy in church and among young people.

In November 1970 he was called to military service. From the very start his faith and faithfulness to the living God were subjected to heavy trials. His prayer life was especially intense, and God strengthened him to continue witnessing among the soldiers and officers, most of whom were very hostile to the young Christian and subjected him to terrible persecution and torture. Once during these hard times, Vanya spent a whole night in prayer to God and in the morning saw a choir of angels singing

> In every corner of wretched earth
> Everywhere there are men
> The message of the Gospel
> Flows as a pure, majestic torrent of faith.

This hymn became his favorite song until his martyrdom.

AUGUST

Following the memorandum signed by 17,054 persons, the *Sovetskaya Litva*, a Russian Communist organ in Lithuania, published an article warning party members against clumsy antireligious action:

"Irreparable harm could be done by administrative attacks and by insults to the feelings of the faithful. Bad methods to combat religion not only do not undermine the basis for its diffusion, but much to the contrary lead to an intensifying of religious fanaticism and clandestine practices, arouse discontent and suspicion among believers, and aggravate the situation."

Western observers interpret this article as an admission that a traditional religious sentiment still prevails over the effects of atheist and Communist indoctrination in that country. By religious fanaticism the author is referring to such acts as the recent suicides by fire. The *Sovetskaya Litva* also warns not to underestimate the danger: "All of this means that we must intensify the combat against religious influence in certain groups, while varying the method."

SEPTEMBER

1. One hundred twenty-four Lithuanian priests sent a letter to Mr. Kosygin demanding freedom for Msgr. J. Stepanovicius, apos-

tolic administrator of the Panevizys and Vilnius diocese. The sixty-one-year-old prelate was confined to his home and prevented from exercising his duties.

"This letter," states the September 7 issue of *The Cross,* "comes after the petition sent last March to Mr. Waldheim, Secretary General of the United Nations, asking him to intervene to stop religious persecution."

2. *Pravda* of the Ukraine, dated September 15, calls for an intensification of the fight against the superstitions of believers. It is absolutely intolerable, the journal declares significantly, that party members or Communist youth attend church, marry in the church, and have their children baptized. Particularly guilty in this regard are the Communists of the Kemerovo, Orlova, and Nikolayevsk Districts.

3. The Swedish Academy published the text of the lecture that Solzhenitsyn should have delivered in Stockholm upon receiving the Nobel prize:

"Our world is torn apart by the same cage-age emotions," the Russian author states. "The primitive refusal to compromise has been raised to a theoretical principle and considered an orthodox virtue. Therefore the rule is to act only in the interest of one's own party . . . Dostoevsky's devils, which seemed to be a provincial nightmare of the last century, are scattering throughout the world before our very eyes. The young jubilantly repeat our Russian blunders of the nineteenth century, thinking they have discovered something new. They acclaim as a joyous example the most wretched degradation by the Chinese Red Guards."

OCTOBER

1. During party sessions held in Erfurt last October 11, Mr. Gerald Götting, General Secretary of the German Democratic Republic, Christian Democratic Party, reminded his hearers that no participation for the betterment of society was to be granted to the churches of the G.D.R. Nevertheless, the working-class party and the state entrust responsible Christians with the opportunity to prove themselves as Christians and citizens in the midst of society.

2. Eight young Catholics arrested after the Kaunas events of last May were condemned to prison terms of from one to three years.

3. According to the Soviet review *Science and Religion,* religious persecutions in the Soviet Union are only a myth. Religious communities loyal to the state have every guarantee of meeting their religious needs. If extremists are pursued, that is because they ignore the laws in force and not because of their religious convictions.

NOVEMBER

1. The Polish church protested against the fact that seminary students had been called to the armed forces despite government assurances and the 1950 agreement between church and state.

2. On November 4 the Soviet writer Yuri Galanskov, thirty-three years old, dies in the Potna camp following an operation.

Born in 1939, Yuri Galanskov worked in the national museum of literature and became noted for his poems published in the typewritten review *Phoenix* (1961). Having participated in the protest on Red Square for the release of the nonconformist writers Yuli Daniel and Alexander Sinyavsky, Galanskov was arrested on January 22, 1967 and sentenced to seven years of corrective labor during the Ginzburg-Galanskov trial in January 1968.

In an open letter to the Presidium of the Supreme Soviet of the U.S.S.R., Yuri Galanskov and other prisoners—among them Yuli Daniel and Alexander Ginzburg—give a glimpse of Soviet camp:

"Under the title 'educational,' of course, must be mentioned certain prohibitions upon believers condemned for religious activities. They cannot receive religious literature (even the Bible is banned) nor subscribe to and receive works and periodicals published outside the Soviet Union, including the Communist press and the press of Socialist countries, the U.N., or UNESCO. It is fitting, no doubt, to tag as 'education' not only physical violence, but this constant attack upon human dignity."

3. Msgr. Paul Golichev, archbishop of Novosibirsk and Barnaul, was dismissed from office. He was accused by the patriarchate for "transgressing canonical norms, unworthy conduct, and inability to lead in church life." In January 1972 he had been transferred to the small Vologda diocese from which he had sent a letter to the patriarch that was not answered for several months. In it he indicated that his pastoral work in Novosibirsk had not pleased A. S. Nicolaev, the local representative of the Council for Religious Affairs, who tried to involve him "in a secret provocation . . ."

Msgr. Paul ended his letter as follows:

"Now I have been assigned to the insignificant Vologda diocese comprising only seventeen parishes. I conclude from this that in the eyes of His Holiness I am no longer capable of occupying a more important position. That is why I shall not reject new and constant transfers in the future.

"Perhaps my education and pastoral experience have even shown themselves to be insufficient for governing a diocese anywhere in the Soviet Union. If such is the case, I am ready to retire completely, if His Holiness will help me obtain a visa to France, where I can peacefully finish my days with my brother in Paris."

Ex-abbot Plojhar, former president of the Committee of Catholic Clergymen for Peace in Czechoslovakia and former minister of health in all the Stalinist governments from 1948 to 1968, gave an especially forceful address over Prague radio, during which he denounced Msgr. Tomasek, apostolic administrator of Prague.

But what is most astonishing is unquestionably his attack against the new Committee of Czechoslovak Clergymen for Peace. He reproaches them with being accomplices of "world clericalism" related to imperialism, militarism, and colonialism . . .

—*The Cross*
December 15, 1972

In the Free World—1972

JANUARY

The Presbyterian Church of Taiwan sent a moving declaration to the World Council of Churches regarding its national destiny. We quote a few momentous lines:

"The Executive Committee of the Presbyterian Church of Taiwan, speaking for the two hundred thousand Christians of Taiwan, wishes to express extreme concern over world events that could seriously affect the lives of all the inhabitants of this island. Founded on the certainty that Jesus Christ is the Lord of all men, the just Judge and Savior of the world, we express our anxiety and our requests and, in so doing, we are convinced that we speak not only for the church, but for all our citizens . . .

"We oppose any powerful nation that despises the rights and desires of 15 million persons, that makes unilateral decisions to its advantage; and this because God has ordained, and the Charter of the United Nations has affirmed, the right of every people to determine its own destiny.

"In world affairs, our country has recently become the victim of political bargaining. If this direction is not reversed, Taiwan may well share, in the near future, the tragic lot of Eastern European peoples oppressed by Communism."

FEBRUARY

1. On February 1, in the Norwegian Storting, discussions were held concerning the persecution of Christians behind the Iron Curtain. On that occasion, Mr. Cappelen, Minister of Foreign Affairs, said:

"The Norwegian people have justly reacted to any form of suppression and discrimination, no matter where it takes place. We know that in many countries relations between religious groups or church communities and the authorities are very strained. All of us have from time to time seen in the press that Christians in Eastern countries consider themselves to be discriminated against by the authorities because of their activities and their religious faith. On many occasions for example to the U.N. and to the European Council, the government spoke against all forms of discrimination. We pointed out that many states have minority groups within their borders that suffer discrimination in one way or another. We said that it was very important for every government with such groups under its jurisdiction to take responsibility for them and also measures to prevent discrimination."

2. Several hundred believers, summoned by Abbot Coache and Father Barbara, met on February 18 near Grenelle Street in order to pray for their brothers of the Church of Silence, persecuted by the U.S.S.R. Marxist regime.

The silent demonstrators carried placards with such slogans as "Pray for our brothers of the East," "Pray for the Church of Silence," and "Pray for the Ukrainians," or "For the Hungarians," or "for the Czechoslovakians."

What was the official reaction? In the No. 6 issue of *Catacombes*, Father Barbara said:

"Collaboration of the general press with the persecutors. The press relates the most insignificant news item. Why then its silence about our demonstration? A whole district in Paris was encircled by police. Hundreds of policemen kept us from nearing the Soviet embassy. There were even, yes, two armed C.R.S. cars! . . .

"And over all that the press was silent! Completely silent! That day, February 22, except for Radio Luxemburg, to which we pay public respects, not one radio or television broadcast and not a single daily paper spoke about our demonstration to echo the call of the Church of Silence."

MARCH

1. On March 18, 1972 Pope Paul VI held a private session with the delegation of the Rumanian Orthodox patriarchate, which had been invited to the Vatican by the Secretariat for Christian Unity. The Pope was thereby hoping to find "the solution to the problems existing today" between the Catholic church and the Rumanian Orthodox Church, problems that according to him "date back to the last century or to more recent years" and are thus "even more deeply felt and more painful."

The small Rumanian Catholic community of Eastern rite residing in Rome had, in fact, vigorously protested the Thursday before the meeting. The community's parish priest, Msgr. Tautu, had recalled the suffering long endured by the bishops and by the 1.5 million faithful of the Byzantine Catholic dioceses of Rumania, which had been forced to rejoin the Orthodox church.

Commenting on the presence of the official delegation of the Rumanian Orthodox church in Rome and especially on the "pained and disapproving reactions" of the Rumanian Greek-Catholic colony, M. Alphonse Menoud wrote in the Fribourg *Freedom* of March 22, 1972:

"We remember the tragedy suffered by Catholics of Eastern rite in many of the countries in the East. This was the case for the faithful of the Ukrainian, Czechoslovak, and Rumanian churches. As for this last, the forced union with the Orthodox church was settled by the arrest of six bishops, three of whom died in prison, the persecution of hundreds of priests, and the confiscation of church property.

"We may understand that these painful memories, still fresh, do not disappear overnight in the hearts of those who have endured this calvary. Now they see the church for which they suffered relink with those who but lately forced them to take the way of exile in order to remain faithful."

2. Cardinal Silva Henriquez, archbishop of Santiago, severely condemned the Christians for Socialism movement founded in Chile in 1971 by eighty priests: "It is anti-Christian and antipriestly to resort to Marxist tools of class struggle because, as the bishops have said, their social and scientific value has never been proved. And besides, Marxist tactics and methods cannot be separated from the global theory of Marxism, which is atheistic materialism . . . Theology cannot be reduced to an ideology . . . Christianity cannot be limited to bringing change only in the social and economic domains."

APRIL

1. Excerpt from the "Paschal Message, 1972" by Pope Paul VI:

"Will our greetings of peace reach the churches of silence today, celebration of the risen Christ? For they still exist, these humble and dauntless communities of the faithful, or rather they languish, in vast and numerous regions of the earth. Though by no means subversive, they are refused a lawful existence; the free establishment and expression of their religious and church life is denied.

"May these isolated souls know, may these oppressed and fettered churches know if ever an echo of this paschal voice reaches them, may they know that they are not forgotten: we assure them of our solidarity in faith and love, with our prayer and with our common hope in the risen Christ: Christ no longer dies."

2. On April 19 in Nice M. Raymond Marcellin emphasized the totalitarianism of all the Communist parties, including the one led by M. Georges Marchais:

"The Communists claim to fight for freedom, democracy and Socialism, but there is neither freedom nor democracy nor Socialism in the countries where they have taken over. In twenty years 15 million refugees of all professional and social classes have escaped from popular democracies surrounded by barbed wire, walls, and border guards."

Mr. Marcellin also explained that "the Communist party strives by means of agitation-propaganda to weaken institutions in order to open the way for seizing power. By infiltrating the press, film, television, and radio, it seeks to weaken the loyalty of citizens in the state and thus the capacity of Western nations to defend themselves. Agitation-propaganda dupes individuals as well as professional groups by exploiting their aspirations or their discontent. In the face of this offensive, led vigorously by the Communist parties in all the Western European states, under cover of numerous associations, the counter-attack is weak and poorly organized . . ."

3. At the eighth congress of the International Bureau of Civic Development in Lausanne, April 29 to May 1, *Catacombes* shared Stand No. 49 with the Brotherhood of Notre-Dame-de-la-Merci, thereby testifying to the Church of Silence and the persecutions behind the Iron and Bamboo curtains.

MAY

On May 3 Msgr. Maziers, archbishop of Bordeaux and president of the Bishops Council, officially turned over to newsmen the document entitled, "First Observations by the Bishops Council for the Working World in Its Dialogue with Militant Christians Who Have Chosen Socialism."

The council declared that "Christian militant workers have demonstrated, sometimes in very difficult situations, that they could really live out their faith in Jesus Christ in their struggle to establish Socialism." And it adds: "The working class as a whole is attracted to Socialism, whether to Communism or to other forms. This constitutes a strong challenge for our pastors. It presents itself as one of the essential tenets of the working class. The church cannot be estranged from the aspirations and struggles of this class. Rather, it is called to discover therein the signs of the Spirit's work and to accomplish the task of discernment . . .

"The working class will not be satisfied with declarations. It awaits a purifying renewal in the behavior of the church. It asks that its institutions meet the demands of a just society. Anything in charitable or social initiatives that manifests paternalism constitutes a counter-testimony.

"The working class wants the church to manifest true simplicity of life and pay attention to the disadvantaged; demonstrate its independence with respect to economic and political powers, and vigorously denounce all forms of human oppression."

JUNE

1. The permanent Synod of the Ukrainian Catholic Church held its first session in Rome June 4 to 8, presided over by Metropolitan Joseph Slipyi. Deliberations centered especially upon the conditions of that church, first in the Ukraine where, officially liquidated in 1946, it exists in the catacombs; and then in other countries, including those of the Western World.

2. The French Council for Solidarity with the Nations of Eastern Europe, in its official statement to the press on June 6, 1972, notes the release of Angela Davis and expresses the hope that after, declaring "help to all the political prisoners," she would be able to intervene for Victoria Smirnova, young Soviet woman confined to a psychiatric asylum for having dared to demand a visa to the West.

The council expressly calls for U.N. intervention on the basis of Articles 1, 4, and 6 of the Declaration of Human Rights, of which the U.S.S.R. was one of the first signers; impartiality requires that the same regulations apply to Victoria Smirnova as to Angela Davis.

3. A project to seize the Orthodox church of the Rumanian Diaspora community was undertaken by the Bucharest authorities. Obviously elaborated with care, the plan hinged on the action of a French community seeking a recognition in Orthodoxy—the consecration of Bishop Gilles Hardy. Father Boldenau, representing the parish council, wrote:

"Thus, on Saturday June 10, about 4:15 in the afternoon, two clergymen's cars stopped in front of the church. In it were Théophile, former bishop, accompanied by Alexandru Ionescu, vicar of the Bucharest patriarchate and representative to the Rumanian National Assembly, and by clergymen of the Orthodox Catholic Church of France. They tried to enter the church premises, where a wedding was being celebrated. The parish council had decided to lock the doors as a precautionary measure. A warning to the faithful had been posted on the door, and council members stationed at the entrance secured the way for Rumanian and French believers attending the wedding. Former Bishop Théophile and his companions tried to force the entrance. Refused, they caused an uproar at the entrance of the lobby, disturbing the last part of the ceremony and assaulting council members as well as guests. The district superintendent of police was alerted and came on the scene to make a report . . .

"On Sunday, June 11 the doors of the Saints-Archanges Church were kept shut; a restrained service was officiated by the clergy. Many believers went to the church to demonstrate their support and solidarity with the parish council."

4. On June 17 and 18 the Council of Western European Bishops of the Russian Orthodox Church met in the Orthodox church of Frankfurt. It was presided by the Archbishop of New York, Metropolitan Philaret.

Admitted to the church were representatives of the German, Swiss, Scandinavian, Russian and Baltic press, the latter two from outside the borders of their respective countries, who send broadcasts over radio to Eastern European countries and over television to Germany.

Metropolitan Philaret drew the assembly's attention to the fact that the functions of the St. Sergius Laura and of the Cathedral of the Vision to Yelokhovo are permitted by the atheistic authorities as a screen to mask the real face of spiritual life in the Russian church.

That true spiritual life to a large extent escapes the control of the authorities and goes underground, where the hearts of the real Orthodox church are formed.

The Frankfurt assembly decided to present detailed documentation to the United Nations and the governments of Western Europe on the violation by the Soviet government of the right of Christian parents to rear their children according to their own religious convictions.

5. Guido Bekker, parish priest of the ancient and illustrious Mayence Cathedral, addressed the people of that town, asking them to help the persecuted Christians in Russia. He called for letters to be sent to the Presidium of the Supreme Soviet of the U.S.S.R. for release of Christians imprisoned, deported, or confined in psychiatric asylums because of their faith.

The Catholic press agency that reported this specified that the call came in response to the appeal of June 18, 1972 sent by the Russian bishops of Western Europe, meeting in Frankfurt.

JULY

On July 28 the assembly of Ukrainian believers "Icon" and the Association for the Establishment of the Ukrainian Catholic Patriarchate launched an appeal for freedom of religious and cultural life in the Soviet Ukraine:

"We continuously receive tragic news from the Ukraine as well as other Eastern European countries on the desperate plight of religious communities, the persecution of believers, priests and hierarchy, as well as the oppression of cultural life in general.

"We wish to call to mind that there is no summer truce for the imprisoned, suspected, and watched in the Ukraine. On the contrary, this period risks being for Westerners a rupture of a solidarity that is so necessary in our world, and it will be used to the advantage of the Soviet government organs to strengthen their control over minds and consciences and to better fabricate the records of those who are to be tried.

"News of persecutions, arrests and religious, cultural, and national discrimination in the Soviet Union—gleaned from underground publications and the writings of dissenters and convicts that have been shipped to the Western world—has been regularly published. Now no one pays any attention to them, no one is stirred, no one echoes the despairing cries.

"In this regard we would emphasize that a spirit of peaceful coexistence should be defined precisely as a corollary to freedom of spiritual life and to peace of mind and that the proponents of this spirit must continually demand its fulfillment."

AUGUST

1. During the Olympics in Munich, the Church of Silence international team was present in order to begin its "fishing for men from the East." Christians originally from countries subject to Communism worked day and night, and the project was fruitful: some 1700 Bibles were distributed to participants, all of whom complained of the dearth of religious works as well as the obstacles to spiritual life and the hypocrisy of the official churches behind the Iron Curtain.

2. The World Congress of the *Anti-Communist League,* held in Mexico City August 25-27, met with great success. In the closing invocation, the members of the W.A.C.L. affirmed their desire to fight with God for a better world, a world of justice and universal brotherhood:

"We want a better world with you, Lord, and not a Communist world without you—we want a better world with social justice, free enterprise, and freedom of expression.

"We, the delegates of the W.A.C.L., who come from sixty countries in the five continents of the world, we make the commitment, oh God, to remain faithful to you as long as we live, in a world ready to reject all morality and all traditional virtues and even to accept collaboration with Communism, which seeks to destroy the world through pornography, drugs, and many other means that ruin and brutalize man.

"Give us, oh Lord, the strength to follow this difficult path of freedom; give us the will to fight for a great cause, especially when heavy clouds threaten the world, particularly now in Asia and the Americas, which atheistic Communism strives to conquer at all costs."

3. Toward the end of the month, Msgr. Mindszenty, primate of Hungary, Archbishop of Esztergom, was guest of Belgian Catholics and of the important Magyar colony in Belgium. He celebrated a pontifical mass in the Koekelberg basilica. Many Hungarian refugees and Belgian believers attended this especially impressive ceremony.

SEPTEMBER

The televised broadcast *"At Equal Arms,"* M. Georges Marchais against M. Alain Peyrefitte, was prelude to the next electorial campaign.

M. Georges Marchais defended socialism and its historical realizations in the U.S.S.R. and in satellite countries. The general secretary of the V.D.R., in contrast, denounced the one-party system, the lack of freedom of expression, the negative aspect of the standard of living, and the totalitarianism of the socialist world.

"In the background," Mr. Peyrefitte concluded, "there's the police. There's the fear of police. There can be no freedom in countries where there is fear."

OCTOBER

Msgr. Nikodim, metropolitan of Leningrad and Ladoga, formerly "in charge of external relations of the Moscow Patriarchate," gave a press conference in Athens, on the occasion of Patriarch Pimen's visit to Greece.

Questioned on Solzhenitsyn's famous "Lenten Letter" to Patriarch Pimen, Msgr. Nikodim answered in his typical manner, dodging acknowledgment of the lack of religious freedom denounced by the writer. According to him, the patriarchate had not hastened to answer the Letter because it contained "many errors" and indicated a "misunderstanding of religious affairs."

NOVEMBER

1. At an international missionary conference Msgr. Phum Quang Than, a bishop of South Vietnam, declared on November 9 in Lyon:

"The Catholics unreservedly support President Thieu; we support Thieu when he refuses to sign because, from the moment of the signing, we would see crimes and assassinations committed by the Communists. We think that peace should not be signed until the fifteen North Vietnamese divisions have gone home. Our refusal of Communism and of atheists will perhaps surprise the French, but making peace with the Communists would be to repeat in Vietnam the history of Eastern Europe: the crushing of the Catholic communities."

2. In an open court on Wednesday, November 15 Pope Paul VI spoke of a presence that is too little recognized, but terrifying for the Christian world: Satan.

"Satan is Enemy Number One," the Pope said, "he is the tempter par excellence. We know that this obscure and troubling being really exists, and that his guile is always at work. He is the hidden enemy who sows errors and woes in the history of men . . .

"The devil is 'the father of lies,' according to Christ's definition; he is the disturber of man's moral equilibrium; he is the treacherous and cunning charmer who insinuates himself among us, by means of the senses, the imagination, lust, false reasoning, or dangerous social contacts, in order to lead us astray. These deviations are as destructive as they are seemingly congenial to our physical or psychic make-up or to our deep yearnings."

DECEMBER

Mr. Valery Chalidze, thirty-four-year-old Russian scholar and dissenter who militated in the U.S.S.R. for another Socialism than that of injustice and labor camps, was deprived of his passport and his nationality. The two members of the Soviet consulate in New York explained to him that the forfeiture was pronounced by the Presidium of the Supreme Soviet "for behavior unworthy of a Soviet citizen."

The *Aurora* of December 15 commented: "This man is first a brilliant physicist, then a very rigorous jurist, and finally an eclectic who has been awarded numerous diplomas. The U.S.S.R. is thus depriving itself of a highly gifted scholar whose renown is already established, the more so because Chalidze is a true humanist, who tries with all his might to serve his country, helping it develop while staying strictly within the law."

9: Calendar

Jan. 1, 1962. Deputy General Kovalev of the city of Minsk, famous for his restrictive measures concerning the religious life in the U.S.S.R., forbids school-age children to participate in worship and in the sacraments.

Jan. 4, 1971. Death of Boris V. Talantov in the prison hospital of Kirov. "A profound type, having existed from all time," wrote Anatoli Krasnov-Levitin in a letter. "He's a hero, but discreet, never obtrusive, serene; he gives his life with simplicity, without affectation, without posing . . ."

Jan. 10, 1970. Brutal, illegal evacuation of the Evengelical Baptist assembly of the city of Krivoy Rog (Ukraine); the benches of the meeting house destroyed by the police.

Jan. 16, 1970. The Verkhnedvinsk court of law took away his last three children from Ivan Feodorovich Sloboda because he was giving them religious education. "You have taken my wife and my five children," he complained to the Soviet leaders, "but the Lord has not forsaken us. Whether I live or die, the Lord is always there!"

Jan. 19, 1918. Indictment of Patriarch Tikhon against "the declared or secret enemies of the truth of Christ": "What you are doing is not simply cruelty; it is really the work of Satan for which you deserve eternal fire after death and the terrible curse of future generations here below!"

Jan. 22, 1934. In a report presented to the Second National Congress of Chinese Soviets, Mao Tse-tung declares: "The Catholic priests and Protestant pastors have been expelled by the masses. . ."

Jan. 25, 1918. Vladimir Bogoyavlensky, the old metropolitan of Kiev, is shamefully assassinated near his residence in the Cryptes monastery. He may be considered the first martyr of the Russian church, an innocent victim of Communist terror.

Jan. 31, 1953. Report of losses suffered by the Catholic church in Poland: (a) archbishops and bishops—7 in prison and 2 dismissed; (b) priests—37 killed, 260 dead or missing, 350 deported, 700 in prison, 900 exiled; (c) monks—54 dead, 200 deported, 170 in prison, 300 exiled.

FEBRUARY

Feb. 3, 1948. Msgr. Georges Volaj, Bishop of Sappa, is shot to death without any semblance of a trial. He is not the only martyr of the Albanian Catholic church. Several days after his execution Msgr. Francois Gijni, Regent of the Apostolic Delegation, was shot in the same manner. Later, in August 1952 Msgr. Nicolai Vincent Prennhushi, head of the Albanian Catholic church, died in prison after unbearable tortures.

Feb. 7, 1925. Founding of the renowned League of the Godless; Soviet atheist Emilyan Yaroslavsky (Gubelmann) is made head of this sinister institution, created to absolve "the struggle against religious prejudices."

Feb. 10, 1964. Soviet police arrest Anatoli Shchur, a monk from the Abbey of Pochaev. In a letter addressed to U Thant, the poor mother of this persecuted and imprisoned monk denounces the violent coercion on the part of the Communist authorities and beseeches the U.N. "to exercise its influence on the Communists so that they restore freedom to the monks and to all the Christians. The case of my son by no means constitutes an exception in Pochaev. It is only a link in the whole chain of crimes committed by the Communists."

Feb. 16, 1950. From the *Report* that the Polish bishops addressed to President Bierut: ". . . We would emphasize that the fight against religion that has been going on in Poland for a long time is conducted with tactics beyond anything the imagination has ever conceived to fight against God."

Feb. 17, 1892. Birth of Cardinal Joseph Slipyi, the great *vladyka* of the Ukrainian church, in Zazdrist in western Ukraine, formerly

Austrian Galacia. Ordained a priest in 1917 and a bishop in 1939, he succeeded Andrei Sheptytski as archbishop. He was arrested by the N.K.V.D. secret police in April 1945 and condemned in March 1946 and again in 1953 and 1957 to imprisonment in Siberia. In 1963, thanks to the intervention of Pope John XXIII, he received the right to leave the U.S.S.R. and has lived ever since at the Vatican.

Feb. 22, 1945. End of the Trial of the Albanian Union, with the following sentences: the Jesuit Fathers Daniel Dajani and Jean Fausti, Franciscan Father Shllaku, and two seminarians condemned to death; three seminarians to life imprisonment; another defendant to ten years of hard labor.

MARCH

Mar. 2, 1971. Evangelical Baptist believer Aron Aronovitch Wibe, 61 years old, is illegally arrested by the Soviet police and condemned with other Christians to five years of prison.

Mar. 8, 1946. A Communist-inspired "Orthodox synod" begins its crushing work. Goal: total destruction of the Ukrainian Catholic church. Obeying Kremlin orders, the Red patriarchate proclaims "the union of the Ukrainian Greek-Catholic church to the Russian Orthodox church." In order better to destroy the "reactionary church," this decision was followed by arrests, sentences, deportations: 11 bishops, 2 apostolic delegates, and 1739 priests and members of religious communities were deported to Siberia: 1090 nuns driven from their convents; 3000 parishes dissolved; 4400 churches and chapels expropriated.

Mar. 10, 1947. Historic protests of Cardinal Hlond, Primate of Poland, against the venomous attack upon the church unleashed by the Communist government: "Those atheists want above all to obliterate all religious principles in the education of the young. All their actions are bent toward stamping out religion in the masses and dechristianizing them. . . . Since the persecutions of Nero the Church has never suffered comparable attacks . . ."

Mar. 18, 1966. Three orders of the Supreme Soviet Presidium of the Soviet Union impose restrictions upon freedom of worship, despite Article 124 of the Constitution, which speaks of the freedom of religious practice. The penalty ranged from a fine of 50 rubles to loss of freedom for three years.

Mar. 11, 1964. Ecumenical meeting of the Committee for Information on the Situation of Christians in the U.S.S.R., in the Palace of Mutuality. Francois Mauriac in a fiery address to the whole world said: "Christ is in agony in Moscow, we must not sleep in such times!"

Mar. 19, 1958. Last day of bishop elections in Wuhan, Red China, according to the popular resolution demanding freedom and autonomy for the Chinese church, with the right to elect its own bishops.

Mar. 25, 1925. Death of Patriarch Tikhon, probably by poison, in Moscow. His last words: "The night will be very long and very dark."

APRIL

Apr. 4, 1968. The Orthodox Christians in Gorki send a letter to the Moscow Patriarchate addressed to Metropolitan Nikodim asking that the church hierarchy intervene with civil authorities to have the churches reopened. It is a stubborn repeat of former letters sent in vain to Patriarch Alexei in August 1966; to the chairman of the Committee for Religious Affairs and to the Executive Committee of the town of Gorki in the summer of 1967; to Comrade V. A. Kuroyedov of the Committee for Religious Affairs serving the Council of Ministers of the U.S.S.R. in January 1968; and to the Supreme Soviet Presidium of the U.S.S.R. in February 1968.

Apr. 10, 1952. Sentenced to 20 years of confinement, Watchman Nee, the great evangelist of China, is imprisoned, first in the municipal prison of Shanghai, then later at hard labor.

Apr. 11, 1945. Five Ukrainian bishops arrested: Metropolitan Joseph Slipyi; N. Budka, Bishop of Stanislaviv, Msgr. Chomysyn and his assistant John Latysevski, as well as Msgr. Carnevski, apostolic delegate from Volyn.

Apr. 12, 1971. A young, courageous Baptist believer, Aida Skripnikova, sentenced July 15, 1968 to three years of prison, is set free. Born in 1941, she became known in the West for her fight for religious freedom in the U.S.S.R., notably for her response to the outrageous article by "atheistic comrade" Valen Ivanovich Kuzin: "Don't be a corpse among the living."

Apr. 13, 1948. In a Collective Letter addressed to the nation's Christian youth, the Polish episcopate condemns the furious assaults of atheism and the hostile attitude of the government in the area of education.

Apr. 18, 1950. Untrue bulletin from the Czechoslovakian government concerning the occupation of all monasteries, convents, and parish houses: "Proof was recently obtained that the Catholic religious orders had become instruments in the hands of enemies outside the Republic."

Apr. 26, 1968. Boris V. Talantov, martyr for the Russian Church of Silence, disputes in an open letter to the attorney general of the U.S.S.R. the accusation of contact with foreigners and of calumny against the social order.

MAY

May 8, 1953. In a Memorandum to the president of the Council, First Cardinal Wyszinski denounces the abusive policies of the Communist government which "arrogates the right to become a permanent meddler in the internal affairs of the church and even in the priests' own conscience, as well as the right to arbitrarily and systematically take over ecclesiastical jurisdiction."

May 14, 1949. The mysterious disappearance of Msgr. Francois Hong, apostolic vicar of Pyong-Yang in North Korea, on his way to the sisters' convent in Se-Po. Before this 123 missionaries from the Wonsan vicarage were taken prisoner by the Communists.

May 15, 1951. In order to put down the opposition of the Hungarian clergy to the atheistic régime, the secret police arrest the archbishop of Kalocsa, Msgr. Joseph Grösz who aimed, according to Radio Budapest, "to overthrow the popular government of Hungary . . . while awaiting the restoration of the Hapsburgs . . ." In addition, he had "put into effect illegal operations in fiscal matters and committed acts of espionage . . ."

May 19, 1971. Declaration by A. Krasnov-Levitin in the Moscow trial: "Christ asked us to defend all the oppressed. That is why I defended the rights of men, whether they were the monks of Pochaev, or the Baptists, or the Tatars of the Crimea; and if one day convinced adversaries of religion are oppressed, I will defend them too . . . No sensible man thinks that to criticize certain terms of the law, to try to amend them, is a crime."

May 22, 1953. The Yugoslav parliament votes for the famous Law Concerning Religious Confessions. According to the journal *Osservatore Romano*, "The Communist-dominated governments want to force the church to renounce its internal laws and conform to state ecclesiastical law, inspired by materialistic and antireligious ideologies."

May 28, 1970. Msgr. Jules Hossu, the last bishop of the United Church of Rumania, dies in the Colentina Hospital of Bucharest, at the age of 85. Arrested the night of October 29, 1948 with all the other Greek-Catholic bishops, he suffered sixteen years of prison and four years of supervision in the Caldarusani Orthodox Monastery near Bucharest. The Rumanians consider him a national hero and a martyr of the persecuted church.

JUNE

June 1, 1956. The cathedral of Ufa, a monument dating from the sixteenth century, is dynamited by Communist city authorities. Thus resumes the fierce battle of Soviet atheists against the Christian Church, carried further in the year 1958 when "liberal" Nikita Khrushchev decides to unleash antireligious forces against the dangerous expansion of the Orthodox church. In order the better to strike at religion—still considered "the opium of the people"—all church construction and restoration are forbidden, those "useless places of obscurantist worship" are closed and confiscated, and above all, churches of historic value are barbarically destroyed.

June 6, 1954. The Belgian Abbot Bruneau dies in Camp D, North Vietnam, having attended the death of his companion Father Künsch in October, 1953. During their entire imprisonment they had been tied together with handcuffs or by foot chains.

June 14, 1955. Publication of a decree by President Ho Chi-Minh concerning "freedom of belief and worship." Article I announces that in their sermons "ministers have the duty to inculcate in the faithful the love of country, the sense of their civic obligations, respect for the power of the people and for the effective law of the People's Republic of Vietnam." As for "freedom of belief and worship," Article 15 emphasizes that these are the rights of the people, to be exercised with the help of the authorities.

June 16, 1971. The newspaper *Kazakhstanskaya Pravda* announces that large quantities of Christian literature have been published in the Soviet Union. At Alma-Ata in central Asia, Ivan and Marie Pavlichenko and four of their friends were arrested for publishing and distributing hundreds of religious works. Police responsible for the investigation were surprised to discover that the forbidden books had been produced, not in a secret den, but in a state printing office, with the cooperation of the printers.

June 19, 1949. In a letter sent to the clergy, the Czechoslovakian Episcopate denounces a whole series of abuses of power and of Communist techniques: the campaign "systematically carried out by radio and in public speeches against the Church"; the disregard of "the right of parents to choose the type of education they desire for their children"; the complete suppression of the religious press, "except in a few insignificant cases"; and "prohibition of any meeting whatsoever outside the church."

JULY

July 1, 1971. According to a news release in the Baptist underground periodical *Bratsky Listok* for Sept.-Oct. 1971, the Russian believer Pavel Frolivich Sakharov, age 49, "departed for eternity," "His chronic illness and ensuing death were only the consequence of torture and imprisonment to which he was subjected in the name of the Lord; for he belonged to that community which, despite hardship and oppression, chooses the path of those who obey the Lord and who consider the reproach of Christ as riches greater than earthly treasure . . ."

July 2, 1951. Imprisonment of John Tong, abbot from the Diocese of Nanking and implacable opponent of the Three Autonomies Movement. His fiery words delivered Sunday, June 3, 1951 from the esplanade of Saint Joseph's Cathedral in Chungking: "Sirs, I have only a soul, which I cannot divide. But I have a body that can be cut to pieces. I think it better to offer my soul to God and to the Church, my body to my country . . ."

July 5, 1922. Russian Metropolitan Benjamin is condemned by a Communist court to capital punishment. Accused of opposing the seizure of valuables, Msgr. Benjamin received the verdict with calmness and dignity, without fearing an end that would be similar to the martyrdom of the first centuries.

July 11, 1964. Saints Peter and Paul Church of Moscow is dynamited. The protests of believers, who assembled on the church *parvis* and broke through police lines, were not able to prevent this illegal act. Speaking of "such methods, used against the clergy and religious communities," even the newspaper *Komsomolskaya Pravda* of May 21, 1963 admitted that "this creates justified discontent among the people."

July 16, 1970. Msgr. Edward Walsh, bishop of Shanghai, freed by Communist authorities after twelve years in prison, declares in the newspaper *Osservatore Romano:* "I must admit that it is difficult for me to understand the severity of the sentence against me, since I was neither an American nor a Vatican spy."

July 14, 1964. A Christian, E. Shchur, of Pochaev, sends a letter to U Thant in which she describes in general the tragic situation of the monks of the Laura Monastery and in particular of her son Anatoli.

AUGUST

Aug. 2, 1937. Following a mock trial that lasted for nine days, Msgr. Alexander Frizon, apostolic administrator of Odessa, is mercilessly shot to death in the prison of Simferopol.

Aug. 4, 1948. The government of Bucharest issues the Decree Concerning the General Procedure for Meetings in order to subject all religious activity to the control of the Communist state, according to the cunning statement of Article I, which demands "obedience to the laws of the state on the part of believers of all religions."

Aug. 6, 1954. Last day of the First National Conference of Protestants of China, held in Peking. Beginning July 20, it was attended by 232 representatives of various churches. They elected a national committee of 150 members, chaired by Wu Yao-tsung, leader of the Three Autonomies Protestant movement.

Aug. 12, 1951. Death of Father Suen, former president of Peking Seminary. Arrested July 25, he was taken just before his death to the hospital of the Peita University in Peking, under the constant watch of an armed guard. With the permission of the local police, one of his brothers dug up the body several months later; the bones still carried the marks of the handcuffs and of foot chains . . .

Aug. 13, 1922. Benjamin, metropolitan of Petrograd, is executed. With him two others die: Archimandrite Sergey Sheyn; G. Novitsky, professor of criminal law; and A. Koncharov, former jurist. Gurevich, Benjamin's lawyer, said: "He was a saint!"

Aug. 26, 1954. Vietnamese seminary student Louis Sinh writes to his benefactors in France: "Since 1945 our mission in Qui-Nhon has been divided in two: one group remains in the Communist zone where many priests are imprisoned and two of them were killed. The seminarians cannot continue their studies. I was there for three years, and escaped in 1953 . . ."

Aug. 31, 1962. Officers of the KGB, attached to the militia of Pochaev and Ternopol . . . entered the precincts of the abbey and forced open the door of Father Joseph's cell. They beat the seventy-year-old man, gagged him, and took him to a psychiatric asylum, where all trace of him was lost. It is said that he was killed . . ." (Extracts from a petition by the parishioners of the Pochaev Abbey, addressed to the Free World.)

SEPTEMBER

Sept. 5, 1965. Evangelistic meeting in Kiev, after which M. Y. Khorev, a Christian, is accused of having incited the young to insubordination to the authorities. "That is not true," Khorev defended himself during his trial in Moscow. "During the meeting we sang hymns, I gave a talk, but all that does not transgress the laws . . . Some of the militia were even present. At the end of the meeting, I thanked an officer for having helped maintain public order . . ."

Sept. 8, 1955. Msgr. Kong, Bishop of Shanghai, is imprisoned with

21 priests and 300 laymen. This was a new, far-reaching scheme against the church in China. In three weeks, 17 more priests, 38 theology students, 5 nuns, and almost 600 laymen were imprisoned. According to the newspaper *Sin Wen Je Pao* of Shanghai, "These counter-revolutionaries have, during their long struggle, acquired vast experience. That is why we must take our enemies seriously and treat them accordingly."

Sept. 9, 1970. The Lithuanian priest Antanas Seskevicius is sentenced to one year of harsh imprisonment for having prepared several children in his parish for their first communion. The clergy of Lithuania stood solidly behind the accused: 72 priests of the Vilkaviskis diocese and 32 from the one in Kaisedorys signed a petition to the Central Committee of the Communist Party.

Sept. 13, 1950. The Polish episcopate, meeting in plenary assembly in the Church of Czestochowa, addresses a letter to the president of the Republic, protesting against a long list of abuses of power and of unbelievable coercion against the church since 1945 by an atheistic and malevolent administration. The letter-document stresses that, "to attain the needed peace of mind and national unity," there must be "an end to the battle against religion."

Sept. 21, 1915. Birth of Anatoli Krasnov-Levitin, in Baku, champion of the Russian Church of Silence, religious writer and civil-rights defender.

Sept. 26, 1962. The Soviet newspaper *Pravda* openly campaigns for atheism: "The old ways will not disappear without struggle. Many Soviet citizens are still prisoners of religious ideology . . . In the homes of the workers, atheistic propaganda is still mildly carried on. Many trade unions stand aside from this great enterprise . . ."

OCTOBER

Oct. 2, 1940. Gladkov, vice-president for Interior Affairs of the Lithuanian Socialist Republic, sends an "absolutely" secret and "extremely" urgent circular to "all the district heads of state security division," with the aim to destroy the church and annihilate the Lithuanian priests accused of carrying on "secret activities hostile to the U.S.S.R."

Oct. 3, 1966. The small Russian Baptist community of Pryval station, led by believer F.B. Makhovitzky, is disturbed by local police using "a propaganda car," equipped with loudspeakers broadcasting noisy music.

Oct. 7, 1948. Collective letter from the Rumanian Greek-Catholic bishops to President Petru Groza, complaining of the official destruction of their church.

Oct. 15, 1953. Death of Father Künsch in Camp B I (North Vietnam). At his bedside, his companion in captivity and suffering, was Father Bruneau. He was buried, wrapped in a mat, somewhere near the camp.

Oct. 20, 1953. Martyrdom, for Christ and his Church, of Franciscan Father Leonida Bruns, missionary to China since 1938. Mistreated by a band of rabid people, he continued repeating, "I want to die poor and naked, like Christ my Master. . . ."

Oct. 24, 1947. In a letter addressed to the Council president, Cardinal Mindszenty reproaches him for the violation of "democratic liberty" in Communist Hungary: forcing "persons to join the Communist party who do not agree with its policies" and attempting to lead the priests, under threat, "to spy on the Catholic orders and bishoprics and report periodically what they have heard and seen."

Oct. 27, 1947. Horrible slaying of Msgr. Theodore Romzha, Ukrainian Bishop of Mukatchiv by means of a "travel accident": soldiers and armed police rammed their car into his with the obvious intention of turning it over and killing him. Since the travelers—Msgr. Romzha was accompanied by two priests and two clergymen—were not injured in the collision, the Communists struck the bishop on the head with iron staves and left. He died on October 31 in Munckacs Hospital.

NOVEMBER

Nov. 1, 1944. Metropolitan Andrew Cheptytskyi dies under strange circumstances. Although Nikita Khrushchev, then first secretary of the Ukrainian Communist party, personally attended the funeral and even delivered a funeral oration, the Communist authorities could never forgive Msgr. Cheptytskyi for resisting both fanatical atheistic propaganda and the violation of children's consciences.

Nov. 7, 1918. Historic "letter" from Patriarch Tikhon to the "Council of Commissars of the People on the first anniversary of the Soviet government": "You promised freedom . . . You have not given that freedom; your kind of freedom consists in encouraging the base passions of the people, in letting murder and plunder go unpunished . . ."

Nov. 11, 1953. Death of the "hero" of Shanghai, Beda Tsang, in a

Communist prison hospital. Arrested August 9, he did not "bend" beneath the worst tortures by brainwashing specialists, namely, electric torture. His martyrdom for Christ greatly upset the Christians of China and of the entire world.

Nov. 20, 1950. Excerpt from the *People's Daily News,* a Chinese government newspaper: "Both Catholic and Protestant religions must become social activities completely free of foreign tutelage and belonging to the Chinese themselves . . . Patriotic Christians must transform the churches into a work appropriate to Chinese Christians themselves."

Nov. 25, 1963. Leonid Ilichev delivers his famous speech against religion before the members of the Ideological Commission of the Central Committee of the Communist Party, calling for the development of anti-Christian propaganda and the reinforcement of atheistic education among the Soviet people. In his opinion, "The way to succeed is through a systematic, well-devised effort, varying in form according to the peculiarities of different social groups and encompassing all sides of human life. Not a single aspect must be left for church people and sectarians to use to penetrate men's souls."

Nov. 27, 1953. Msgr. John Herrigers, from the diocese of Yung-pingfou, is arrested and accused of the following: (1) communicating with nationalist officers; (2) sending out Chinese priests as spies; (3) turning the young away from Communist organizations; (4) forbidding children to carry the "red handkerchief"; and (5) sabotaging the Independent Church Movement.

DECEMBER

Dec. 1, 1970. Lidia Mikhailovna Vins, president of the Council of Relatives of Baptist Prisoners in the U.S.S.R., is arrested. She is the mother of Ghiorghi Petrovich Vins, secretary of the Council of Dissident Baptist Churches, and wife of Piotr Yakovlevich Vins, who died in a Siberian camp.

Dec. 5, 1922. Arrest by the Soviet police of John Cieplack, archbishop of Mohilev; Leonidas Feodorov, Russian Catholic Exarch (Byzantine); Msgr. Butkiewcz, as well as twelve priests and a layman; all accused of resisting Red government orders and opposing "the normal activities of Soviet institutions."

Dec. 11, 1918. Birth of Aleksandr Solzhenitsyn, the great Russian writer, in Kislovodsk in the beautiful Caucasus. Arrested and condemned in 1945 to eight years of hard labor for "anti-Soviet agitation among his acquaintances," Solzhenitsyn is an Orthodox believer and zealous member of the underground church. His works bear the mark of his Christian faith and of his free spirit.

Dec. 15, 1965. Two Orthodox priests, N. P. Eshliman and G. P. Yakunin address an "open letter" to "Comrade President of the Supreme Soviet Presidium of the U.S.S.R." in order to protest against "the illegal conduct of the leaders and legal representatives of the Council for the Affairs of the Russian Orthodox Church, serving the Council of the Ministers of the U.S.S.R." It deals expecially with participation in the campaign to close the churches and convents, brutally preventing worship, interfering in the administrative and financial life of the religious communities, illegally limiting the number of priests, and violating the principle of freedom of conscience with regard to children.

Dec. 26, 1948. Cardinal Mindszenty, primate of Hungary, is arrested. After forty days of unimaginable torture, he begins to accuse himself and pleads guilty to espionage, treason, and unlawful traffic in currency.

Dec. 31. 1970. Msgr. Thomas F. Quinlan, former Bishop of Chun Cheon, Korea, dies in the Saint-Colomban Sisters Hospital in Samchok, on the east coast of Korea. Captured with many other missionaries of all faiths by invaders from the North when the Korean War broke out, he endured the terrible March of Death (more than 160 kilometers in the dead of winter) and remained in prison for two years and six months . . .

Appendix I.

ASSOCIATIONS, MISSIONS, ORGANIZATIONS FOR THE CHURCH OF SILENCE

(Material help, Bible shipments, radio broadcasts, publications, etc.)

ACTION EVANGÉLIQUE POUR L'ÉGLISE DU SILENCE: 40, rue du 22-Septembre, 92—Courbevoie, C.C.P.-M.C.E. 10.334-15, Paris.

AIDE À L'ÉGLISE EN DÉTRESSE: B.P. 1, 78-Mareil-Marly, C.C.P. 22.223-50, Paris.

CENTRE ORTHODOXE D'INFORMATION: 46, rue Abel-Vacher, 92-Meudon, C.C.P. Archip. A. Troubnikoff, 10.228-66, Paris.

PRESENCE DES PERSECUTÉS: 25, rue de Bois-Colombes, 92- Bois-Colombes, C.C.P. Marcel Mocquais, 13.937-92, Paris.

ACTION CHRÉTIENNE DES ÉTUDIANTS RUSSES: 91, rue Olivier-de-Serres, Paris-15e. C.C.P. 2441-04 Paris.

LA CHAINE (Association radiophonique pour l'Église du Silence): B.P. 79, 92405—Courbevoie, C.C.P. 30.746-20 La Source.

ASSOCIATION DU VOEU POUR LE VIETNAM: 11, rue Tronchet, 75008—Paris.

PRO FRATRIBUS (Mission catholique slovaque): C.C.P. Paris 18.703-77.

EUROPE

ACTION SUISSE EN FAVEUR DES DROITS DE L'HOMME: Postfach 167, 8029 Zürich, Switzerland.

ASSOCIATION CHRÉTIENNE POUR L'ÉGLISE DU SILENCE: rue de Foxhalles 17-19, 4800 Verviers, Belgaum.

BROTHER ANDREW: P.O. Box 147, Ermelo/Holland.

CENTRE FOR STUDY OF RELIGION AND COMMUNISM: 34 Lubbok Road, Chisiehurst, Kent BR7 5JJ/, England.

CENTRO STUDI RUSSIA CRISTIANA: Via Martinengo 16, 20139 Milan, Italy.

COMMUNAUTE DE SECOURS AUX ÉGLISES MARTYRES (C.S. E.M.): Case 57 Stand, CH-1204 Geneva, Switzerland.

EUROPEAN CHRISTIAN MISSION: 24 Elm Grove, London, N. 8 9AL, England.

FOYER ORIENTAL CHRÉTIEN: Avenue de la Couronne 206, 1050 Brussels, Belgium.

HILFSAKTION MARTYRERKIRCHE (HMK): Postfach 250, 5802 Wetter 2/West Germany. Postfach 169, 3601 Thun/Switzerland Postfach 12, 8043 Graz/Austria.

INSTITUT SUISSE DE RECHERCHE SUR LES PAYS DE L'EST: Jubiläumstrasse 41, 3000 Berne 6/Switzerland.

LICHT IM OSTEN: Postfach 1340, Kullenstrasse 1, 7015 Korntal/ West Germany.

MISJON BAK JERNTEPPET: Vidarsgt 20 B, Oslo 4/Norway.

POSSEV: Flurescheideweg 15, 6230 Frankfurt/M. 80/West Germany.

SLAVISKA MISSIONEN: P.O. Box 15037, S 161 15 Bromma/ Sweden.

ST STEPHEN'S MISSION: PL 019, 00300 Helsinki 30/Finland.

UNITED STATES
EASTERN EUROPEAN MISSION: 232 North Lake Avenue, Pasadena, Calif. 91101.

JESUS TO THE COMMUNIST WORLD (J.T.T.C.W.): P.O. Box 11, Glendale, Calif. 92109.

RUSSIA FOR CHRIST: P.O. Box 30,000, Santa Barbara, Calif. 93105.

SLAVIC GOSPEL ASSOCIATION: 2434 N. Kedzie Blvd., Chicago, Ill. 60647.

UNDERGROUND EVANGELISM: P.O. Box 808, Los Angeles, Calif. 90053.

Appendix 2.

BOOKS OF GREAT INTEREST

Alliluyeva, Svetlana. *Only One Year*. Trans. by Paul Chavchavadze. New York: Harper & Row, 1969.

Amalrik, Andrei. *Will the Soviet Union Survive Until 1984?*. New York: Harper & Row, 1970.

Andrew, Brother. *God's Smuggler*. Westwood. N.J.: Revell, 1968.

Benson, David. *Christianity, Communism and Survival*. Glendale, Ill.: Regal, 1967.

Bourdeaux, Michael. *Faith on Trial in Russia*. New York: Harper & Row, 1971.

Caucher, Roland. *Opposition in the U.S.S.R., 1917-1967*. Trans. by Charles Markmann. New York: Funk & Wagnalls, 1969.

Divomlikoff, Lavr. *The Traitor*. Trans. by J. F. Bernard. New York: Doubleday, 1973.

Fletcher, William C. Nikolai. *The Russian Orthodox Church Underground, 1917-1970*. New York: Oxford, 1971.

Goffman, Erving. *Asylums: Essays on the Social Situation of Mental Patients and Other Inmates*. Chicago: Aldine, 1961.

Labin, Suzanne. *Fifty Years: U.S.S.R. vs. U.S.A.* New York: Twin Circle, 1968.

Marchenko, Anatoly. *My Testimony*. New York: Dutton, 1969.

Noble, John. *I Found God in Soviet Russia*. New York: St. Martin's Press, 1959.

Solzhenitsyn, Aleksandr. *The First Circle*. New York: Harper & Row, 1968.

Solzhenitsyn, Aleksandr. *One Day in the Life of Ivan Denisovich*. Trans. by Ralph Parker. New York: Dutton, 1971.